Whig Organization in the General Election of 1790

Whig Organization in the General Election of 1790

Selections from the Blair Adam Papers

Edited by

Donald E. Ginter

Berkeley and Los Angeles
UNIVERSITY OF CALIFORNIA PRESS
1967

University of California Press
Berkeley and Los Angeles, California

Cambridge University Press
London, England

Copyright © 1967, by
The Regents of the University of California

Designed by Jorn B. Jorgensen

Library of Congress Catalog Card Number: 67-13999
Printed in the United States of America

Contents

Preface

In the spring of 1962 I was fortunate in being granted permission by Captain C. K. Adam of Blair Adam to assist him in sorting and arranging his family papers. I was surprised and gratified to find that these are one of the more remarkable collections of British papers remaining in private hands. None of these papers had ever been systematically used, and it is hoped that the entire collection, which is an unusually large one, will eventually be arranged and made available to scholars. Meanwhile I had the pleasure of spending several months at Blair Adam putting the papers of one generation of the family, those of William Adam, into some sort of order, so that they may now be used. I wish to express my deepest gratitude to Captain Adam and his gracious family, who accepted me into their home with a warmth and generosity which I shall always remember.

I should like to express my appreciation to Earl Fitzwilliam and the Trustees of the Wentworth-Woodhouse Estate, and to the staffs of the Sheffield City Library, the Northamptonshire Record Office, the Department of Palaeography and Diplomatic of the University of Durham, the British Museum, the National Library of Scotland, the Scottish Record Office, the University of Nottingham, and Duke University Library who gave me permission to consult and to quote from manuscripts which have been placed in their keeping.

A special word of thanks must be extended to the

Woodrow Wilson Foundation and to the Social Science Research Council, whose generous financial assistance supported three years of my research in Britain.

I am also deeply indebted to Professor George H. Guttridge, my mentor, and to Mr. John Brooke, who first suggested that I work on Opposition politics of the late eighteenth century. Both have continually been most generous with their time and knowledge.

Finally, I must express an indebtedness to the late Sir Lewis Namier and to his team of researchers, which included John Brooke, that made the resources of the *History of Parliament* available to students of the latter eighteenth century. These volumes have saved me an incredible effort, and my use of them has been so extensive that with a few exceptions I have found it impracticable even to cite them in my notes.

In accordance with the rules of transcription adopted by the editors of the Burke correspondence, a description of which may be found in Professor Thomas Copeland's preface to the first volume (Chicago, 1958), I have retained the spelling, capitalization, punctuation, and paragraphing of the manuscript. In addition, I have followed the Burke editors in making three exceptions to this rule. Antique or commonplace abbreviations, about which there is no ambiguity, have been expanded without editorial comment, unless these abbreviations occur in proper names, date lines, or addresses. Punctuation has been added at the end of sentences only when there is no doubt of a break and when the next sentence begins with a capital. Similarly, if a stop is clearly present between two sentences, a capital has been added to the beginning of the second. Angle brackets indicate words or phrases which are illegible or doubtful, or which are missing from the manuscript. Square brackets indicate editorial insertion or comment. Endorsements and postmarks have been retained only if they add to our knowledge of the document and its circumstances, but not if they simply repeat information obtainable in the text. Unless otherwise indicated, all endorsements are in the hand of Adam or his clerk. Italics throughout indicate underlined words.

The documents included in this volume are from the Blair Adam papers unless otherwise indicated. But they are by no means a comprehensive collection of letters and papers relating to the general election of 1790. Nor do they include every item on that subject in the papers of William Adam at Blair Adam. It has been my intention, however, to include a selection of documents which fully illustrates the scope and quality of the electoral activities of the Opposition organization during that period.

Introduction

This volume is specifically concerned with one aspect of one party in the late eighteenth century, that is, with the development of an electoral organization by the Whig Opposition during the years leading to the general election of 1790. But since our larger concern is with the origins of modern British parties, this essay will therefore not be confined to an analysis of the Whig electoral organization. It will attempt to place the developments of 1784–1790 in the larger context of British party history and to clarify our usage of the term "party" when writing of periods before the late nineteenth century. Finally, we will attempt to define and discuss the causes of the emergence of party organization in the late eighteenth century. Unfortunately definitive answers must await more research and critical discussion. But it is hoped that this essay will at least provoke the latter by raising the questions in this context. Before analyzing the election and the problem of origins of party, however, it may be well to begin by discussing what we mean by the terms "party" and "party system."

The whole debate over the origins and continuity of "party" in English history touched off by Namier's work, has tended to center on such questions as whether there is "mind" in history, whether the forces at work in political conflict are ideological or personal, or both— and in what proportion. Historians asking these questions have frequently assumed that ideology is a test for the presence and reality of "party" without making clear or even carefully considering precisely how essential a test it is, or if it is the only or most important one.[1] Indeed there is clearly no agreement, and certainly there has been inadequate discussion, of what we mean when we employ the terms "party" and "party system." One distinguished historian recently suggested that the only alternatives were either to restrict the term "party" to those complex organizations which developed in the peculiar political and economic conditions of the late nineteenth century, or else to apply it indiscriminately to all political groups of any description operating in any period.[2] But there is no reason to limit ourselves to these

1. Perhaps the most influential definition of "party," that by Edmund Burke, significantly included ideology as an essential and determinative ingredient: "Party is a body of men united for promoting by their joint endeavors the national interest upon some particular principle in which they are all agreed" (*The Works and Correspondence of the Right Honourable Edmund Burke*, ed. Earl Fitzwilliam and Sir Richard Bourke [London, 1852], III, 170). It may well be that ideological expression is essential to the nature of "party," though some historians would wish to dispute that contention. But is it necessary to insist that the ideological expression of parties always be sincerely felt and meaningfully phrased? May it not be useful to allow a political group the name party even if they are united fundamentally to promote their personal ends, whether or not in the national interest, or even if their ideological expression is no more than a superficial façade for their real convictions and intentions? For example, by 1792 the Whig Opposition found to their dismay and discomfort that the traditional toasts of the Whig Club— toasts which expressed an adherence to "the principles of the Glorious Revolution" and which had been blandly and unthinkingly mouthed by generations of politicians of every description— had suddenly become patently ambiguous and even dangerous in the context of the French Revolution. Ideology can be an anachronistic and meaningless cliché to an even greater extent than the politicians themselves realize.

2. J. P. Kenyon, *History Today* (December, 1961), 863–865: "a great deal of time has been wasted in recent years in sterile

two extreme alternatives. If we can agree upon basic definitions of the terms "party" and "party system," then we should be able to apply them usefully and intelligibly to a large spectrum of political groupings and situations which more or less measure up to a minimal standard.

The meaning of our terms must be determined by the prototypes we inevitably have in mind, the parties and party system of the later nineteenth century. In any case much of our interest in studying earlier political organizations presumably arises from a desire to trace the origins and development of these later institutions; otherwise we must admit to being antiquarians and not historians. But recognizing our prototypes does not solve the problem. It is admittedly difficult to contrast an earlier political grouping or situation which is in an elementary stage of development with the highly complex and sophisticated modern political party and party system.[3] Much of this difficulty disappears, however, if we recognize the complexity of the modern party and party system, define what is peculiar to its nature, and distinguish the essential elements of its structure.

The political party of the late nineteenth century was a multifarious phenomenon. Perhaps its most essential attribute, however, and that which distinguishes it decisively from the personal political groupings of the mid-

---

discussions as to whether the name 'party' can be applied to this clique or that. We have two alternatives. We can resume the old-fashioned habit of labelling any coherent group of M.P.'s a 'party,' right back to Sir John Neale's Puritan 'choir' or even beyond; or we can retain that title for the national organizations which arose with and by means of such nineteenth–century inventions as the telegraph, the railway and the rotary press. There is no middle course."

3. This is one difficulty which a historian has in utilizing the work of sociologists or political scientists who have normally given insufficient attention to the fundamental problems of identification encountered by students of earlier historical phenomena.

eighteenth-century Opposition, is its outward orientation. The inner group of a modern political party, for whatever reasons it is bound together (and for the purpose of determining "party" these seem less fundamental than the question of orientation), seeks the sources of its power to a large and significant extent outside itself. Whatever means its members choose to employ, or not to employ, to pursue its ends, or for whatever motivation, the modern political party does not rely simply upon the resources of its own inner and professional or semiprofessional group. It is not essentially introverted. It seeks to make itself indispensable to the continuance of government by generating massive support from outside its own ranks, that is, by winning elections and numerically dominating the House, or by generating a protest outside the House sufficient to lend irresistible weight to its own arguments within.

But even if it is possible to agree that outward orientation is an essential—perhaps the one essential—quality of a modern party, this awareness will not in itself clarify the discussion of its historical origins. Outward orientation manifests itself normally in commitment to ideology and in organization; in fact it is these features which we have always employed as tests for the existence of party. It is quite right to employ them as tests, and indeed it is difficult to see how we could detect party without the presence of one or the other to some degree. But in defining "party" these features must be seen as ancillary to outward orientation.

In seeking the origins of the modern party, then, the historian must concern himself with the two dimensions through which outward orientation is manifested, the ideological dimension and the organizational dimension. In its ideological dimension, party may be defined as a group of men acting together in Parliament [4] because of

4. By restricting the term to those groups who act "in Parlia-

ideas they hold in common or because these ideas may to some degree and at various stages have been imposed upon them. The second dimension of party may be defined as that organization which enables these groups to translate their principles into a legislative program, to enlist support for it from the country out of doors, and to muster sufficient strength within doors either to push their program through the legislature and into law, or themselves into power, or both.

To distinguish between these two dimensions of party is not of much use unless we also recognize the fact that they need not occur simultaneously. However much it may seem to a twentieth-century observer that the organizational dimension of party must arise as a natural extension of the ideological, so that whenever you find the one you should find the other as a natural corollary, nevertheless the two dimensions in fact seldom seem to have coincided in any highly developed form before the late nineteenth century. Whenever the one developed at all it did so in most cases alternately or even in the total absence of the other, and not on every occasion as the result of the same stimulus.[5]

The ideological dimension is undoubtedly the more

---

ment," we exclude those organizations which act exclusively out of doors; for surely, in order to avoid confusion, the term "political party" should be restricted to those organizations which were "political" in the sense of operating within the framework of Parliamentary politics. This would not necessitate excluding groups which aspired to parliamentary membership but had as yet secured no seats in the House. But undoubtedly this point will require further discussion.

5. Perhaps the reason for this sporadic and uncoordinated development was that whereas the first dimension was sometimes forced upon men by conscience and moral necessity, the second was a question of expediency and efficiency which could arise at any given moment, equally well from personal and not particularly altruistic motives.

difficult to analyze as well as the more dangerous to employ as a test. Close examination of a larger group which we may wish to call a "party" may reveal that the party is actually a coalition of smaller ideologically formed groups among whom there may be the most decided disagreement on the most deeply felt issues of the day. It is difficult to say, under these conditions, whether a party as such is seeking to project a meaningful image or program into the country. Ideological evidence may in this instance argue against party. In the last analysis it may be decided that outward orientation depends upon a sense of identity within the group, and this identity, if it seeks to project itself outward must do so through either a common organizational activity or a shared ideological expression, or both.

It may be well to emphasize, too, that the shared ideological positions should ideally be involved in intrinsically *party* issues. These issues may be defined as those which are so fundamental, pervasive, and persistent that they take precedence over and color one's reactions to lesser issues or problems. If the cohesiveness of a group is to be based on shared principles, then these principles must be felt by its members to be of such importance that all other likely issues are subordinate to them; otherwise the shared principle may be anti-party insofar as it creates a wholly artificial situation in ideological terms and prevents the formation of potentially more permanent and politically useful groupings. This is not to say that a political group which is outwardly oriented and bound together by transitory issues is not a party. But the distinction here made will assist in explaining why such parties—by perhaps being dependent upon temporary situations—frequently dissolve quickly and therefore tend to leave little permanent impression on national political alignments.

In the period before modern political parties have

fully evolved, then, we should be willing to speak in terms of degrees or levels of party development among groups which have a sense of common identity and a demonstrably outward orientation. This identity and orientation may be expressed organizationally or ideologically. There is no reason, however, why we should consider the ideological element to be the more essential or significant factor in the history of party development. Indeed the organizational is in some ways more significant, because it is the sophisticated product of a conscious effort; and since the history of party has shown it to be the last to appear, it presumably requires the more fundamental change in political attitude.

The use of the phrase "party system" also becomes clearer if we employ the above distinctions. By party system we mean a condition in which political groups are competing not only among themselves but also for the attention and support of the political nation as a whole. Thus a party system implies the existence of more than one outwardly oriented group. Ideally, the two or more groups, if we may be permitted a rough metaphor, should competitively fill up the political space of the nation. To the extent that they fail to do so, a party system does not obtain. If they aspire to do so, but unsuccessfully, a party system may be said to be incipient. Thus, for example, the existence of a Court of Ministerial party, however much it seeks the support and good wishes of the nation, does not constitute a party system if it is merely in competition with introverted factions which do not seriously compete with it for support out of doors.

The scholarship of the past thirty years on British politics of the middle decades of the eighteenth century has indicated that the opposition groups of that period were not political parties. They were not outwardly oriented nor were they significantly organized. Taking electoral activities as an example, those of even the largest and most sophisticated political connection of the 1770's, the Rockingham Whigs, were restricted both in character and in scope. While Burke had assisted Rockingham in finding suitable candidates for seats and had gone to great lengths in assisting friends such as Lord Verney in his contest for Buckinghamshire, nevertheless the seats with which Burke and Rockingham were concerned were those in which Rockingham and his immediate friends and relations had a personal interest, the candidates suggested were known friends who were to be associated with Rockingham's personal political group, and men such as Verney, who was not a Rockinghamite but had been an early patron of Burke and had long acted with the group in the House, had personal claims on their assistance. Burke helped Rockingham organize his resources and those of his friends and put them to best use; but the Rockinghams did not normally employ their resources to support candidates outside the circle of their own intimate political or family connections. Nor did they normally compete for seats where they had no personal interest. There were rare occasions when they did so, and there is no intention here to draw too fine a line between the 1780's and the two preceding decades. But when they did so—when they approached Edward Eliot for seats in 1780, for example—it was as a last resort and on behalf of persons closely associated with Rockingham's personal connection. It is worth noting, too, that even in this significant exception Rockingham himself displayed the greatest reluctance and inefficiency in the negotiations, much to the exasperation of the Duke of Portland, through whom the contact had been made. While Rockingham was alive his group did not, on the whole, think of a general election as an opportunity to expand the bases of their political power beyond the bounds of their connection, and their eyes were normally turned toward those constituencies where their personal political interests gave them their best opportunities rather than toward opportunities in the country as a whole.

Where, then, are we to place the origins of modern British parties? Historians writing in the late nineteenth century believed modern political parties originated in the seventeenth century. They thought of the Whigs and Tories of the Stuart period as organized bodies enjoying some degree of ideological homogeneity, and assumed they evolved without serious interruption or discontinuity into the Liberal and Conservative parties of late Victorian England. This view of the continuity of party development was destroyed several decades ago by the writings of Namier and others, who insisted on the discontinuity of party in the middle decades of the eighteenth century. Since the Namierite revision, historians have laid increasing emphasis upon the period of the Reform Bill as that in which modern parties, in the sense here employed, had their origins. It is not clear what has been generally thought of the period from 1784, which is the end of the period of Namier's special competence, to 1832, but most historians have felt that Namier's generalizations would continue to be applicable at least until the latter part of the third decade of the nineteenth century, when the agitation leading to the Reform Bill had gained momentum.

A preliminary study of the papers of William Adam at Blair Adam, and of other related collections, makes it clear that the decisive shift in political attitudes and atmosphere, the shift toward an outward orientation and competitive spirit which made possible the fuller development of political parties and the emergence of forces leading to a party system, occurred for the first time not in the late 1820's or early 1830's but rather some fifty years earlier, during the closing years of the American war.[6] The disunity which characterized the opposition before that date had enhanced the impression which was so widespread in the country of a scramble for power at Westminster by self-seeking factions. Under those conditions it was difficult for an independent country gentleman with Country sentiments to identify with any particular professional group of politicians. But for nearly a decade after 1783 every opposition group of any significance within Parliament identified itself to some degree with the Whig party headed by the Duke of Portland and Charles James Fox. The "Whig interest" became correspondingly more attractive in the country as it became the only alternative—and a less personal and more public one—to the Government in power. It was therefore potentially more capable of attracting the talents, energies, funds, and good will which previously had been dissipated among a myriad of opposition and independent Country interests. Moreover, coincidentally with its assuming an image of comprehensiveness and enhanced respectability, the Whig party began to evolve an organizational structure which would enable it effectively to utilize its potential strength both within and out of doors; and, almost from the outset, it found within itself the will so to use it.

By the later 1780's the Whig opposition had centralized and organized itself under the formal leadership of the Duke of Portland to an extent unprecedented and indeed inconceivable in the middle decades of the century. Its organizational activities had come under the central direction of a political manager, William Adam. A per-

6. This proceeded by stages. For the transition from a period of "personal" to a period of "political" parties in the 1770's, and for easily the most penetrating and authoritative analysis of the development of "party" as a political phenomenon in the middle and later decades of the eighteenth century, see John Brooke's introduction to the *History of Parliament*, I, 183–204.

manent establishment had been erected for the sending of circular letters and for parliamentary canvassing, and the party's whips were employed in these activities not merely at the beginning but from time to time during each session of Parliament. Every effort was made to increase a sense of identity with the party and its immediate objectives, and these efforts were not confined to personal contact with one's friends, nor even to members of the two Houses. Political clubs with both a parliamentary and a broad extraparliamentary membership were established in the metropolis and in the counties, and were specifically designed to increase the party's strength among the electorate.[7] Addressing and petitioning movements were organized and partially directed by the party's men of business in London and Edinburgh.

7. For political clubs before the 1780's, see note 30, below. The most important of the party's political clubs was the Whig Club of Westminster, which was founded in May, 1784, as an election club in the interest of Charles James Fox. Similar Opposition clubs were founded in Britain and Ireland during the following decade, particularly in the home counties, and especially after the general election of 1790. All were consciously modeled to some degree on the Westminster club. Because the Whig Club was Fox's own; because it was located in the seat of Government and at the hub of national social life; and because its membership came to include nearly all the more important members of the party as well as much of the professional and wealthier mercantile interest of the metropolis, the club quickly transcended its local significance and became an institution of national importance. Its meetings were held on the first Tuesday of each month during the sitting of Parliament, and its proceedings, which came to be regularly reported in the Whig press, were taken throughout the country to be accurate reflections of party sentiment. After the outbreak of the French Revolution the more liberal elements within the party attempted to capture the party imagery and organization by placing a series of resolutions before the club; and it was the proceedings at the Whig Club from December, 1792, to February, 1793, which were the most decisive events leading to a dissolution of the old party alliance.

Pamphlets were written and distributed at the party's expense at moments of political crisis, while the party's subsidized press spread propaganda throughout the country on a more regular basis. A headquarters for these propaganda activities was established in the apartments above the shop of Thomas Beckett, a bookseller, in Pall Mall. All these activities in turn supported the party in the most critical, and at the same time the most political of all political situations, the general election.

The general election of 1784 was the first in which an eighteenth-century opposition electoral organization showed signs of developing an apparatus like that of a modern political party. The Opposition approached the general election of April, 1784, with more than the usual apprehension. In December the king had personally canvassed against Fox's India Bill during its passage in the House of Lords. This open confirmation of the disfavor toward the Coalition, which everyone knew must exist within the Closet, was made even more blatant when Fox and North were dismissed. But the leaders of the Coalition did not expect to remain long out of power. They were confident of retaining their majority in the lower House. They fully expected Pitt's government would be outvoted and thus unable to pass the necessary Mutiny Act and the legislation for supplies, and would therefore be forced in turn to resign. In that event the king would have no alternative but to accept the Coalition back into office. Above all, they hoped to forestall a general election until the issue with Pitt had been settled. Unfortunately they were unable to achieve any of these objectives. Pitt was finally able to pass his measures as the Opposition majorities dwindled, and by March the party found itself forced into a general election with less than a month in which to make final preparations.

Like all eighteenth-century opposition groups, they had a greatly exaggerated fear of Treasury influence in general elections. But Treasury funds and the lure of possible government patronage were not negligible factors when opinion in the country also swung strongly against the conduct of the Opposition, as it did increasingly in early 1784. By March, 1784, it was already clear that the Opposition could expect to lose much of its talent and many men of influence in the House of Commons unless it provided them with alternative seats which were at the disposal of various members of the party or of their friends. William Adam was delegated to coordinate this pooling and apportionment of seats on behalf of the party, and his efforts represent a more elaborate and calculated approach to the problems of a general election than had characterized those of the opposition groups in the previous decade.

William Adam (1751–1839) was the eldest son of John Adam of Maryburgh, a prominent architect. His grandfather and three uncles were also members of that profession, one being the well-known Robert Adam. Educated at Edinburgh and Christ Church, Oxford, William Adam was first returned for Gatton in 1774 on the interest of a friend of the family. Adam was an ambitious young man, and he was convinced that the road to preferment and respect in the House for a young Scotsman relatively without connections was through a display of abilities and studious independence. Although early attracted by the personality of Charles Fox, by 1780 or 1781 he had become a close political adviser of Lord North and an intimate companion of North's eldest son, George Augustus. Once he had formed this connection, his political character seems to have altered abruptly, and he remained steadily loyal first to North until the latter's political retirement in the later 1780's, and increasingly after 1783 to Portland and Fox. From the outset of his career Adam had pursued a reputation as a parliamentary man of business, specializing in election committees. By 1783 he was one of the principal men of business of the North group and one of the negotiators of the Fox–North coalition. His career was continually diverted and hindered by the most extraordinary series of financial disasters, and for brief periods following 1785 and 1796 he was forced to retire largely from public activity. But on the whole he was the most important man of business within the Portland and Foxite Oppositions during the last two decades of the eighteenth century.

Much of Adam's correspondence for the general election of 1784 does not appear to have survived. From what is extant, however, we may gain some idea of the scope and character of his activities. At least forty-five candidates looked to Adam for seats either with or without a contest. It is important to note that a large percentage of these men do not appear to have been closely connected with the leaders of the party or their closest friends, and that many of them were new to politics and were seeking to enter Parliament for the first time. A number of the constituencies which appear in Adam's list, moreover, were not pocket or close boroughs which were "within the power" of members of the party "to dispose of." We may conclude, therefore, that Adam's activities extended beyond the limited scope he indicated in his letter to Aberdeen, included in the documents that follow. How much farther they extended does not appear in the evidence; but we do know that he seems to have been particularly interested and active in six Scottish constituencies, in the election of the Scottish representative peers, in Fox's Westminster contest and in securing an alternative seat for Fox at Knaresborough, in the Kirkwall Burghs, and in the Orkneys.

But one can easily go too far in speculating about the scope of Adam's activities in this general election. He was not yet the principal political manager of the party.

The duties of management seem generally to have been widely distributed within the party at this time, and much appears to have been left to the initiative of the principal men of business. Much work of the type performed by Adam in the general election was also undertaken by other members of the party—and not only by men of business—outside the constituencies in which they normally had an interest as individuals.[8] In any case—whether due to organizational deficiency, the influence of the Crown, or to issues and general unpopularity—the Coalition fared badly in the general election of 1784.

At the end of 1788 the Regency Crisis broke upon a Whig Opposition which was beset with lassitude, despondency, and petty quarreling. The fortunes of the party had diminished considerably after the frenzy of 1784. By the later 1780's the younger bloods within the party, Grey and his friends, were becoming increasingly exasperated with Burke's prosecution of Hastings, which was draining the political resources of the Opposition and distracting public attention from issues which they believed would more immediately serve their political ambitions. Fox himself had left the country in the early autumn for an extended tour on the Continent, and there was every expectation that the parliamentary session of 1788–1789 would be a fruitless one for Opposition. Even the most sanguine member of the party would have found it difficult to believe at that moment that they were about to come into power; for not even the striking successes of recent years on the Irish propositions and the shop

8. On 18 April the Duke of Portland wrote to Adam, who was in Scotland seeing to his own election and to the interests of the party in other constituencies: ". . . as I am at this moment employed in the service of Our Friends who are engaged in Contests in Herts, Bucks, & Middlesex, & have as I hope just launched an efficient Candidate for Cambridgeshire I must confine myself as much as possible to those subjects only which lay within the compass of Your Actual Sphere" (Blair Adam MSS).

tax had brought them perceptibly closer to storming the Closet or even to destroying Pitt's normal majority in Parliament. In the session of 1788–1789 a determined Opposition might expect to effect alterations in various pieces of legislation; but if these were reasonable alterations, they could probably be carried by Opposition speakers by force of argument and without a full attendance of their supporters. Successes of this description did not bring down governments in the eighteenth century. Incentive for organization was at a low ebb.

In November, 1788, the prospect for the coming session radically altered, and the political atmosphere, which had before been languid throughout the country, suddenly became electric. George III entered his first prolonged period of mental incapacity. For the first time in thirty years the Ministerial system seemed certain to be reversed by the placing of sovereign power in new hands. The Opposition was jolted into a frenzy of activity both by the prospect of acceding to office within a few short weeks and by the necessity of planning the tactics and securing an attendance for the battle with Pitt which was certain to form the prologue to the establishment of a regency. In the event, the battle with Pitt was more prolonged than was expected; and the Opposition, having lost the initiative in proposing the terms of the regency, soon found that the natural inclination of the majority of both Houses was to favor the restrictions Pitt proposed to place upon the power and patronage of the Prince's administration.

As in 1783, the highest expectations by the Opposition of at last acquiring durable power were frustrated unexpectedly, in this case by the recovery of the king in March, 1789, before the passage of the Regency Bill. Again, as in 1783, the party was faced with the odium in the country, which inevitably resulted in that period from a seeming attempt to encroach on the legitimate dignity and power of the Crown. As it also became increasingly clear that a general election was imminent, the party strained every resource to sustain and recoup its credit in the country, not only in order to secure future support for its activities out of doors or to gratify the dignity and sense of propriety of its members, but more importantly to prevent another disaster at the polls such as the party had suffered in 1784. Thus the Regency Crisis of 1788–1789 and the general election of 1790 precipitated the second period of accelerated development in the organizational dimension of Opposition politics.

The general election of 1790 was far more elaborately organized by the parliamentary Opposition than had been any previous election of the century; full-scale preparations were begun more than eighteen months before the dissolution of Parliament in June of that year. In the eighteenth century, as in other periods, a number of contests were usually decided months or even years in advance of the general election. In relatively close constituencies, particularly in Scotland, elections were not so much openly fought at the time of the poll as settled by negotiation during the periods between elections. Negotiations among borough patrons and between patrons and candidates began in many instances at least three years in advance of the general election in 1790. Indeed in some constituencies the struggle for an increased electoral interest was incessant after 1784. In April, 1787, the ambitious F. H. Mackenzie was already engaged in a heated dispute over the boundaries of electoral interest in Ross-shire, and from this date he prepared for a general election at a brisk pace. In December of that year William Adam approached his own patron Lord Findlater for assurances of his return at the next election. In June, 1788, having received his answer in the negative, he immediately went to Fox to consult on obtaining another seat. By October Findlater had quarreled with Henry Dundas, and Henry Erskine suggested that Adam open the question with him once again. This too failed, and Adam had to look further. Evidence of this pattern of almost continual intrigue and bargaining is to be found for innumerable constituencies throughout Britain for the six years preceding the general election in 1790.

During the Regency Crisis the preparations for a general election suddenly assumed massive proportions, for it had gotten about Whig circles that the Regency Government would probably consolidate its strength in the House by dissolving Parliament in the summer or autumn of 1789, provided the terms of the regency were as it desired. Sir Gilbert Elliot explained further contingencies to his wife, which must also have occurred to politicians not so well informed: "It might possibly happen . . . that this Parliament should be so entirely devoted to Pitt as to disable the Prince from carrying on even the ordinary business, in which case it might be necessary to dissolve it immediately." [9]

By the time Elliot wrote these words the party was in a far stronger position for fighting a general election than it had ever been while in opposition; for, so confident were its leaders that they were on the threshold of power, they had already begun to act like a Government. Much of their energies were devoted to anticipatory appointments to office, and the organizational functions which had been common to Government since the days of Walpole were being distributed in advance to the

9. Sir G. Elliot to Lady Elliot, 25 December 1788, Minto MSS, National Library of Scotland. By mid-January the partiality of the House for Pitt made it appear that a dissolution would be indispensable to the success of the Prince's Government (Sir G. Elliot to Lady Elliot, 20 January 1789, *The Life and Letters of Sir Gilbert Elliot, First Earl of Minto,* ed. Countess of Minto [London, 1874], I, 267, and Minto MSS).

party's men of business. Most importantly, toward the end of 1788 William Adam was asked to undertake the office of patronage Secretary to the Treasury. He thus became the political manager of the party and, by immediately and conscientiously taking up his duties, proceeded to centralize and regularize the organizational activities of the party to a degree unprecedented in opposition politics since the Hanoverian succession.

When it became clear that the Regency would not assume the unrestricted form at first envisaged by the party, and that it was likely Adam would not receive a proper financial remuneration for his efforts, he nevertheless persisted in his duties. As he explained to his father:

the king was thought to be in a way not to live. . . . Since then much has been to be done & who was there to do it. I could not Stand by & let the cause suffer. I was as it were called forth by all descriptions, from the Prince who is to reign to the lowest person in the Party. I could do nothing less than act. Without doing it neither any thing within or without the House of Commons would have been brought forward or executed.

Even when the king recovered and the prospects of the Opposition for office again receded, Adam continued in his duties as secretary to the Duke of Portland and political manager of the party. The elaborate and more sophisticated organizational structure which he managed and helped to develop during those hectic months was also maintained by the party, until it was partially disrupted and readjusted by the dissolution of the old party alliances in 1793 and 1794.

Adam managed a variety of activities both within and outside the Houses of Parliament; but attention must here be focused upon his role in preparing the party for the general election. From the beginning of 1789 when it was known that he was to manage the election, and particularly from the summer of that year when the political world returned from London to their seats in the country, Adam began receiving periodic and detailed reports of the state of interests in their constituencies from a large number of possessors of interest, candidates, and their agents. In late March and early April, 1789, London was convulsed with excitement at a rumor that Pitt had persuaded the king to dissolve Parliament immediately.[10] Adam rushed to town from his circuit and began final preparations; but this activity died quickly as it became evident that the king would not dissolve the House for some months. Nevertheless the trumpet had been sounded and the troops were already in process of formation. The Duke of Portland and Adam began their close and frequent consultations and inquiries in July. The intensive preparations, which had scarcely begun before they were forced to fruition in 1784, were in 1790 permitted almost a year to ripen before the dissolution was finally announced.

The activities of Adam and Portland in 1790, while not in every case different in kind from those of 1784, were immensely extended and more systematically un-

10. According to Elliot, whose information was that of the Opposition leaders, the rumor was "owing partly to the Stir amongst the Ministerial Election agents, partly to information given by some of the inferior people employed in the offices, & partly to the Idea that Pitt has wished for some time past to secure a favorable Parlt. for seven years more while his popularity lasts," Sir G. Elliot to Lady Elliot, 17 March 1789, Minto MSS. After the great fear of April, rumors of dissolution continued to flourish sporadically, thus maintaining the intense interest in preparation. Windham, upon his return from Paris in September, immediately hurried off to Norfolk amid a flurry of rumors (William Windham to Edmund Burke, 15 September 1789, Wentworth Woodhouse MSS, Sheffield City Library). Rumors were again general in March (William Elliot of Wells to Sir G. Elliot, 15 March 1790, Minto MSS). Parliament was not dissolved until 12 June 1790 (Debrett, XXVII, 712).

dertaken; and there were a number of highly significant innovations which make the later election a major breakthrough in the development of modern party organization. The qualities which Adam and Portland principally contributed to the conduct of the election were coordination of resources and dissemination of information. Adam seems to have operated out of his legal chambers in Lincoln's Inn Fields during most of the months of preparation, and while he was out of town his mail was forwarded by his clerk. But during the more hectic months—during the Regency Crisis, or when rumors were flying in April, 1789, and as the summer of 1790 approached—the addresses on his correspondence indicate that he had set up offices in Burlington House, the Duke of Portland's palatial residence in Piccadilly.[11] Between the two of them, Adam and Portland planned an electoral campaign which literally extended to every corner of Britain.

It is a common mistake to regard Fox as the principal leader of the party in this period. He was not. The correspondence which follows clearly indicates that the Duke of Portland, far from being a cipher, as he is invariably portrayed, was both in title and in effect the leader of the party. It should be emphasized, in fact, that Fox could not in this period have been the formal leader of a party which included the old Rockinghams. He did not have the aristocratic pretensions for such a role. And it is worth noting in the correspondence the number of instances in which people out in the counties, people personally unknown either to Fox or to Portland, expressed their attachment to "the interest of the Duke of Port-

11. Most of the letters to Adam in January, February, March, and April, 1789, and occasionally during the following year, are addressed to Burlington House, even when the sender knew Adam's private and professional quarters were in Lincoln's Inn Fields.

land" without any mention of Fox whatever. Fox was in many ways the most colorful and attractive figure within the party. His warm and open personality exerted a powerful influence upon the House, and he was immensely popular in the metropolis and increasingly so among the Dissenter and reforming interest. But much of the growing "Whig interest" in the country was aristocratic, or was reassured and flattered and encouraged by the respectability of a man such as Portland, or simply took more seriously than have later historians the fact that Portland possessed the formal leadership of the party.

On the other hand one must not go to the other extreme by underrating the role of Fox within the party. He was the leader in the House of Commons, and particularly in the midst of political debate was frequently decisive in altering the course of party strategy and tactics. His relationship with Portland and the aristocratic leadership was warm and close, and he was always consulted when important decisions were to be made. He was exceptionally good at the role he played within the party, and the role was a paramount one; but the dimensions of that role must not be exaggerated. He was not the final authority, however much weight his opinion carried. Nor did he attempt to offset his inferior position to Portland by activity or industry. He was temperamentally unsuited to the daily business of politics and actively avoided it. People came to him with information and sought his opinions on political activity outside the House, but he rarely took the initiative in such matters. Through a great personal effort he would rouse himself at election times to appear in Westminster or to undertake some unpleasant activity on behalf of a friend. But the day-to-day business of politics outside the House of Commons for the most part was left to others and passed him by. The efficient leadership of the party when viewed outside the narrow context of the House of

Commons—as it ought to be viewed—was exercised by the Duke of Portland, a man of limited capacities undoubtedly, but utterly devoted to his responsibilities, untiring, warm and generous in support of his friends, and with an impeccable private life which inspired the confidence of the country, and even to some degree of the king. But while a national figure such as Portland, along with his principal man of business, comprised the center of the electoral organization and exercised the limited authority that went with formal political leadership in that period, a number of subsidiary centers of organization and authority were essential to the successful functioning of the larger structure. Most notably, a group of politicians resident in Edinburgh, many of whom were not in Parliament, had formed around the leadership of Henry Erskine, the Lord Advocate under the Coalition, in the days of the Coalition Ministry. These men were extraordinarily ambitious for the fortunes of the party; and, luckily for their cause, they were gifted with political imagination as well as energy. Since 1784 they had been looked to, above and below the Tweed, as the principal men of business and the organizational center for Opposition activities in Scotland. It was they who had founded the Independent Friends in 1785.[12] It was they again who had organized the extraordinary campaign in Scotland in opposition to Pitt's Irish propositions. They

12. The club had deliberately been given this innocuous name in order to draw into its membership men who were normally disposed to oppose Government but who would not wish to identify themselves publicly with any particular political group. The founders of the club hoped to bring such men gradually into habits of public cooperation with Opposition leaders. This was a more subtle approach than that adopted by the comparable Whig Club in Westminster, and was dictated by the relatively greater popularity and influence of the Government interest in Edinburgh.

seem continually to have fed information on Scottish affairs to the leadership in London which could be used
against the Government on the floor of the House. In
1789 they organized the Scottish addresses on the Regency at the same time that they were preparing for the
impending general election.

A number of individuals also played an essential role
in the party's organization. Sir Thomas Dundas, along
with Adam, seems to have been the principal inter-
mediary between Opposition interests in Scotland and
England. Reputedly the greatest purveyor of ecclesiastical patronage in Scotland, with extensive property and
interest in both parts of the kingdom, and the brother-
in-law of Lord Fitzwilliam, he was naturally looked to
as a man of weight and confidence within the party. In addition, and not to be underestimated, there were the local
magnates, men like F. H. Mackenzie or even the sometimes untrustworthy Sir Francis Basset, who, while essentially interested in furthering their family influence,
were willing to varying extents to associate their interests
with those of the party and to assist the party with information, influence or—the real test—funds, even when,
on occasion, they could foresee no immediate profit to
themselves.

The problems of coordination and evaluation were
greatly eased by the preparation of political surveys.
There is no evidence that Adam and Portland undertook
the preparation of a grand survey of the entire kingdom,
such as John Robinson had formerly made for the Government. The Opposition surveys were instead concen-
trated on certain areas of England and Scotland. In at
least one instance, Hill's survey of the political state of
Scotland, a survey, not drawn up on the party's initiative,
was offered to Adam and Portland by an obviously ambitious young man who was unknown to them. In other
instances the information of the more active magnates,

such as Mackenzie in northern Scotland, amounted in effect to a survey of their area of interest. But by far the most extraordinary case, and the one most significant because of its indication of a shift toward a more modern political attitude, is that of J. Jackman, a former newspaper editor, who was employed by the party as an agent to survey the state of interests in the cinque ports. In this instance the party itself seems to have taken the initiative, in an effort to secure a foothold in constituencies where they had no natural political interests or connections.[13]

The party was also active in the writing and distribution of election literature, through the metropolitan and county press and in the form of pamphlets. But the extent of such activity is not clear. We know that during the Regency Crisis the party undertook a broad distribution of literature on a plan suggested by Lord Porchester. There is evidence, too, that payments were being made to county newspapers during the months preceding the general election. But it is not always clear whether such payments were being made for services recently or yet to be rendered, or whether they were for services already rendered during the Regency Crisis. Nor is it clear what the content of the literature might have been. There is no indication that the constituencies in which the party took an interest were contested on the basis of national issues.

Many of these activities were made possible by what were the most significant organizational developments of the decade: a general party fund and two special election funds. The general fund originated sometime

13. Other agents were sent down from London by Adam and Portland to assist party candidates in their elections, while still others, such as Walsh, were employed as messengers and writers. See the index for references to Walsh, Richardson, Jackman, Whiting, Hodgson, Reid, Kent, Carpenter, Morthland, and Hill.

during the early 1780's and was annually subscribed by a few of the more prominent and affluent members of the party. It was originally conceived as a newspaper fund; but while the greater portion of it was disbursed as subsidies to the party press, another sizable portion was used to offset the expenses of Frederick Walsh, who wrote the party's circular letters for attendance, and for quarterly payments to Joseph Richardson, the playwright, who was a party agent and nonparliamentary man of business. The subscription was never sufficient for the purposes of the fund and had never been designed to meet election expenses of any description. In 1788 Lord John Townshend was returned for Westminster in one of the most hotly contested bye-elections of the century. The expenses were staggering, something in excess of thirty thousand pounds, and because Townshend had been called in as a party candidate and a large number of influential people in the party had actively engaged in the campaign, the feeling ran strong that the debt was a party rather than a personal one. A special subscription was initiated on a very wide basis, and within the next two years it succeeded in paying the debts of the bye-election in full. A similar subscription was subsequently initiated with a few to a general election fund, and it enjoyed considerable success. But some of the debts of the general election were eventually inherited by the general fund, and this fund continued until the disintegration of the party in 1793. Some of the debts of the general election may never have been paid.[14]

The reader of the following documents may well receive the impression that the Whig Opposition, while organized, was nevertheless rather inept and that the

14. The development and administration of party funds has been described in detail in my article "The Financing of the Whig Party Organization, 1783–1793," *American Historical Review,* LXXI (1965–1966), 421–440.

fruits of its labors seem hardly spectacular. Some of the more significant episodes, such as Jackman's mission to the cinque ports, read even ludicrously at times and somewhat in the strain of comic opera. But questions of the Opposition's ability and success are quite beside the point in studying the origins and development of party and of party organization. The substantial significance of the Whig organization lay in the very fact of its existence and implementation.

Let us examine, then, the quality and extent of the party's organizational activities during the general election of 1790 and the bye-elections which immediately preceded it. The reader should be cautioned that, although the evidence always points strongly at specific organizational activity, many times the limited nature of the reference does not allow certainty. A number of categories have been established and arranged in the order of their significance for party organization.

Some effort has been made to be conservative in placing constituencies within these categories but the serious student is advised to pursue each constituency through the footnotes and index. More particularly, it should be noted that the figures do not include those constituencies whose seats were at the disposal of patrons closely associated with the party but which were disposed of privately by the patron in the normal way without specific reference to the wishes of the party leaders in London. Such activity was normal throughout the eighteenth century, and the figures are only intended to demonstrate the extent of activity which was qualitatively new. Thus the boroughs of Lord Fitzwilliam are excluded, although Fitzwilliam and Portland were doubtless of one mind; the seat of the Duke of Bedford at Okehampton is included, as Bedford applied to Portland for a list of candidates who might be available and interested. Bye-elections which occurred before 1788 are also excluded.

During the years 1788 to 1790 the Duke of Portland

and Adam are known to have become involved organizationally, and in their capacity as leader and manager of the party, in at least eighty-three constituencies in England, Wales, and Scotland. Of these eighty-three, some forty-five had at least one incumbent member with an Oppositionist voting record in the Parliament of 1784,[15] another thirty-eight constituencies did not.[16] Thirty-seven of the constituencies were brought to the attention of the party by candidates who had elected to try their fortunes there on their own initiative, or by a local patron whose personal interest was involved;[17] forty-six of the constituencies were not brought to the party's attention by such a candidate or patron but were sought out on the initiative of Portland and Adam, or alternatively by the Edinburgh group or by such local magnates as Mackenzie or Morshead.[18]

15. Aberdeen Burghs, *Aldeburgh,* Arundel, Bath, *Bletchingly,* Bridport?, *Bucks, Caithness, Carmarthen borough,* Christchurch, *Cockermouth,* Colchester (bye-election), Cornwall, *Dover,* Dumfriesshire, *Durham co., Exeter, Gloucester?,* Haslemere, *Helston,* Honiton, Horsham?, *Hythe,* Lincoln, Linlithgowshire, Malmesbury, *Morpeth* (bye-election), *Newport* (I.o.W.), *Norwich, Okehampton,* Pembrokeshire, *Petersfield, Renfrewshire, Rossshire,* Rye, *Seaford, Stafford, Surrey,* Tregony, *Wareham, Wendover, Westminster,* Weymouth and Melcombe Regis, Winchelsea, and *Wootton Bassett.* Those constituencies in which at least one candidate who subsequently supported the party was successful have been italicized in this and subsequent footnotes. A question mark has been placed after cases where the evidence for the constituency is particularly unclear. These figures do not in themselves measure the effectiveness of the party's organization; successes are not necessarily due to the party's intervention. They only confirm a general impression of the effectiveness of the organization formed by an examination of the documents.

16. Appleby, Ayrshire, *Bristol,* Canterbury, *Carlisle?,* Carmarthenshire, Chester, Dysart Burghs, *Evesham,* Fowey, Fife, Glasgow Burghs, Grampound, Hastings, Hertford, Invernessshire, Ipswich, Lymington, Milborne Port, New Romney, *Northampton,* Northern Burghs, Peeblesshire, Perthshire, Pontefract?,

The specific activities undertaken by the party within each constituency will be divided into five categories, which will be given in ascending order of significance.[19] In the first and lowest category fall six constituencies from which reports of difficulty or progress were sent in to Adam and Portland, and not simply in order to satisfy curiosity but with the implication or an indication that some assistance might be in order. But the evidence does not reveal that any assistance was given or offered.[20] The second category comprises some sixteen constituencies in which the activity undertaken by the party was limited to the writing of letters or to canvassing voters directly or indirectly, or to employing a messenger to deliver the

---

Reading?, Rochester, Roxburghshire, St. Mawes, *Sandwich,* Shaftesbury, Southampton, Stirling Burghs, *Sudbury?,* Suffolk, Sutherlandshire, Taunton, and *Thetford.*

17. Aberdeen Burghs, Arundel, Ayrshire, Bath, Bridport?, *Bristol, Bucks, Carmarthen borough,* Christchurch, Cornwall, *Dover, Durham co., Exeter,* Fife, Glasgow Burghs, *Gloucester?, Hythe,* Lincoln, Linlithgowshire, Malmesbury, *Morpeth* (bye-election), Northern Burghs, *Norwich, Okehampton, Renfrewshire?,* Roxburghshire, *Sandwich, Seaford,* Southampton, *Stafford, Sudbury?,* Suffolk, *Surrey,* Taunton, *Wendover, Westminster,* and Weymouth and Melcombe Regis.

18. *Aldeburgh,* Appleby, *Bletchingly, Caithness,* Canterbury, *Carlisle?,* Carmarthenshire, Chester, *Cockermouth, Colchester* (bye-election), Dumfriesshire, Dysart Burghs, *Evesham,* Fowey, Grampound, Haslemere, Hastings, *Helston,* Hertford, Honiton, Horsham?, Inverness-shire, Ipswich, Lymington, Milborne Port, *Newport* (I.o.W.), New Romney, *Northampton,* Peeblesshire, Pembrokeshire, Perthshire, *Petersfield,* Pontefract?, Reading?, Rochester, *Ross-shire,* Rye, St. Mawes, Shaftesbury, Stirling Burghs, Sutherlandshire, *Thetford,* Tregony, *Wareham,* Winchelsea, and *Wootton Bassett.*

19. Constituencies placed in the more significant categories may also show evidence of organizational activity appropriate to the less significant categories.

20. *Caithness,* Carmarthenshire, Christchurch, Inverness-shire, Pembrokeshire, and Suffolk.

writ.[21] In the third category, which is far more significant, are placed some ten constituencies in which the
party undertook to strike some kind of bargain, or to
offer some type of patronage, or to send down from
London an agent to assist in the return of the Opposition
candidate.[22] But it is the final two categories which are
easily the most significant and which reveal the most
startling expansions of political vision and activity. The
fourth category comprises some forty-three constituencies, in the majority of which the party attempted to
bring a constituency and candidate together, either by
seeking a suitable candidate for a known constituency or
by seeking a likely constituency for a known candidate.
It also includes those constituencies which were the objects of political surveys, either on the initiative of Adam
and Portland (in which case the survey might be financed
out of party funds) or of one of their associates, or in
which Adam and Portland attempted to find a friend who
would purchase an interest which was for sale.[23] In the

21. Aberdeen Burghs, Bridport?, *Bristol, Bucks, Carmarthen
borough, Gloucester?,* Lincoln, Linlithgowshire, *Norwich,* Perthshire, Reading?, *Renfrewshire, Seaford, Sudbury?, Surrey,* and
Wendover.

22. Ayrshire, Cornwall, *Durham co.,* Dysart Burghs, Fife,
Hythe, Northern Burghs, Roxburghshire, *Sandwich,* and *Stafford.*

23. *Aldeburgh,* Appleby, *Bletchingly, Carlisle?,* Chester, *Cockermouth, Dover,* Dumfriesshire, *Exeter,* [Fowey], Grampound,
Haslemere, Hastings, *Helston,* [Hertford], Honiton, Horsham?,
Ipswich?, Lymington, Malmesbury, Milborne Port, *Morpeth* (bye-
election), *Newport* (I.o.W.), New Romney, *Northampton, Okehampton,* Peeblesshire, *Petersfield,* Pontefract?, Rochester, *Ross-
shire,* Rye, St. Mawes, Shaftesbury, Southampton, Stirling Burghs,
[Sutherlandshire], Taunton, *Thetford, Wareham,* Weymouth and
Melcombe Regis, Winchelsea, and *Wootton Bassett.* Constituencies in which activities, initially undertaken by others, were vetoed
or disapproved by the Duke of Portland are placed in square brackets. None of the Scottish counties analyzed by Hill in his *Political
State* have been included unless specific reference has also been
made to them in other documents.

fifth category are some eight constituencies which provide the ultimate test of the Opposition's character as a
party, for in these constituencies Portland and Adam
offered, or were persuaded, to underwrite out of the
subscribed general election fund a portion of the Opposition candidates' expenditures.[24]

Two final sets of figures will be of interest. Fifty-seven
persons found themselves without seats and looked to
the party for likely constituencies. Of these, thirty-five
were not returned at the general election or during its
aftermath,[25] and indeed less than half of these thirty-
five seem to have found constituencies. Another six were
finally returned for constituencies where they had a natural interest and where they seem to have decided to
stand without the party's suggestion.[26] But as many as
sixteen were returned at the general election or during its
aftermath for constituencies which had been suggested to
them by the party.[27]

The final set of figures are the most tenuous of all, for
they attempt to answer the inevitable question, who won
the election? This is probably a question which should
never be asked of eighteenth-century general elections.

24. Arundel?, Bath, Canterbury?, *Colchester* (bye-election),
Evesham, Glasgow Burghs, Tregony, and *Westminster.*

25. T. Assheton Smith, H. Aston, A. Blair, F. Calvert, Sir G.
Cooper, E. Cotsford, G. Craufurd, Sir W. A. Cunynghame, Lord
Daer, J. Fletcher Campbell, Sir J. Frederick, W. Fullarton, Gifford, C. Greville, Harford, Horseley, Hume, Ironside, R. P.
Jodrell, R. Mackey, E. Morant, W. Nedham, J. Ord, G. Osbaldeston, Sir P. Parker, Sir R. Payne, Pembroke, Pocock, Prescott, J. Purling, R. Scott, T. Scott, Tempest, W. Tollemache,
and W. Wrightson.

26. W. Baker, G. Byng, Lord Clive, G. A. North, B. Tarleton, and M. A. Taylor.

27. J. Anstruther, W. Braddyll, Lord Downe, Sir G. Elliot,
W. Ellis, P. Francis, T. Grenville, Lord Grey, S. Lushington,
Lord Melbourne, Lord Palmerston, J. St. Leger, Lord R. Spen-
cer, J. Tarleton, T. Thompson, and Lord Titchfield.

The ultimate test of a man's political allegiance is not what he professes in private, or even on his feet in the House, but rather how he tends to behave when the members of the House are called into the division lobbies. But published division lists are still rare in the 1780's; and their value as evidence of political allegiance is further diminished by irregularity of attendance and by the almost total absence of party discipline. Moreover, while there was a rough notion of what normally constituted party and non-party questions, there was still a certain fuzziness about the matter, and the more independent members in particular would frequently find some point of principle which would cause them to divide against those whom they normally found themselves following into the lobbies. But despite these difficulties—and they should be emphasized most strongly—some tentative figures on the comparative voting potential of the Opposition in the House of Commons both before and after the general election will be offered. On the basis of voting records [28] the Opposition potentially was able to draw the support of some two hundred twenty-nine members during the Parliament of 1784. After the general election of 1790, during the sessions of 1791 and 1792 and before the split in the party, Opposition was able to draw upon the support of some one hundred ninety-

---

28. For references to the seven extant division lists for the Parliament of 1784, see the *History of Parliament,* I, 534. Emphasis has here been placed on how members voted on the Irish commercial propositions, Richmond's fortifications plan, and particularly on the Regency questions. There are two—but only two—good party divisions during the Parliament of 1790, one for each of the two first sessions. For the division on Grey's motion on the state of the nation, 12 April 1791, see *Morning Chronicle,* 13, 14, 15, 16 April 1791; Debrett, XXIX, 154–157. For the division on Whitbread's motion relative to the armament against Russia, 1 March 1792, see Debrett, XXXI, 399–400; Cobbett, *Parliamentary History,* XXIX, 1000–1001.

three members. The resultant loss of thirty-six members cannot be taken as a very exact figure, particularly since it is based on only two divisions—although very good ones—for the Parliament of 1790. The safest conclusion is that the Opposition, while it lost slightly, did remarkably well in holding its own, particularly when one remembers that the general election followed rather closely on the Regency Crisis, which had left the party in bad repute and with newly dampened and even bitterly disappointed hopes. They were fortunate not to have experienced a repetition of 1784. Given some timely mistakes by the Ministry and some unfortunate incidents abroad, which in fact occurred at Nootka Sound and Oczakow, the party was in a position to prosper, and might well have done so had it not been torn asunder by the ideological tensions generated by the French Revolution.

Rather paradoxically, the period from 1792 to 1796 saw both the extension and the disruption of Opposition organization. While much of what has been described above, and particularly party finance, was temporarily disrupted when the Portland and Windhamite wings broke from Fox and his young friends, nevertheless it was in this same period that Charles Grey and those associated with the Friends of the People undertook a most ambitious and promising expansion of the extraparliamentary organization. But this ambitious new Foxite organization went into eclipse in its turn as the Pittite repression of all reformist extraparliamentary agitation became more severe. Shortly after the turn of the century, however, as the Foxite secession from Parliament broke down under the prospect of new political opportunities, organizational activity revived. Research is not yet sufficiently advanced to permit delineation of this later development in any detail, but it is already clear that the Whig organization continued to expand gradually throughout the first three decades of the nineteenth century, until the Reform Bill provided the impetus for the next period of highly accelerated development.

The shift in political attitude which occurred during the closing years of the American war and which made possible the emergence of an organized Opposition party is surely one of the most intriguing and yet elusive phenomena in English political history. A historian's task is not merely to describe it and its results, which is an important and preliminary duty, but to explain it, if he can. But how does one explain such a thing? The answer is not yet clear, but it may move us closer to an answer if some effort is made to define the problem. In order to feel the full weight and significance of the change which occurred some attention might first be given to the special situation in which a parliamentary opposition found itself during the mid-eighteenth century and the mentality which prevented its overcoming the disadvantages of that situation. It is from this context and the limitations of this mentality that the Fox-Portland Opposition freed itself to some degree in the last two decades of the century.

In a political world roughly divided between Court and Country it may be seen that every political group which formed an administration in the eighteenth century enjoyed, temporarily at least, a distinct advantage over the parliamentary opposition in enlisting support for its measures both within and outside the doors of Parliament. The attitude underlying the conduct of the Court interest within Parliament was positive: it was to support whatever measures might be proposed by Administration so long as that Administration retained its confidence. Thus Administration could normally rely on a broad support for its measures in the House, provided it could persuade its supporters to attend their duties in Parliament. The Court interest out of doors was potentially

—if only potentially—a unified party capable of identi-
fying itself with the Government in power and upon
whom encouragements, inducements, and even pressures
could be applied by that Government with some vestigial
sense of propriety and some hope of success.

The parliamentary opposition did not enjoy these advantages with respect to the Country interest. Whereas
a man who reflected the Court interest could succumb to
Government pressures and inducements with a relatively
clear conscience, knowing that he was taking the line of
his principles, as well as of his interest, a person who reflected the Country interest was not always prepared to
follow the line of a particular, or indeed of any group
within the parliamentary opposition. The political conduct of the Country voter and politician emanated from
negative instincts. He distrusted the power of the Crown
and the ministers who wielded it. He resented interference with local interests and administration. He clung
tenaciously to the inviolability of his property and of his
privacy, and proclaimed the sacredness of the latter in
support of the former in his opposition to excise. In
sum, his inclination was not normally to support any
particular program or any particular set of politicians.
His attitude with regard to national politics was essentially negative. At his worst he was a destructive force
in British politics; at his best, which was more normal, he
was like Sir William Wyndham or Sir George Savile, a
useful, disinterested, and responsible critic of government
policy.

Throughout the middle decades of the eighteenth century there is not much evidence that the parliamentary
opposition was particularly inclined to overcome these
disadvantages and to give attention to improving their
strength out of doors, or at least they were not inclined
to do so by a sustained, extensive, and systematic effort.
The efforts of opposition groups were on the contrary

almost wholly oriented toward Parliament itself. Thus far it has not been possible to trace any widespread out of doors propaganda campaigns initiated and financed by an opposition group of this period after the collapse of the opposition to Walpole. County addresses and petitions were the result of exclusively county activity and were not stimulated by opposition central committees. General elections throughout the period were organized, fought, and financed by individuals through local *ad hoc* committees rather than by parliamentary opposition groups as such, while between elections there was little effort in the more open constituencies, apart from occasional patronage, to sustain an active interest with a view to the next election.[29]

Moreover, the parliamentary opposition from the fall of Walpole to the final years of the American war was characterized by a disunity which dissipated its energies and resources and operated strongly against any one of its groups gaining substantial and firmly committed support either in or out of doors. National government in the eighteenth century was almost exclusively concerned with war, foreign policy, taxation, and various enabling legislation which was purely local in interest. There was not much scope within this framework for the elaboration of a party policy which would be a distinct and appealing alternative to that of Government or of other opposition groups, and what scope there was

29. For example, local election clubs which were closely connected with professional parliamentary groups were exceptional before the 1780's. I know only of the Rockingham Club in Yorkshire. Such organizations as the Steadfast Society and the Union Club in Bristol, and one can find many similar organizations in the first volume of the *History of Parliament,* were purely local in their connections and inspiration and seem to have had no direct significance for the emergence of nationally based political parties. In some instances, in the more close constituencies, they were no more than organized agencies for electoral extortion.

was not much utilized by eighteenth-century politicians. Except in time of national crisis parliamentary politics tended to be dominated by the manipulation of private interests and maneuvers for the realization of private ambitions, however much these maneuvers might be clothed in ideological anachronisms or myths and however much such politicians as Burke sincerely believed their country's best interests would be served by utilizing the peculiar talents of their own group.

Opposition politics were conducted in a relaxed and informal, at times even despondent and pessimistic manner. There is as yet no evidence that an opposition group employed a formal whip on the floor of the House of Commons before the 1780's. Occasionally they may have sent letters requesting attendance at the opening of a session, and in rare instances for an important division during a session; but these letters were sent by individuals to their friends without system. There was in fact no organizational machinery with which the opposition groups of the mid-eighteenth century could have made themselves efficient and effective either within or out of doors. There was no one but the busy politicians themselves to write circular letters or to canvass for divisions. There was no opposition counterpart of John Robinson to coordinate and efficiently utilize efforts and funds in a general election. Nor was there a general fund which opposition groups as such could employ to finance an organized endeavor of any nature either inside or outside Parliament. So long as they relied wholly upon individual efforts and refused or neglected to create an organizational machinery even comparable to that which Government had employed at least since the administration of Grenville, the opposition groups could not hope under normal circumstances to defeat the Government either at the poll or in the division lobby. Their only possibility for power was to await a public calamity of such magnitude as to destroy public confidence in the present ministers and then to sweep their particular opposition group into power as an alternative Government.

It must be clear, then, that the eighteenth century Opposition was at a severe disadvantage in competing for political power within the state. Yet it must strike the student of this period even more strongly that mid-eighteenth century Opposition politicians did not normally take what may to us appear to be obvious measures to overcome this disadvantage, namely, to broaden the bases of their power by extending their political resources more widely and deeply into the country. There is evidence that many of them recognized their problem, and that it distressed and frustrated them.[30] Men of business like Burke occasionally suggested appropriate remedies, but they were rare and were not heeded. Extensive political involvement with the masses, or even with people "unknown" to the leaders of the party, was shied away from as somehow degrading or unnecessary by the Whig aristocrat who felt his "character" alone earned him the attention and respect of his countrymen. There seems indeed to have been a psychological barrier, an attitude deeply imbedded in the mid-eighteenth century personality, which prevented Opposition politicians from acting in a manner which, while they felt it to be decidedly inappropriate and perhaps degrading, they must themselves have half-consciously recognized to be essential for the realization of their ambitions.

Nevertheless a decided shift did take place in their political attitudes toward the end of the American war.

---

30. For example, see Archibald S. Foord, *His Majesty's Opposition, 1714–1830* (Oxford, 1964), especially pp. 171–175; and the well-known letter from Burke to C. J. Fox, 8 October 1777, in *The Correspondence of Edmund Burke,* ed. George H. Guttridge (Chicago, 1961), III, 380–388.

By 1784 the newly unified Whig Opposition stopped relying entirely on its own resources and began to seek its strength in the country at large. The student is left with two related questions: Why did the shift occur at all, and why did it occur when it did?

In answering these questions one may employ the traditional mode of explanation by listing the relevant factors which coincided with and seem to have caused a change in the situation. The Rockinghams had been conditioned somewhat to the advantages of party by Burke. Moreover, after nearly twenty years in the wilderness it was a bitter disappointment to be cheated of the gratifications and emoluments of office first by fate, in the death of Rockingham, and then by the king, who dismissed the leaders of the Coalition in a manner which they considered both vindictive and unconstitutional. The Northites could scarcely have been less displeased and frustrated by 1784, for the contrary reason that they were accustomed to office and the favor of the king. The implacably hostile attitude of the king, which was made startlingly clear in the months following December, 1783, added intensity to an already frustrating situation; and ironically, the central role within the party of the strangely lovable and talented Fox made him at once the party's greatest single asset and—by focusing the hostility of the king—its most serious liability. In the negotiations of 1784, and again in 1792, it was clear that Fox was unacceptable to the king (or at least that excuse was easily employed against him, as it had been employed against Pitt's father by Newcastle) and that his indispensable position as the party's leader in the House of Commons threatened to prevent indefinitely his party's return to office.

The experience of 1783 and early 1784 had also given the Coalition's men of business an intensive lesson in political management and perhaps a taste of what might be accomplished by it. During the wildly competitive months of early 1784 they felt compelled to turn to the country, first to publicize a constitutional position in which they felt secure, and then to justify themselves in the face of a mounting tide of public hostility and outrage. To some extent the Whig organization of the later 1780's seems to have been the result of sheer inertia emerging from the struggles of the earlier part of the decade. While organizational activity became increasingly more sporadic after the spring of 1784, it nevertheless continued and increased in variety and sophistication, until it received its next great impetus in the Regency Crisis and the general election which followed in 1790.

Then, finally, the historian can turn to the larger context and note that the development of party organization coincides with and may be related to the humiliation of the American war, the growing sense that something fundamental was amiss in the British political system, and the emerging parliamentary reform and revitalized economical reform movements which aimed at purifying the political life of the nation. If he wishes to wander farther afield in search of explanation, he can further note the contemporary expansion of industrial activity and technology with the accompanying social dislocation and breakdown of traditional patterns of behavior and responsibility. He might suggest that all of this is also linked somehow with the increasingly prominent and obvious role which the Dissenting community, with its deep involvement in the economic, scientific, and technological life of the country, was beginning to play in the constitutional and humanitarian reform movements. Indeed the reform movements, every variety of them, were developing and employing on a national scale a sophisticated array of organizational devices which were difficult to ignore. The movements—while they were not

1

strictly parliamentary—were outwardly oriented and sought their strength in organized and vocal public opinion; and their success made a deep impression upon such politicians as Fox, Sheridan, and their associates, who themselves became caught up in these movements and tried with limited success to divert these energies partially to their own political ends.

But how much have we explained by listing these factors? Have we really explained why the shift occurred at all, and why it occurred when it did? Surely our explanations are partial. We have described conditions which taken together make a shift understandable or, perhaps, possible; but what happens if we take our factors separately? The possibilities for returning to power must have seemed desparate to the Opposition after 1784, as they had to the elder Pitt before 1756; but Pitt's reaction had not been to organize massive strength in the country or to look for his chance to bring in dependable friends at a general election. On the contrary he and his Cousinhood remained introverted. Their field of battle continued to be the House of Commons, and their object was, in the characteristic pattern set by Walpole toward the end of the second decade of the century, to storm the Closet by making the conduct of Government impossible without their support. But significantly, their strategy failed. While they paralyzed debate in the House, they found themselves unable to win divisions. It was the loss of Minorca, a national disaster resulting from an obvious Government blunder, which destroyed the confidence of the House—at least so Newcastle was convinced—and brought the Government down.

Burke's advocacy of party is weakened as explanatory evidence if we remember how early he began to advocate it—more than a decade before the organization began its full development—and how proportionately little weight he carried in the inner counsels of the party after the death of Rockingham, which is the critical period. Indeed the problem becomes more perplexing when we note that since at least the late 1760's the Opposition had been exposed both to the advocacy of coordinated and extended effort and to the examples of organized activity practiced by the Government. Granted that ideas sometimes take a long time to win acceptance, but not invariably. Why should they have in these circumstances? It is not sufficient simply to emphasize that the political pressures of the early 1780's were unusually intense, unless one is then prepared to suggest that political pressure by its nature tends to generate party organization. Sheer pressure surely does not dictate direction of development.

It may be necessary, then, to rely upon all of these factors taken together in the larger context in order to explain the emergence of party organization. For we must note that the shift in political attitude and atmosphere was not peculiarly confined to professional politicians in this period. The entire country was awakening and coming alive politically in the late 1770's and early 1780's—not to mention the 1790's—in a way which was wholly foreign to the middle decades of the century. The taste and style of politics during the last quarter of the century was moving away from that of the 1750's with an increasing rapidity. And, perhaps simply because it was coincidental, this change seems intimately related to comparable changes in the economic, social and even religious life of the nation. But nevertheless, even considering these larger factors, we are left with one further matter for explanation, namely, why did all of these factors converge in the late eighteenth century? It is surely the larger context, in fact, which is the most laden with significance, but which is also the most resistant to adequate explanation.

A historian may at this point turn to comparative studies in order to broaden his context still further. It is perhaps useful and highly suggestive, for example, to learn that during this period party organization began significant development in the former American colonies as well as in Great Britain.[31] R. R. Palmer has indeed suggested that much of the political activity of the later eighteenth century was part of a fundamental change which was at that time occurring throughout the Western world. But comparative studies, while invaluable, are not in themselves sufficient; for the causes of change, even in the expanded context, remain unexplained by sheer enumeration of similar phenomena.[32] With some trepidation it must be admitted that the changes in the quality and forms of political life which we are here considering bear the classic characteristics of a Gestalt shift.[33] People began to see and understand their problems differently, while the elements of their problems remained essentially the same—rather as one suddenly reconstructs the elements of an optical illusion. It may be that in attempting to solve the problem of this shift, as with so many of the problems which confront the historian, it will be necessary to turn increasingly to methodologies and forms of explanation which have been developed outside our own discipline.

31. A foundation for such a comparison has been laid by Noble E. Cunningham's *The Jeffersonian Republicans: The Formation of Party Organization, 1789–1801* (Chapel Hill, N.C., 1957) and *The Jeffersonian Republicans in Power: Party Operations, 1801–1809* (Chapel Hill, N.C., 1963).

32. R. R. Palmer, *The Age of the Democratic Revolution* (Princeton, 1959–1964), 2 vols., where more is in fact attempted than sheer enumeration, but with limited success. *Cf.* J. Godechot, *France and the Atlantic Revolution* (London, 1965).

33. For an interesting application of the principles of Gestalt psychology to a problem of historical change, see N. R. Hanson, *Patterns of Discovery: An Inquiry into the Conceptual Foundations of Science* (Cambridge, 1958).

It may be helpful to conclude this essay with a brief outline of the emergence of party as a permanent feature of British political life in the light of what we now know of politics in the late eighteenth century, and to place this outline within the theoretical framework proposed in the opening pages of this essay. If we begin with the proposition first put forward systematically by Namier and his associates that there were no political parties properly so-called in the middle decades of the eighteenth century, then we must look to the closing years of the American war as the first decisive period of modern party development. But while the transition was dramatic enough, it should be emphasized that it was not altogether abrupt. For example, it could be argued that the Government interest during the earlier period gave indications of being a modern party within the terms discussed in this essay. It displayed rudimentary organization and had a program which it wished to pass into law. But the danger here is in equating "Government" with professional groups in power. The outward orientation displayed to some degree by Government was not necessarily a characteristic of the professional groups, and one should be cautious of assuming that it was when it is recalled that these same groups failed to display outward orientation when returned to the ranks of Opposition. Moreover, there was no real sense of group identity between the Chatham connection, for example, and the Court and Treasury interest. Government was a term comprehending a number of disparate interests and loyalties. Elements of the change which occurred after 1780, then, are to be found during the two preceding decades, and particularly among Government and the Rockingham Whigs; but the broad change itself did not occur until the closing years of the American war.

It should be emphasized, moreover, that the political

change which occurred in the 1780's was organizational. While it is true that the country was undergoing a broad ideological revolution from the late 1770's, the effects of that revolution did not make themselves fully felt on political party alignments and policy until after the outbreak of the French Revolution. The Fox-North Coalition had come, or rather had been thrown together, partly through sheer political self-interest, but also as a result of the American war. Indeed by 1783 the American war had become a good example of what is termed in this essay an anti-party issue. It had temporarily brought together under a single leadership a number of political groups which had nothing in common ideologically. If one looks at the Whig Opposition of 1784–1792 in ideological terms one finds the entire spectrum of contemporary parliamentary opinion, from the ultra-conservative Northites on the right to the liberal and reformist Fox and later Grey and his friends on the left. When the tensions produced by the French Revolution and war forced British political society to realign itself and to act more rigidly in conformity with constitutional principles, the organized but ideologically heterodox Whig Opposition shattered.

The first important phase in the development of modern party, then, occurred during the 1780's, and it was almost wholly an organizational phase. During the early 1790's the Whig Opposition split, and the Foxite remnant, while it continued to develop organizationally, also found itself with a rather high degree of ideological homogeneity on what were to be the fundamental political and constitutional issues of the next four decades. For nearly a decade after the fall of Pitt in 1801, however, and largely due to the resultant shattering of the political right, British politics tended to revert to the personal and factional pattern of the mid-eighteenth century. But from the second decade of the nineteenth century party became an increasingly pervasive factor in British political life, and both organizational technique and ideological polarities continued to develop. The second important phase in the emergence of party occurred in the wake of the first Reform Bill. Even more than the first phase, the second introduced little that was fundamentally new in organizational terms. The significance of the 1830's lay in the extent and intensity with which organizational techniques were developed and applied. Finally the third phase in the emergence of party occurred during the last two decades of the nineteenth century, when British parties entered the classic period of their development.

Two points should be particularly noted from this outline of party development. First, a good deal of stress has been placed on the development of party among the parliamentary opposition. This emphasis is of course partly due to the accidents of research. But it is also a calculated one, for it is surely of far greater significance that a parliamentary opposition should become outwardly oriented and organize itself than that the same should occur within Government. Government has the human and financial resources at its disposal with which to organize, and is constantly under public pressures which should incline it to do so. The same cannot be said for an opposition group, and political organization among such groups must be considered proportionately more significant in that it is less natural and easy to accomplish.

Secondly, it should be noted that the organizational and ideological dimensions of party tended to develop out of phase with each other and not invariably as the result of the same stimuli. This means that the political groupings of the earlier periods are not going to display many of the characteristics which we normally associate with the parties of the late nineteenth century. The Whig Opposition of 1784–1792, for example, was developed organizationally but was totally lacking in ideological homogeneity. Does this mean that it should be placed in a class with the personal groupings or factions of the mid-eighteenth century? Surely not. It was decidedly a different sort of thing, and it had far more in common with the political party of the late nineteenth century than it did with the Bedford or Grenville connections of the earlier period. It is far more useful, and meaningful, to describe it as a party which was in a rudimentary stage of development. Nothing would be served by creating a third category of political phenomena. Nor, so long as important distinctions are kept in mind, is there any real danger of reading back into history what we know of a later period.

Abbreviations

Adam, *Pol. State*

View of the Political State of Scotland in the Last Century. Edited by Sir Charles Elphinstone Adam. Edinburgh, 1887.

Add. MSS.

British Museum Additional Manuscripts.

Debrett

John Debrett, *The Parliamentary Register.*

DNB

Dictionary of National Biography. Edited by Sir Leslie Stephen and Sir Sidney Lee. 22 vols. Oxford, 1921–1922.

Furber, *Dundas*

Holden Furber, *Henry Dundas, First Viscount Melville, 1742–1811.* Oxford, 1931.

H of P

History of Parliament: The House of Commons, 1754–1790. Edited by Sir Lewis Namier and John Brooke. 3 vols. London, 1964.

Mackenzie, *Pol. State*

A View of the Political State of Scotland at the Late General Election. [Edited by A. Mackenzie.] Edinburgh, 1790.

Official Returns

[*Official*] *Return of the Names of Every Member of the Lower House of Parliaments of England, Scotland, Ireland, 1213–1874. Parliamentary Papers, House of Commons,* 1878, vol. LXII, part ii.

Universal British Directory	*Universal British Directory of Trade, Commerce, and Manufacture.* Compiled by Peter Barfoot and John Wilkes. 5 vols. London, 3rd ed., [1797].
Whig Club	*Whig Club, instituted in May, 1784.* London, 1788 and 1792 editions.

The Blair Adam Papers

Lord Elphinstone *to* William Adam
15 *March* 1784

Endorsed: Lord Elphinstone / 15 March 1784— / Concerning
managing / the D of P's Interests in / Scotland

John, 11th Baron Elphinstone (*c.*1739–1794), had estates and
electoral interests in Stirlingshire and Lanarkshire; in Dunbarton-
shire his was the largest interest of the county. Laurence Hill noted
in 1789 that Elphinstone habitually supported Pitt's ministry, but
Hill also observed that "his connections are almost all in Opposition" (Adam, *Pol. State,* pp. 89, 96). His brother, G. K. Elphinstone, was an intimate friend of William Adam and supported
Opposition in the House, while in 1777 his sister Eleanora had
married Adam. The family was also deeply involved in East India
Co. politics through Lord Elphinstone's brother William, whose
successful contest for a directorship of that company in 1786 was at
least partially organized by Adam. In 1784 Lord Elphinstone was
standing his first contest for a seat as a representative Scottish
peer.

Edinburgh Castle 15 March 1784

I wrote you some time ago how much I thought it necessary some person of a certain consideration, and who
was known to be sufficiently attached to the Duke of
Portlands interest should come down & take a lead here
as I was well assured by the activity of the other party,[1]
and the want of such a person the Dukes interest in this
Country suffered considerably. I then mentioned Lord
Stormont [2] as a proper person in my idea for many obvious reasons, failing him I thought Lord Mount Stuart [3]
was very likely to gain friends and give infinite satisfaction. Lord Kelly [4] who is strongly attached to the Portland party has been with me urging the necessity of some

one haveing the entire confidence of the Duke Lord North & Mr Fox being sent without delay as he as well as myself is very confident they have already suffered much and must do much more the nearer it approaches an election. Lord Kelly thinks that should Lord Stormont not be able to come down, Lord Cassillis [5] would be a proper person as he is generally known here. Lord Kelly is to write his own sentiments on this business this night, I have only to say I do wish you would communicate this my oppinion on this score it is evident it can proceed from no interested idea and I am very sensible it must be attended with salutary consequences. I can not tell you how much I am flattered by the success I have mett with on my canvas many more than you could conceive when I tell you I have not wrote but one letter not knowing I should be the object of the attention of either party, I do entreat you as far as you can move in this matter it is of great consequence not only to the return of the Peer's but Burroughs in particular I shall write you tomorrow.

Ever yours
ELPHINSTONE

NOTES

1. Note in this and subsequent letters how "the Duke of Portland's interest" (that is, the political interest of the Fox-North Coalition) is taken to extend potentially throughout the country and to contests which in earlier decades would have been considered quite personal and local. The "other party" refers to the Government.

2. David Murray, 7th Viscount Stormont, later 2nd Earl of Mansfield (1727–1796). Representative peer of Scotland 1761–1793. Diplomatic posts at Dresden, Vienna and Paris. Secretary of State for the southern department, 1779–1782, resigning with North. Stormont was perhaps the most important of the Northite political peers after 1782; he adhered to Opposition until the party split, becoming President of the Council in 1794.

3. John Stuart, Lord Mountstuart (1744–1814). Eldest son of John, 3rd Earl of Bute, the early favorite and minister of George

III. Offensively arrogant and lacking perseverance, but with an ability to inspire confidence in some, he had attempted to assume the leadership in Scottish politics while a member of the lower house in 1775–1776. The attempt failed, but he continued to feel an intense competition with Henry Dundas and the Duke of Buccleuch, who became two of Pitt's principal supporters in Scotland. Perhaps partly because of this rivalry, he supported Opposition after 1784, despite both his own intense dislike for Lord North and his father's strong predilection for any government enjoying the support of the king.

4. Archibald Erskine, 7th Earl of Kellie (1736–1797). Kellie fared very badly the following May in his contest for a seat as a representative peer, see William Robertson, *Proceedings Relating to the Peerage of Scotland* (Edinburgh, 1790), pp. 422–423.

5. David Kennedy, 10th Earl of Cassillis (*c.* 1730–1792). Described by Boswell as "a good honest merry fellow" but no legislator or man of business, he had inherited an important interest in Ayrshire (Adam, *Pol. State,* pp. 19 ff.).

EPILOGUE

The cry of Lord Elphinstone for coordinated Opposition management in Scotland increased during the 1780's, seemingly in proportion to the increasing reputation of Henry Dundas in that sphere. Francis Humberston Mackenzie of Seaforth (1754–1815; M.P. Ross-shire 1784–1790, 1794–1796) was one of the more powerful as well as ambitious political magnates of the north of Scotland. In 1788 William Adam asked him for his support should Adam stand for the Northern Burghs during the next general election. Mackenzie heartily agreed, but in his letter of 8 October (Blair Adam MSS) he hastened to point out the difficulties which every Scottish Opposition magnate faced in returning their candidates. The difficulties were "owing to our party being in total want of any one in Scotland to unite our friends in one common mode of exertion & in short to superintend & manage our politics, while the opposite party have that indefatigable manoeuverer Dundas always at work, never missing the slightest opening for interference, & too too often successfull. Witness Sir J[ames]. G[rant]. who if tolerably managed had been ours till Doomsday—he left us merely as he has because we have no System or regular cooperation in *out Door* business & because individuals unsupported had

5

no chance against individuals supporting & supported." (Regarding the loss of Grant, see Holden Furber, *Henry Dundas, First Viscount Melville, 1742–1811* [Oxford, 1931], pp. 206–214.) On 15 Oct. Mackenzie again wrote to Adam (Blair Adam MSS): "Why do you not spirit up our friends to some active *out door* exertion. Harry Erskine will do me the justice to tell you I have long ago & often urged it & offered to chalk out the way in my part of the world—I have also long ago told him the situation of the Burroughs & Countys in the North—he begins to find me right—Lord McLeod is at the point of Death. It is worth while to consider in that case if we cannot do something in Cromartyshire. At least a little activity & information can do us no harm."

R. Aberdeen *to* William Adam
28 *March* 1784

Aberdeen's identity, the precise nature of his activities on behalf of the Coalition during the previous winter or of Lord Mountstuart's promise to him have unfortunately not been determined. But the following sentence appears in a letter from C. J. Fox to an unknown correspondent, dated St. James's Place, 6 Dec. 1783 (Duke University Library): "You may depend upon my inclination to obey your commands with respect to Mr. Aberdeen, but I will fairly say that I doubt much whether there will be any opening at present, as all the Officers of the India Company [added above line: "in the line for which you recommend him"] will probably be continued." The remainder of the letter—which expresses gratitude for favorable sentiments expressed toward the Coalition Administration and requests an attendance for a division on 8 December—clearly indicates that the recipient was an independent supporter of the Coalition in the lower house, and certainly not William Adam.

Park Lane—Sunday *28th. March 84*

Dear Adam—I received Yours of last night, about an hour ago—The Declaration you made yesterday, did in truth so astonish me, & was so irreconcilable to my own feelings, as well as unexpected from the longest habits of friendship & intercourse, that I am not now surprized at any warm expressions which may have escaped me on the occasion—

Your line of Conduct being now adopted, I have only to contrast my own behaviour, in a political situation, where you was personally engaged—

Some time ago, a proposal was made to me, to stand for Genl. Morris's Seat,[1] on the idea of my having many respectable friends and connections in that quarter, & having formerly had an interference with those Burghs, at Mr. Lockart's[2] election—Independent of interest from my own friends, I was made certain of the late Advocate's[3] fullest wishes & exertions—Being naturally averse to any connection with Scots Burghs, I indeavoured to find out the chances of opposition, & learned to a certainty, you was to be a Candidate—The moment I did so, Did I not go to you, & gave you every friendly information & assistance—One powerful reason that influenced me, previous to that discovery, was the idea of quitting friends & principles, to which I had professed an attachment—Though never manifested by any publick situation—but these were not so powerful with me, as the Opposition to a private friend, with whom I had been connected from the earliest infancy—The return that friend makes to me, is a declaration, "that I must stand the last for even the chance of a seat being provided, & till all the friends of the party are served—" When I said yesterday, "that your party would repent it," You could not do me the injustice to think of my holding an idea of that nature, as *from myself:* Nobdy is more sensible of their own thorough insignificance—but I said so, & trust still, that if no attention is paid to Lord Mountstuarts promise, he & his connections would resent it—Had it even not been an *engagement,* but only a *wish,* I perhaps too vainly imagine, some further consideration might have been due to him—

You flattered me, in the course of the Winter, that my trivial services had been so useful, that I had the best claim on Mr. Fox's favor, when oportunity occurred—if my zeal had not been so forward, I should not have met the displeasure of several friends, who thought it then, as it now proves, in my situation, ridiculous:

One thing I may draw to your recollection, that on Tuesday evening I pressed you to obtain a final & positive answer from Mr. Fox—Your answer was, "I cannot answer it to night, or even tomorrow; but in 48 hours, Depend on it, as your situation with all its circumstances shall be fully laid before them"—

If this affair terminates in disappointment, I stand neglected & deserted by your party, & have justly (from interference) lost the confidence & friendship of the other —If it shall be so, I have to wish you complete satisfaction in your publick friendships, & hope that you may never regret the loss of private attachments—When the hour of publick business subsides, private reflection may tell you, that I am an ill used Man—

Yours &c &c

R: ABERDEEN

Wm. Adam Esqr

NOTES

1. Staats Long Morris (1728–1800) was M.P. Elgin Burghs 1774–1784 on the Gordon interest. He was succeeded in that seat by Adam in 1784.

2. Thomas Lockhart (1739–1775) had been elected in March 1771 on the Government interest, but was defeated by Morris in 1774.

3. Henry Erskine (1746–1817), second son of Henry, 10th Earl of Buchan, and elder brother of Thomas, later first Lord Erskine and Chancellor under the Talents Ministry. Henry had been Lord Advocate of Scotland under the Coalition. Oddly

enough, though he was a highly personable man of great talents and wished to enter Parliament, he was able to sit in the House for only a few months during 1806–1807. After the fall of the Coalition in December 1783 he was thought of by Oppositionists in Scotland as the party's principal man of business residing continuously in the North. As a result he was looked to and did tend to take the lead in managing the Opposition interest in that area.

William Adam *to* R. Aberdeen
30 *March* 1784

Draft in an unknown clerk's hand with ms corrections by Adam.

30th. March 84.

Dear Aberdeen

I received your Letter on Sunday Evening when I was at Elphinston's at dinner, & have not since had time to write—

As the conversation which passed between us gave rise to my first Letter, it is a natural consequence that your Letter should give rise to this, First of all I must say that I shall be extremely sorry that any altercation should arise between us by Letter or otherwise; or that upon a clear understanding of the case our intercourse should not be as cordial as ever.

I am ready to acknowledge your personal kindness to me to any extent, in rejecting a proposal to oppose me, but I cannot admit that there is any parrallel between that and my Situation as acting for others, For had I by any underhandealing or partiality perferred you to those I described in my last Letter (and I could not have done it otherwise) I should have deserved every degree of Reprobation from so Glaring a breach of Trust—

As to my declarations "that you were to stand the last

9

of all the friends of the Party for even the Chance of being provided in a Seat," Neither my Letter nor any expression in Conversation authorize such any explanation of my meaning. My Expressions are "My first rule therefore was to take care that those who had lost their Seats in the last Parliament should upon equal terms, by preferred in the next, to any other Person. After those such as I knew to be attached to the Party, & whom from Private friendship I wished to succeed because I knew their Principles, Keeping this rule in View I can assure you I always had your Name uppermost in my thoughts and Suggestions. But I could not without an Absolute Breach of Trust Put it before many Persons who were in the Situation I have discribed." My Situation is different from what you seem to conceive it, Had I any Place of my own to dispose of Your Reasoning might have some foundation, But I am Not disposing of what is my Own, I am only indeavouring to the best of my power to assist in the regulation of what may fall within the power of others to dispose of.

I can assure You I think now as I thought then, that I did You no more than justice, when I said in the Course of the Winter that your Services had been very usefull, nor did I confine that declaration to Your Self only, I said it where I thought it could realy Serve You, and had the Change of Administration not taken Place I can assure You that you would have found that I had kept back the eager Sollicitations of some of my Nearest connections, that you might have no Competitor (as far as in me lay) to the object you then had in view.

I faithfully fullfilled my promise in speaking to Mr. Fox and put into his hands your Note on Wednesday last; And stated every circumstance of your Case, From that time till Sunday Night he was so much engaged, that I did not see him, But in the interim I mentioned you repeatedly to the Duke of Portland, on Sunday

Night again to Mr. Fox, But while Sir G. Elliot,[1] Mr. Beckford,[2] Mr. Tollemache,[3] Sir R. Payne,[4] Mr. Lushington [5] & many others, all of whom have lost their Seats, and are willing to go farther than You to be returned again, And the last of whom paid a very great sum for a three Months Seat only, are unprovided. I cannot Possibly think I should be justifyed in Any degree, or by any Person in Acting otherwise than I have done, And I am sure a contrary conduct would have rendered me undeserving of any Private friendship whatever, I can assure you therefore that my Opinion Cannot alter when the hour of Public Business Subsides, nor will private reflection tell me that you have been an ill used man as far as I am concerned, My Conduct is founded on mature reflection & as I am convinced on the immutable principles of rectitude. I wish to make no Observation upon Your Reflection that you wish me Complete Satisfaction in my Public friendships and hope I may never regret the loss of private Attachment, Because I am perfectly conscious that no Circumstance bears you out in making it, And to observe upon it might encrease that difference which I wish to ⟨see⟩ allayed.

NOTES

1. Sir Gilbert Elliot had withdrawn before the poll in Roxburghshire. He subsequently tried Leominster, Bridgwater, Berwickshire, Forfarshire and Newtown without success and was unable to return to Parliament until September 1786.

2. Richard Beckford (d. 1796), the West India merchant and 1st (illegitimate) son of alderman William Beckford (the supporter of Chatham), had been member for the expensive and unpredictable Bridport. He did not stand during the general election of 1784 (H of P), though he was prepared to do so (see the following document) ; but in June 1784 he was returned unopposed for Arundel when Lord Surrey chose to continue sitting for Carlisle. Surrey—later 11th Duke of Norfolk, like Beckford a staunch Foxite and a supporter of parliamentary reform—had been elected for Arundel and Hereford as well as his old seat at Carlisle.

3. Wilbraham Tollemache (1739–1821), 2nd son of the 4th

Earl of Dysart, had sat for Northampton 1771–1780 on the interest of his cousin, Lord Spencer. In 1780 his uncle by marriage, Shelburne, had obtained him a seat from Edward Eliot at Liskeard; but in 1783 he followed his Spencer connections into opposition to Shelburne and support of the Fox-North Coalition. As a result Eliot refused to return him in 1784. He was never subsequently provided with a seat, despite the occasional concern of Opposition to do so.

4. Sir Ralph Payne (1739–1807), eldest son of an old established West Indian family, had been a staunch supporter of the Grafton and North governments. In 1780 he had been returned for Plympton on the Government interest and at considerable expense. In 1784 he was a supporter of the opposition to Pitt and thus found himself without Government support. He failed to secure another seat until 1795.

5. Stephen Lushington (1744–1807), a director of the East India Company almost without interruption from 1782 to 1805, several times chairman, and a leading supporter of the Portland interest in the company. In December 1783 he had been returned for Hedon at the recommendation of Portland and Fitzwilliam on the interest of the Rockinghamite Beilby Thompson. In 1784 he contested Hastings, but without success.

Memorandum—[1784]

Endorsed: List of Persons desiring / Seats in Parliament / 1784
The memorandum and endorsement are in Adam's hand. The list cannot be dated precisely; but the absence of Sir G. Elliot and Tollemache suggests an original date earlier than 30 March, while the placing of Wrightson at Marlow rather than Aylesbury indicates a date earlier than 27 March.

Of the forty-four persons listed on this memorandum, seven had held Government or Pittite seats during the Parliament of 1780 and were now forced to look elsewhere. Sir Gilbert Elliot and Wilbraham Tollemache should be added to this number. The pressure to seat these people, and the insecurity which most Northites must have felt in finding themselves suddenly Country rather than Court at the time of an election, may go far in explaining the immediate impetus toward organization in the spring of 1784.

Eleven of the forty-four found seats at the general election or shortly thereafter. One, John Stephenson, turned out to be Pittite and was crossed off the list. Thirty-two were not returned.

Persons who will not stand a Contest

Mr Beckford 3000. or 600 a yr.
Lord Melbourne [1]–
Lord Maitland [2]
Mr Aberdeen [crossed out]
Mr Lushington–Ld Fitzm.[3]
Sir R. Payne–3000
Sir G. Coopar [4] £1000
Ld Grandison [5]–
Conway [6]–
Mr Stephenson [crossed out] [7]
Major Gale.[8]–3000 or 3500 possibly
Mr Ord [9] 2500.
Mr Snow–2500.
Mr Mackay.[10] 2500. London Fields Hackney
Mr Aberdeen 2500
Mackay 2500 [name and figure crossed out]

Persons who will stand a Contest.

Lord C. Fitzgerald [11]
Mr Cotsford– [12]   Hindon
Mr. R. Wilbraham [13]
Col: Keating [14]   Wallingford
Sir G. Webster [15]   Aylesbury.
Genl Dalrymple [16]   Ipswich
Sir A. Hammond [17]
Mr Salt [18]   Aldborrough
Mr Parkyns [19]   Stockbridge
J. Wilkinson [20]
Mr Snow [crossed out]   Sudbury [21] [crossed out]
Mr Adey [22]

Mr Birt   Wells [23]
L. Damer [24]
Mr Fisher–
Sir N. Nugent [25]   Aylesbury [crossed out]
Mr Trecothic 2500
Mr O'Byrne–any money [26]
Mr Stephenson [crossed out]
Mr Baillie– [27]   Honiton
Lord Grandison [crossed out]
P. Wyndham– [28]   Taunton
Major Gale [crossed out]
Bond Hopkins. 3000 G^s [29]
Mr Beckford [crossed out]
Lord Templeton [added later] [30]
Genl. Fletcher–   Mibourne [sic] Port
Mr Blair £2500 [31]   Wells [crossed out]
Mr Bruce 3000
Mr W. Elphinstone [32]   Stirling &c—lost.
Mr Aberdeen 2500 [name and figure crossed out]
Mr Bond any money   Honiton
Mr Wrightson– [33]   Marlow
Major Webber 3000
Lord Macdonald [34]   Milbourne Pt
Mr Taylor–   Aylesbury.

NOTES

1. Peniston Lamb, 1st Viscount Melbourne (1745–1828), a Gentleman of the Bedchamber to the Prince of Wales and supporter of the Coalition. He had been member for the Pittite George Selwyn's pocket borough of Ludgershall. In 1784 he was returned unopposed for Malmesbury, where the patron temporarily deserted Government and sold both seats to Opposition.

2. James, Viscount Maitland, later 8th Earl of Lauderdale (1759–1839). An outspoken supporter and intimate friend of Fox, and perhaps for this reason he did not stand again for the Duke of Northumberland's borough of Newport (Cornwall) in 1784. He was instead able to negotiate an unopposed return at Malmesbury.

3. William Wentworth Fitzwilliam, 2nd Earl Fitzwilliam

(1748–1833), nephew and heir to the estates and local political interests of Lord Rockingham. He was the most intimate of Portland's personal connections.

4. Sir Grey Cooper (c. 1726–1801), Secretary to the Treasury 1765–March 1782 and a lord of the Treasury April–December 1783, had sat in the House since 1765 on either a Treasury or Admiralty interest. In December 1783 he had followed North into opposition and was thus without a seat at the general election. He was again brought into Parliament only in 1786 for one of Sir Thomas Dundas's seats at Richmond.

5. George Villiers, 2nd Earl Grandison (1751–1800), had supported Government while member for Ludlow 1774–1780, though he was frequently absent. He declined standing in 1780 because he was abroad. The *H of P* describes him as "a spoilt only child" who "early developed extravagant tastes." He married a daughter of the 1st Earl of Hertford, which perhaps helped to incline him toward Opposition in 1784.

6. Probably one of the Seymour Conways, sons of the 1st Earl of Hertford. George, Hugh, or Robert seem most likely, since Henry and William stood contests in 1784. All were returned but William, to whom Henry gave way in 1785.

7. Probably John Stephenson (?1709–1794), London merchant in the Spanish and Portuguese trade and a seeker of government contracts. He had closely identified himself politically with Lord Sandwich since his political debut in the 1750's. Returned for Tregony on Treasury interest 1780–1784, he supported North, opposed Shelburne, and supported the Coalition. He suddenly deserted Sandwich when the Coalition fell and supported Pitt; thus he is crossed off this Opposition list.

8. Possibly Henry Richmond Gale of Bardsea Hall, Lancashire, who was promoted Lt. Col. in 1794 (*Universal British Directory*, I, cxviii). Gale joined the Whig Club in April, 1790 (*Whig Club*, 1792 ed.); he was never returned to the House.

9. John Ord (1729–1814), who had been returned for Midhurst 1774 and Hastings 1780 on Administration interest. A consistent supporter of North's government, he voted for Shelburne's peace preliminaries and for Fox's East India bill and went into opposition with the Coalition. In 1784 he was returned for Wendover after a contest; the electors of that borough were in revolt against the financially embarrassed Lord Verney and the margin at the polls was overwhelming. Ord reportedly paid £3000 for the seat. Although he had opposed the Portlandite Verney in this contest, he supported Opposition in the Parliament of 1784.

10. Robert Mackey of London Fields, Hackney, was a livery-

man of the City of London and a member of the Joiner's Company (*Universal British Directory,* V, 89). A Robert Mackey of Tawin, Herts, joined the Whig Club in April, 1786 (*Whig Club,* 1792 ed.). He never sat in the House.

11. Lord Charles James Fitzgerald (1756–1810), second surviving son of James, 1st Duke of Leinster, one of the leading Irish Whig families. It is not known if Lord Charles stood in 1784; he sat only briefly in 1807.

12. Edward Cotsford (1740–1810), a nabob, returned to England in 1781 with a considerable fortune. He contested the expensive Hindon in December, 1783, and again in 1784, but was badly defeated on both occasions. Returned for Midhurst without a contest when a vacancy occurred in June, 1784, he voted consistently against Pitt.

13. Roger Wilbraham (1743–1829) was connected with the erratically ambitious and volatile Sir Francis Basset (who normally supported the North government and later the Portland opposition) and in 1784 contested both Truro and Mitchell on Basset's interest. Defeated at Truro, he gained a double return at Mitchell, but lost on petition. He was returned for Helston in April, 1786, and actively supported Opposition.

14. Thomas Keating unsuccessfully contested Wallingford at a bye-election in January, 1784. He joined the Whig Club the following June (*Whig Club,* 1788 ed.). According to the *H of P,* Wallingford was not contested during the general election. Keating stood at Great Marlow instead and was again badly defeated.

15. Sir Godfrey Webster, 4th Bt. (1748–1800), was a prominent figure in the reform movement in Sussex and was by this period connected with Fox. In 1784 he canvassed Bedford on Lord Upper Ossory's interest and unsuccessfully contested Hastings against Treasury candidates. In 1785 and 1786 he contested Seaford on the interest of Lord Pelham, who was trying to wrest control from the Treasury; he was seated on petition in 1786. The *H of P* describes Aylesbury as "squalid and venal, and without an established patron." In 1784 the Government and Opposition each returned a member for the borough, the Foxite being William Wrightson, who is listed in this document for Marlow.

16. William Dalrymple (1736–1807), younger brother of the 5th Earl of Stair. Upon returning from the campaign in North America he stood a successful contest at the general election for the Wigtown Burghs on his brother's interest, an interest which had returned William Adam for that constituency in 1780. He was listed as "doubtful" by Adam in his analysis of the Commons in

May, 1784, but he voted with Opposition on the Regency. An Opposition candidate does not appear to have come forward at Ipswich in 1784, though the "yellow" interest was at that time in search of a gentleman to contest the second seat.

17. Sir Andrew Snape Hamond, 1st Bt. (1738–1828), son of a shipowner and himself a naval officer. Governor of Nova Scotia 1780–1783 and Commander-in-chief at the Nore 1785–1788. His political sentiments in 1784 are unknown. He was not returned to the House until 1796.

18. Samuel Salt (c. 1723–1792) of the Inner Temple. He was the legal agent to Edward Eliot of Port Eliot and sat on his interest at Liskeard 1768–1784. Salt deviated from Eliot, who supported Shelburne and Pitt, by voting against Shelburne's peace preliminaries and for Fox's India bill. Perhaps partly for this reason (though Salt had been permitted to support Opposition while Eliot held office under North), Eliot did not return Salt in 1784. Instead Salt bought a seat at Aldeburgh from P. C. Crespigny, to whom Salt may have been introduced by Crespigny's brother, who had been a director of the South Sea Company during Salt's governorship (but see note 21 below). Salt supported Opposition during the Parliament of 1784.

19. Thomas Boothby Parkyns (1755–1800). "A friend of the Prince of Wales and connected with the leaders of Opposition, Parkyns carried his election at Stockbridge [1784] against the Government; and voted against them in the House" (H of P).

20. Jacob Wilkinson (c. 1716–1791), a wealthy London merchant and heavy speculator in government loans, director of East India Company 1782–1783. M.P. Berwick 1774–1780, Honiton 1781–1784. He voted with the Opposition to North's ministry, against Shelburne's peace preliminaries, and for Fox's India bill in which he was named as one of the nine assistant commissioners. He resigned his India directorship during the furor over this bill, and the H of P finds no evidence of his having stood during the general election of 1784.

21. Philip Champion Crespigny was thought to have a substantial interest in Sudbury at this time. He had supported North's government, opposed Shelburne's peace preliminaries, supported Fox's India bill and was to oppose Pitt in the Parliament of 1784. Sudbury's having been temporarily considered as a seat for Snow suggests that either Adam or someone in the party approached Crespigny for support in returning Opposition candidates at Sudbury and Aldeburgh (see note 18, above).

22. Stephen Thurston Adey (d. 1801), a banker in Pall Mall,

M.P. Higham Ferrers 1798–1801. On 17 November 1783 Portland proposed both him and Lushington to Lord Fitzwilliam as suitable candidates for Hedon, explaining that Lushington would be the more useful candidate "by his being able to assist us with his voice as well as his vote" but urging deep obligations which he felt toward Adey (Milton MSS, Northamptonshire Record Office). He joined the Whig Club 7 March 1785 (*Whig Club,* 1788 ed.).

23. William Beckford of Fonthill and Clement Tudway, who by this period controlled one seat in the borough, were returned for Wells in 1784, apparently without a contest.

24. Lionel Damer (1748–1807), 3rd son of Joseph, 1st Baron Milton. Damer and his brothers were close friends of Fox and particularly of Lord Fitzwilliam, voting with Opposition after 1784 despite the politics of their father and his relations, the Sackvilles. Lionel had been seeking a seat since 1783, but was brought in for Peterborough by Fitzwilliam only in 1786.

25. Probably Sir Nicholas Nugent, Bt., who joined the Whig Club in June, 1784 (*Whig Club,* 1788 ed.). He did not sit in the House.

26. Not identified, but see *The Historical and Posthumous Memoirs of Sir Nathaniel William Wraxall, 1772–1784,* ed. H. B. Wheatley (London, 1884), V, 381–382.

27. A John Bailey contested Honiton in 1784, but was badly beaten.

28. Percy Charles Wyndham (1757–1833), 2nd son of Charles, 2nd Earl of Egremont, was returned for Chichester in 1782 on the Duke of Richmond's interest. In 1783 he deserted Richmond, who remained in Shelburne's and Pitt's governments, and followed Fox. The 1st Earl of Egremont had possessed a considerable interest in Taunton. There appears to have been no contest in the borough in 1784; Hammet and Popham, the two members returned, represented the independent interest, which had opposed Government candidates in earlier contests. Wyndham was not returned until 1790.

29. Benjamin Bond Hopkins (?1745–1794), son of a Turkey merchant and inheritor of the considerable Hopkins estates through his wife. An unsuccessful candidate in 1780 at Oxford and in 1783 in Surrey, where he had substantial property, he successfully contested Ilchester on the Lockyer interest in 1784. He was classed as "Opposition" in Adam's analysis of May, 1784, but voted with Pitt on the Regency (his only recorded "party" vote).

30. Clotworthy Upton, 1st Baron Templeton (1721–1785). He was not returned.

31. An Alexander Blair, of Portland Place, joined the Whig Club in January, 1785 (*Whig Club,* 1788 ed.), but Blair is a common surname.

32. William Fullarton Elphinstone (1740–1834), 3rd son of Charles, 10th Baron Elphinstone, and a brother-in-law of William Adam. He was elected an East India director in 1786 with Adam's assistance. He was not returned in 1784.

33. William Wrightson (1752–1827). Portland recommended him to Sir William Lee on 27 March 1784 as a candidate for Aylesbury, describing him as "a gentleman of as independent principles as fortune." He was successfully returned for that borough without a contest and supported Opposition in the Parliament of 1784. A contest at Marlow fell instead to the luckless Thomas Keating (see note 14, above).

34. Alexander, 1st Baron Macdonald (*d.* 1795), possessed large estates and interest in Inverness-shire. Described by Hill in 1789 as "quite independent," Macdonald had some Opposition connections, though his younger brother, Archibald Macdonald, had married into the Gower family and followed their political lead (*H of P;* Adam, *Pol. State,* 172). T. H. Medlycott, the patron of Milborne Port, returned two Government candidates in 1784. Lord Macdonald was not returned.

Laurence Hill *to* William Adam
4 *January* 1789

Address: William Adam Esqr / M.P. Lincolns Inn fields / London
Endorsed: L. Hill / 4th. Jany 1789 / on The Rolls of /
Scotch Counties

The following correspondence of Laurence Hill reveals that he was the unidentified compiler of the *View of the Political State of Scotland in the Last Century, a Confidential Report on the Political Opinions, Family Connections, or Personal Circumstances of the 2662 County Voters in 1788.* The *Political State* was edited and published in Edinburgh by Sir Charles Elphinstone Adam in 1887. The contents of this invaluable compilation run to 353 published pages and include not only political data on a high percentage of the enrolled freeholders listed but also contain prognostications and evaluations of future contests in the counties, indicating the nature and extent of the principal county interests, how they may be expected to align themselves and, in some instances, how they might be increased or attacked at a Michaelmas meeting of the county head court.

Dear Sir

I have been employed for several weeks past in preparing a political state of every county in Scotland showing the names of the several freeholders distinguishing the absolute & confidential voters and by whom the confidential votes are made with a short scale at the end of each county showing at one view the present political force of each individual.—This work is in considerable forwardness; twelve of the counties I have already completed and in the course of a month or perhaps less I hope I shall be able to complete the whole. It has been attended with much trouble & a good deal of expense for access to the Rolls & Minutes of Freeholders but I do not in the least grudge this.—When completed it will form a neat octavo volume and I mean to interleave it for notes & remarks on the circumstances situation & connections of each freeholder which may influence his political conduct —there are men of business here who have a pretty general acquaintance in each county and through their information I do not despair in a very short time of making these notes & remarks pretty complete.

I dare say you will be sensible of the great advantages of this state to any Minister or Secretary who is to have a superintendance of the government & affairs of Scotland —It is only however a man of business who can make the proper use of it—It is a book for a desk and not for a table or a parlour window—I intend one copy for you another for the Dean of faculty [1]—additions & alterations must be made on it after every Michaelmas head court [2] and therefore I mean to renew it every year in the humble expectation that in the arrangements your friends when in power may have occasion to make it will be thought proper to make some provision for a service of this kind —which must indeed be equally beneficial to a party whether in or out of power—and I hope you will not think there is any meaness or impropriety in my mentioning this—

Indeed the state I am now preparing forms but a part of a much larger & more comprehensive plan I have had for some time in contemplation viz. to show in one view not only the *present* political state of each county but what force each Individual *might* exert by splitting & subdividing his estate—Two of the counties viz. Renfrew & Dunbarton I have already laid down on this great scale and I have made great progress with ⟨Stirlingshire⟩ and have made notes & extracts from the ⟨Records⟩ respecting other counties but in the present uncertain state of the political law of Scotland there is perhaps little occasion to look farther than the Rolls as they now stand, besides the larger state I have mentioned will require a very long time to bring it to perfection and will be attended with so heavy an expense and would take me so much off my profession that I am afraid to think of it—At any rate the other work which I expect to complete in a month is of more immediate use, and indeed can alone be of use if an election comes on before Summer 1790.—

> I have the honor to be
> very respectfully Dear Sir
> Your most obedient humble Servant
> LAURENCE HILL

Edin 4 Jany 1789.

NOTES

1. Henry Erskine had been elected Dean of the Faculty of Advocates in December 1785, succeeding Henry Dundas.
2. In Scotland the rolls of county freeholders were made up and

subjected to revision each Michaelmas at the meeting of the county head court. The Scottish electoral franchise before the reform of 1832 was so complex that the county rolls were continuously either undergoing or being threatened with revision, and the meetings of the Michaelmas head court were annual trials of political strength in the county, their outcomes frequently being decisive and therefore of more political significance than the electoral contests which followed.

William Adam *to* John Adam of Maryburgh—[8 *January* 1789]

Address: London Jany Ninth 1789 / John Adam Esqr. / Edinr / W Adam
Postmarked: JA 9 89 *and* JA 12
Endorsed: W. A. Junr. / Londo. Jan 9. 1789 / S.
The eighth of January, 1789, fell on a Thursday.

The office of Secretary to the Treasury, which Portland intended that Adam hold in the event a Regency Government was established, was the same office held during North's administration by John Robinson, whose organizational activities on behalf of the Government during general elections have long been well known (see Thomas W. Laprade, ed., *The Parliamentary Papers of John Robinson, 1774–1784,* Camden Society, 3rd series, Vol. XXXIII [London, 1922]).

Thursday Night

My Dear father

I am absolutely determined to delay writing You no longer, & rather curtail a little Sleep than do it. Things have been so strange that a description of the to's & fro's is impossible. But what you may have heard from Report was actually fact & I meant long since had not things so broke in upon it to have told you so—The Whole party

with one voice & the Duke of Portland with the greatest
affection said no person could do so meritorious an act as
I would if I would undertake the Office of Secretary to
the Treasury. The many handsome things that were said
as to my Capacity to discharge that office need not be
enumerated, nor the flattering things as to my having
higher pretensions in point of Rank—as to profit there
are few better for it is little short of £4000 per Anm. I
considered that I had a Profession to quit that I had a
family to take care off. I found my situation such as to
make it improper to attempt to take Rank in My Profession, & my political Knowledge & Society such as would be
drawing me perpetually aside from my Legal pursuits until things were well settled. My Old Place [1] beneath me
—and place of more dignity incompatible with the Law.
Much time likely to be spent in the same way as if I were
Secretary to the Treasury without profit but with Loss, &
without the same effect & good consequences. I found no
Bar or difficulty to Securing to my family such Sinecures
as I was well entitled to from Labouring in the Office &
quitting a Profession. I found too that that Profession
was not so enlivening as it had been & that I considered it
to be rather like a Stagnate Water which was evaporat-
ing or at least fed with Small Springs than as a very Plen-
tifull & continually flowing Spring. All these things were
before me when the King was thought to be in a way not
to live & all these had made me take my determination.
Since then much has been to be done & who was there to
do it. I could not Stand by & let the cause suffer. I was as
it were called forth by all descriptions, from the Prince
who is to reign to the lowest person in the Party. I could
do nothing less than act. Without doing it neither any
thing within or without the House of Commons would
have been brought forward or executed.

In short I have been Secretary to Treasury Since this
Stir began without a Salary. The consequence of which

has been our exertions in the City, our Exertions in Surry Our Exertions at Dover. A Thousand Subordinate Arrangements & Businesses—& the keeping together even such a House as we have had.

Things however are so far Altered & are on a footing less secure & yet You will see I think that I cannot be the Person to object now or to change even if it were adviseable—I am told by all that I alone can do the duties of the Station. The Parliament is likely to restrain the Prince from granting reversions. Can I, because I cannot be adequately secured owing to Pitt's infamy not my friends fault withdraw from a Station because I am less Secure & it becomes more difficult. In proportion as its difficulty encreases I feel More necessity to go on & more delicacy about withdrawing. Now as to the real State of Things. You may have heard for I understand the Doctrine is Dundas's that we are not to last six Months. If so it is but a short interruption to the Profession. But that is not my speculation. The Restrictions render Government weaker. But they don't render it so weak in reality as in appearance. The Court Places chiefly affect the House of Lords. There are but few in the House of Commons affected by it. The state of the Country is much Changed & much within a few Years. The funded interest the Trading interest the Manufacturing interest much overbalance the Landed interest & have sunk it. The Court governed this last. The Treasury governs the former. The great annual Revenue to be collected is a powerfull Engine. The interests [of] those Classes flow all from the Political Places—Revenue—Navy—Army. Therefore in this country now, Power & Popularity must go together & unless We are powerfull we shall never be popular. When Mr Pitt is no longer Powerfull he will not be so popular, & he will find it very difficult, if we go on prudently & wisely, to raise an opposition on any principle to a Government which he has crippled. These things lead me to think that we shall be more Permanent than they are

24

willing to believe & I am sure whatever the other side says they think so too otherwise there would not have been all this Stir about restraining. They know what the Aversion or favour of a reigning Prince can do. And the[y] Must dread that when united to The Talents we have—The Blood & the Property. 5 Powerfull Dukes ² & Many Earls.

I would have gone into private Affairs but I must leave this for another occasion it is now very late & I have discussed all the Most interesting Matter—So May God Bless & preserve you all of all Descriptions & Ages

W.A.

NOTES

1. Adam had been Treasurer of the Ordnance September, 1780–May, 1782, April–December, 1783.

2. The Dukes of Norfolk, Bedford, Portland, Devonshire and (after having struck a bargain for his supporters, the Armed Neutrality) Northumberland voted with Opposition on the Regency question (John Stockdale, *Debates in the House of Lords on the Subject of a Regency* [London, 1789], p. 190).

Lord Sandwich *to* [Duke of Portland?] [10 *January* 1789?]

Endorsed: Lord Sandwich / January 9th.

The only election to occur on a Wednesday in January from 1784 to 1790 was the bye-election for Dover which was held on 14 January 1789. The preceding Saturday was 10 January. Henniker's Dover connection seems to confirm this subject and date.

My Lord

In consequence of a letter I recieved a few hours ago from Mr Adam I enclose a letter for Sir R : Pearson,¹ I know not his direction.

I have not the least objection to writing to Sir J : Hennicker,² but he is I believe, at Thornham near Ipswich & it seems to me impossible that any letter written to day can be of any use in an Election that is to come on next Wednesday. I wish these intimations had come to me sooner, as I think I could have been of much use in this Election if I had had timely notice. I am

Your Graces

Most faithfull

Humble servant

Saturday evening   SANDWICH

NOTES

1. Perhaps Sir Richard Pearson (1731–1806), a naval officer (*DNB*).

2. Sir John Henniker (1724–1803), M.P. Sudbury 1761–1768 and Dover 1774–1784 on the Government interest. A wealthy Russia merchant and government contractor, he had remained loyal to North after his fall. Sandwich had been writing letters of this type to Henniker and a small group of M.P.'s with East India interests since 1761.

Richard Troward *to* William Adam
[11 *January* 1789]

Endorsed: Mr Troward. / 12th Jany 1789. / Laid before the / Duke. Same day / answered— / Parliamentary Investig[ation]s / His own Object

Richard Troward was a prominent London solicitor who seems to have specialized in parliamentary practice and was well known to the leaders of the party and its men of business. He was solicitor to the Managers of the Hastings impeachment and was also currently representing George Tierney on the Colchester committee of the House of Commons.

Dear Adam,

My time must be yours, as yours is so much more important—I think you will approve the plan I propose to set going, and the more so as it will save you a great deal of trouble—I find it will be very useful to know who are the agents in town for the Attorneys ⟨below⟩ in the different Countys (as they generally are the people who influence the open Boroughs.) I have therefore collected them all from the Common Bail and appearance Rolls into my Pocket book, distinguishing which are Under Sheriffs.

The Maps too I have got done which I find very useful, as it shews names and situations without opening a book.

It was not my intention to have said a word about myself 'till it had been seen that my Services would apologize for it and then perhaps it might have been unnecessary—If Mr. Walpole [1] does not accept the office I spoke of before, namely Secretary and Register to Chelsea Board, it is what we shall be very glad of; I say we, for Mr. Wallis [2] and I are equally interested in all business matters—this office is less an object to others than us, as it vacates a Seat and the constant acting Governors (Mr. Molleson & Sir John Dick) are our particular friends.

If you think it proper, pray do me the favor to mention this to the Duke, and what makes me trouble you on the subject now is, that I may not be too late—

Dear Adam
Yours most truly
RD. TROWARD
Pall Mall Sunday morng.

PS. Mr. Molleson dines with me, I am sorry we are not to see you.

NOTES

1. Horatio Walpole (1752–1822) of Wolterton, a connection and supporter of the Duke of Portland, had been secretary and registrar of Chelsea Hospital in 1783.

2. Albany Wallis was the law partner of Troward (*Universal British Directory*, I, V).

Henry Erskine *to* William Adam
14 *January* 1789

Col. Hugh Montgomerie, a Pittite, had been returned for Ayrshire in 1784. The "long promised office" was the inspectorship of military roads in Scotland. According to Laurence Hill in early 1789 the leading interests in Ayrshire were the Earls of Eglintoun, Glencairn, and Dumfries, Sir Adam Fergusson and Sir John Whitefoord. The Earl of Cassillis also carried great weight. Although Ayrshire had more voters than any county in Scotland (200), the politics of the county depended to a large extent upon the shifting pattern of alliances between these principal interests. In January, 1789, it appeared that Glencairn and Dumfries would go with Opposition. Cassillis was strongly in support of his cousin, Sir Andrew Cathcart, who was to be the Opposition candidate at the general election (Cathcart had declared his candidacy by mid-October, before the Regency Crisis had begun [Henry Erskine to William Adam, 19 October 1788, Blair Adam MSS]). Eglintoun was said to have "lately divided with H.R.H. the Prince of Wales's friends against Mr. Pitt, but he was bound by a previous agreement to support Sir Adam Fergusson," who at this date was expected to be the Pittite candidate at the next election. (John Stockdale, *Debates in the House of Lords on the Subject of the Regency,* p. 191, lists both Eglintoun and Cassillis with the Opposition on 26 December 1788). Laurence Hill noted that Whitefoord "has separated from Sir Adam, whom he once supported, and is desirous of representing the County himself." In the event Montgomerie did not receive his office till the late summer, when a bye-election was held. Cathcart, Whitefoord, and James Boswell of Auchinleck then declared themselves to be candidates, but Government was able to bring in William MacDowall as a stop-gap for Fergusson, who was returned for the seat at the general election in 1790 without a contest. See Adam, *Pol. State,* pp. 18–42; *H of P;* Mackenzie, *Pol. State,* p. 60.

Edinr. Jany 14. 1789

My Dear Adam.

It is strongly rumoured here that Col. Montgomery is immediately to have the long promised Office which is said can be given by the Treasury alone without the

Kings Sign manual. If this be true We shall have an *immediate* Election for Ayrshire—Our Situation there is very critical. I meant to have communicated it to Ld. Cassilis But for reasons that will readily occur to you I rather wish to say nothing to him till the opening shall be certain. If you find it to be so I beg you will immediately see the Peer, and let him know that I am perfectly certain that if Sir Jn. Whiteford goes against us we shall be beat & that if he be with us we are secure.—I have done all I can to prevail with Sir John to give Sir Andw Cathcart an unconditional Support. But in vain. He insists on his original proposal to Lord C. of having the two or three first Sessions of the next Parliament. And says without this he will however unwillingly join the foe.—

I am clear that were Sir John ensured of being speedily provided for he would give up this Idea. Should this be impossible Ld. Cassilis must determine whether rather than lose all he would not promise Sir John the two first Sessions and trust to these two Contingencies[1] either providing for him before a General Election or its turning out impossible to carry him from Sir Andws. Friends refusing to transfer—And if this plan be adopted it is to be stipulated that if Sir John cannot be carried he must Support Sir Andrew.

Sa[y][2] to the Earl that the day of writi[ng] [b]y post *directly* made me take [th]is mode of Communication & for heavens sake bring him to a speedy decision Because Our hopes in Ayrshire may be ruined if a Canvass shall come on before I am in possession of Lord Cassilis Authority to settle matters with Sir John on whom I repeat it *All* depends—

I write this in great haste not to lose the Post

Yours ever truly
HENRY ERSKINE

1. MS. Contengices.
2. The letters in square brackets are torn out of the ms.

Laurence Hill *to* George Keith Elphinstone—[24 *January* 1789]

Address: The Honble / George Keith Elphinstone / Hertford
Street / M.P. London
Postmarked: JA 24 *and* JA 27 89
Endorsed: Edinr Jany 24. 1789 / L. Hill to K. Elp: / Glasgow
Burghs.

Hill was apparently acting as an election agent for George Keith
Elphinstone in his contest for the Glasgow Burghs at the same time
that he was compiling his *Political State*. It is barely possible that
one activity led naturally to the other, though which to which
cannot be determined. George Keith Elphinstone (1746–1823),
the younger brother of the 11th Lord Elphinstone and brother-in-
law of William Adam, was a distinguished naval officer (later
created Baron Keith), a favorite of the Prince of Wales and Scottish secretary to the Prince since 1783. He was to be offered assistance from party funds for his contest in the Glasgow Burghs
(see *infra*, Adam to K. Elphinstone, [March or April 1789?]). It
should be remembered that Hill was asking for his two clerkships
during the height of the Regency Crisis, when it appeared that such
offices would soon be at the disposal of Portland's party.

Dear Sir

I had the honor of your last—The Dean of faculty [1]
was of opinion that your letter to the Provost [2] should
not be forwarded till after the Regent was appointed.—

Blythswood [3] has now declared himself and therefore
I took it on me to send 20 guineas to the Poor of Renfrew and as much to the Poor of Rutherglen being the
first expense to which you have been put respecting these
burghs.—and no more shall be distributed without your
order—

I beg to return my most grateful thanks for your
goodness in thinking of the clerkship—It is an office
which I would be extremely desireous to possess not only
on account of its independance but of the leisure which it
affords. and which I would have it in my power to dedi-

cate in a great measure to the service of my friends private & political—the present vacancy however I understand is filled up as I heard Mr Fergusson [4] the other day declare in a mixed company that he had got through the Dean and Sir Thos. Dundas [5] a promise from the Duke of Portland. Indeed at any rate I could not think of your interfering on my account with any recommendation of the Dean to whom I never yet have ventured to hint at any provision of that kind though I think he may see that I have been and can be of some service and that I cannot in my circumstances afford to allow politics to interfere so much with my profession as they have done & must do till the plan I have on hand is accomplished—

The office of clerkship to the admission of Notaries is at present held by an old man a Mr Robertson Barclay W.S.—I believe it yields from £150. to £200. a year—if it was not presuming too far & would not interfere with the arrangements here to which I am an entire stranger I would solicit you to request that *no* promise might be given to renew this commission to another or to give away the next clerkship of the Session till I had an opportunity of showing the services which I am willing to render if appointed to one or other of these offices—Do you think you could learn whether any promise had yet been given—

As you say nothing of your health I presume you are better & shall allow myself to think so till I hear from you—

Write to ⟨Holinshead⟩.—& press ⟨Houstoun⟩ [6] for his answer—

> I am with sincere respect
> My Dear Sir
> Your obliged Servant
> LAURENCE HILL

NOTES

1. Henry Erskine.
2. Which is not certain, but probably of Renfrew or Rutherglen. For Rutherglen and Provost White, see *infra,* J. Morthland to William Adam, 9 February 1789.
3. John Campbell of Blythswood. "A Lieutenant-Colonel in the Army. Connected with the Prince of Wales, and Dukes of York and Clarence. A batchelor; of an independent estate. A popular officer, and well respected" (Adam, *Pol. State,* p. 223 [the section on Lanarkshire]). Blythswood does not appear in the published correspondence of the Prince for this period, and no pressure seems to have been applied to him from that direction.
4. Fergusson of Craigdanoch. Serious competition also came from Charles Innes of Edinburgh, who had been forward in the party's electoral management.
5. Sir Thomas Dundas, 2nd Bt. (1741–1820), eldest son of Sir Lawrence Dundas, the great Scottish political magnate. In 1788 Alexander Carlyle described Dundas as "the Greatest Lay [ecclesiastical] Patron in Scotland" (Carlyle to William Adam, 19 April 1788, Blair Adam MSS). Dundas and Adam seem to have been the two most important and active political links between the Scottish Opposition leaders and the Portland–Fox leadership in the south.
6. Andrew or Robert Houstoun? But both are listed in Adam, *Pol. State,* pp. 213, 220, 222, 226, as being closely connected with the Duke of Hamilton in Lanarkshire politics.

John Morthland *to* William Adam
7 *February* [1789]

Endorsed: Morthland / Glasgow Burghs

The correspondence which follows on the contest in the Glasgow district of burghs illustrates at close view the variety of difficulties which the Opposition often encountered in attempting to capture largely hostile constituencies, even when the central organization of the party took an active interest in a strong and well-managed candidate, provided broad support by writing letters and canvassing and—the ultimate test of concern—provided some amount of funds to supplement the private means of the candidate and his local supporters and relations. The correspondence also helps demonstrate the impact of the Regency Crisis on electoral activities. For the parliamentary history of the district, see *H of P*. Suffice it to note that in the contest of 1784 Ilay Campbell, the Pittite Lord Advocate for Scotland until October, 1789, had captured the votes of all four burghs (Glasgow, Dumbarton, Renfrew, Rutherglen). Elections in Scottish burgh constituencies were in the first instance fought in the councils of each burgh. Each council decided which candidate it favored. It was then required by law to cast only one vote in favor of that candidate at the final poll for the district. An exception was made in districts composed of four burghs in order to avoid a tie (five out of the fourteen districts had only four burghs rather than five) ; each burgh in rotation was designated the "returning burgh," and the burgh performing that function was given a second vote. Thus the Glasgow district could be won by capturing one burgh plus the returning burgh. The returning burgh of the Glasgow district for the bye-election of February, 1790, was to be Renfrew and for the general election of the following July, Rutherglen. John Morthland was a prominent Edinburgh attorney (Adam, *Pol. State,* p. 215).

7th Feby

My Dear Friend

The instant I understood your Brother-in Law's intentions respecting my district (which by a strange and inexpedient *husbandry* of confidential communication) was by mere accident, I wrote to the *governour-general* of Rutherglen to hold himself disengaged, & his immediate return was such I could wish—The person I allude to is Mr David Scott writer [1] in that Burgh, who from particular circumstances which arose in a *ten years* judicial contest for the sovereignty in the town-council, in which I was his Counsel & ultimately prevailed, would do more for me than for any other person in the world—I need not here add that he knows I would never ask him to do any thing contrary to his *interest*—

While things were in the best possible train, an address

to the Prince [2] was moved in the Council the other day, and carried 12 to 6, as you must have learnt—The first notice I had of this being even in agitation, was by a very angry letter sent me the day after the event, by a Capital fellow, known to Lord Maitland, a Robt Park writer in Glasgow, on supposition the measure had been taken with my knowledge, and condemning it as precipitate & prejudicial—

The fact is this, which I well knew,—

Major Spens, Scott's brother-in-law, *made* present Provost by the latter, has a beneficial lease from Duke H.[3] near expiring, for a renewal of which he has been treating with Mr Davidson here, the Dukes chamberlain —Spens's *heart* was with us, but the *dependence* of that treaty tied his tongue *for the present*—upon it's being finished, he was to have been ours decidedly—But by the address being unseasonably pushed, *he* necessarily was *pushed* to a *Declaration,* & accordingly voted in the minority with all the Common–counsellors he could carry with him and has since been obliged to be our *declared ennemy*—Now My *good Adam,* you have just one course to take—Let the major understand that his *military prospects* with us, are brighter than his civil ones against us, and, my word for it, the Burgh is *unanimously* yours. —The 5 other minority men are of little importance & can at any rate be easily disposed of—As to Renfrew, I had occasion, when there, as Mr Craufurd's [4] Counsel, at the General Election 1784, to observe with perfect accuracy, that there is just *one,* & *but one* method to secure it's Delegate—our friend Speirs [5] is unfortunately *raw,* and on the whole a damned bad canvasser—but his wealth & near residence give him much personal *good will* at least, & the all-powerful instrument weilded by a more practised & dextrous hand, must ensure your success in that quarter—

The above is all that occurs in the moment, in answer

to yours of 4th current—But your business is to suggest whatever you wish, & fear not that I shall fail to move heaven & Earth for accomplishing it—

Your letter stopped me just as I was stepping into a post-chaise for Glasgow, to concert measures with *John Millar* [6] for frustrating as far as possible, *our Duke's* [7] purpose of addressing Pitt from Lanark-shire next tuesday—

You shall see Scotch Addresses presently!—& Pitt shall see them with a deserved vengeance—O damn him! damn him damn him! damn him

NOTES

1. *I. e.,* an attorney.

2. An address supporting the Prince's position during the Regency Crisis.

3. Alexander, 9th Duke of Hamilton (1740–1819), premier peer of Scotland, had a predominant interest in Lanarkshire (43 out of 124 votes according to Adam, *Pol. State,* pp. 212, 226, where it is described as "the controuling interest").

4. John "Fish" Craufurd of Auchenames (?1742–1814), old and close friend of Fox, had been member for Renfrewshire 1774–1780 and for Glasgow Burghs 1780–1784. His return in 1780 had been on the interest of the Duke of Argyll; when Craufurd followed the Coalition into opposition in 1784, that interest was withdrawn. There was no poll in the burghs in 1784, so that one concludes Craufurd withdrew early.

5. Archibald Speirs of Elderslie (1758–1832). Hill (Adam, *Pol. State,* pp. 279–280) noted he had, "it is believed, the largest property estate in the County [Renfrewshire], and can make fifteen votes. He is steady in Opposition."

6. John Millar (1735–1801), professor of law at Glasgow University, a man with decided reformist sentiments. He generally supported Fox's politics out of doors.

7. Hamilton.

John Morthland *to* William Adam
9 *February* 1789

Endorsed: Edinr / 9th Feby 1789 / J. Morthland. / Glasgow Burghs

Glasgow 9th Feby
1789

Well I closetted Scott yesterday three whole hours—
and now you shall know every thing material with
precision—Your friend [1] had opened his campaign naturally enough by applying to the family's man of business
George Smith, writer here—But said George was the
agent all along in the business mentioned in my last for
the Burgh Party in Rutherglen *hostile to Scott,* and of
course is utterly obnoxious to the latter—Scott assured
me that from the time of getting my letter, he had resolved to prefer your friend; but on finding Mr Smith
interfering so much (which he could not suppose was
without authority and communication with all concerned)
he saw he must look not merely to his advantage, but to
his *very political existence in the town* & his Brother-in-
law Spens had concurred in sentiment with him—That
the address was most irregularly gone about, the counsellors being called at 8 in a morning to meet that day, and
no notice given to him the *Clerk,* without whom no meeting can regularly be held; & the vote was carried accordingly in his absence & without the knowledge of either
himself or Spens—That this not only provoked them
both, but demonstrated the imminent danger of their
being effectually undermined & ousted of all their significance in the town Council, and of the detested hostile,

36

and *formerly routed* party obtaining the superiority
again—And they thereon took their ground, & determined to *listen* to the other side, when that side should
speak—

In this critical ferment, arrives post from Edinr *on
Saturday* last Lord Advocate,[2] followed soon after by
her gentle Grace from Hamilton and (quid multa?)
bound fixed nailed irrecoverably both Spens & Scott—In
the hurry of my last I believe I called Spens the *Provost*.
He is the town's *Treasurer*, & not ex officio a councillor.
Mr *White* is Provost—I know him well—one of the
most flexible of men—all means were tried with him—he
promised—but he has already been of at least a dozen
minds on the subject—he may be of a score more before
the election, & we have our chance for the last mind being
to our mind; assiduity and never ceasing importunity
watching & *praying* are the best methods with him—I do
not know that his views have ever been pecuniary—he is
wealthy & unambitious—good natured—tolerably stupid
with all—totally ignorant of *men,* credulous & easily
moved—then just as easily moved the contrary way *voici*
Monsr Prevot!—Lord Adv. returned to Edr last night
being to attend a Justiciary trial to day—& in his absence,
the *Dutchess* gives a splendid entertainment this day at
Rutherglen, to which, besides the whole councillors, every
person in the Burgh, or of the neighbourhood *having any
thing to say in it,* is invited—This somewhat surprizes
me, as I am informed the *Duke* has assured your friend
he has given no authority to any person to canvas, or use
his name—This is a most important point *to be instantly
cleared up*—Campbell Blythswood is here an active
ennemy & I am told Cochran,[3] the Duke's Minister for
Scotland, is an *ennemy* also not *inactive,* though behind
the curtain—I shall soon know this,—I went to him be-

fore leaving Edinr, (being his very old acquaintance) to put him on his guard respecting the County-Address— He assured me his opinion was that, *propriety in the abstract* required his *inaction* in all such matters, independent of immediate views of interest, and that he would take no part whatever in that business, or any of the sort, *and that he had written so to the Dutchess*—If, after this, I find he has been stirring mala fide—you shall know of it, and his merits & deserts shall be left for your future consideration—The above conference I desire you will consider as imparted strictly to *yourself* in confidence—

After turning the matter in all lights with Scott, I at last thus took upon me;

"To be at a word with you, Mr Scott, I come here not merely as J.M. but as *ministerially* authorised—(well pushed) No mortal shall ever know what passes betwixt us—tell me Mr Spens's *ultimate wish, and your own*— your objects, whatever they be, are within your reach"— He turned red and pale & faltered and sweated—at last he quavered scarce articulately "that I was just *24* hours *too late*"—for that yesterday (saturday) at the meeting with Ld Adv. & her Grace, "both Mr Spens & he were absolutely & unalterably bound"—He added he *feared* Provost White was fixed too, but he could not answer as to that, and the councillors at large were open to both parties, & probably would stick by the best bidder—And then expressing his regret that his influence must in this case be exerted contrary to his predilection, concluded with this epilogue "that his engagement was solely *pro* ⟨*haec*⟩ *vice,* and I might command him *next* election"—I shut the door—

The Adv.'s language is uniformly, "That he goes out to be sure at present, but comes in two or at most three months hence, never to go out again. That the King is greatly better, & *will certainly* be on his throne before May next; and the other party driven from all sight of power, during the King's life which will be long—and meanwhile Fox is *certainly* dying, on which event the party will instantly crumble to pieces, and Mr Pitt necessarily be assumed even by the Regent, and all the present opposition-leaders excluded, before the King's reassuming the reins—

Now, My friend, I must entreat you will tell me your *real* belief as to both those points—I know well enough what *my language* ought to be on the occasion, stand the fact as it may;—but, depend upon it, as a truth immutable as any in the Bible, that the malignants of this Country are kept together, high & low, wise & foolish, from no earthly considerations else than those of *the kings speedy recovery, and fox's apprehended bad life*—In this large & populous City, where I now write, *including* the College, you will not find *six* avowed Foxites—I believe some concealed ones there are, but the universal torrent over awes & stiffles them into silence—I have ventured to traverse the streets in blue & buff—& could you imagine it, a relation seriously told me "he thought it a dangerous dress in this town"—The first toast every where is "The king & his speedy recovery"—the 2d "Mr Pitt"—and the name of "Mr Rolle" which I had always felt on my ear as the parole of riducule—as the expressive sound of the quintessence of all that is stupid callous and gross in nature, is here mentioned without a laugh or wry face! [4]

"Kill Fox—recover the King"—that is the mark on the foreheads of 50,000 beasts in this Royalty—And there is not any thing that could so effectually turn the tide all over Scotland as to impress a conviction (if there is ground for it) that the King's situation is desperate—& Fox's health re-established—verbum sapienti— [5]

NOTES

1. G. K. Elphinstone.
2. Ilay Campbell.
3. William Forrester Cochrane of Arran.
4. John Rolle (1756–1842), the rather independent member for Devon who tended to support Pitt in the House, and whose violent dislike of Fox and Burke following the fall of the Coalition had earned him the place of honor in the great Whig lampoon, the *Rolliad*.
5. In early February the rumors of the king's recovery could still have been only wishful thinking, but by the middle of the month the situation was to change entirely. Public and medically undisputed announcements of the king's convalescence began to appear by 17 February. By 23 February even the Prince of Wales and the Duke of York were permitted to see their father (John W. Derry, *The Regency Crisis and the Whigs, 1788–9* [Cambridge, 1963], pp. 187–188). But neither was Fox at this time in any real danger. He had been forced to return full tilt from a tour in northern Italy at the outset of the Regency Crisis, fell ill almost immediately with dysentery, and by 27 January had retired to Bath. But whether he was in reality near death or not, many well-informed persons—indeed Fox himself—feared his physical decline would be permanent and terminal, and this fear was given wide publicity (see *ibid.,* especially pp. 56–57, 106–107).

John Millar *to* William Adam
9 *February* 1789

Address: William Adam Esqr / M.P. / London
Postmarked: FE 12 89

My Dear Friend

It gives me great pleasure to learn that so near a connection of yours, and so good a man as Mr. K. Elphinston, is a candidate for our boroughs. I can only say that I wish I could contribute any thing besides good wishes. The Town Council of Glasgow I look upon as immoveable on the other side. The dispute will probably turn upon Rutherglen and Renfrew. And every thing will depend upon attention and prudent management in those quarters. After an appearance in our favour by the majority of the Council in Rutherglen, which produced an address. The Ld. Ad—te [1] dined with them on Saturday, and I understand boasts of his success. The difficulty lies in their being people of very inferior rank and therefore very wavering.

Your ever
JOHN MILLAR

Glasgow 9th. Febry 1789

NOTE

1. Ilay Campbell.

John Morthland *to* William Adam
10 *February* 1789

Endorsed: Edinr 11th Feby 89. / Mr Morthland. / The Glasgow Burghs
Adam misread Morthland's date, which was faintly penned in places.

Edinr 10th Feby
1789

After writing yesterday I saw the *Provost*—he assured me of his being with us—& that he should certainly preserve his *majority* in the Council—I was happy to learn that Spens had been his competitor for the Dignity of Provost, & on being beat, swore, that he, White, might be Provost, but by God he, Spens, should be *Delegate* [1]— This impolitic & intemperate conduct has produced a *happy personal animosity* between the Treasurer & Provost, & their respective adherents, which will con-

41

tribute powerfully to our aid, & I hope will even ensure absolutely our success, by keeping our friends steady;— the *bad* part of them supplying all defects of the good. I also saw Mr Smith, who along with some persons of weight & popularity in the town, will keep up the right spirit till the election—all this very good—As to Renfrew—you know, I presume, that in case Blythswood stood, Speirs was to take no active part against him—It seemed odd that Ld Adv. should be the ostensible Candidate, & Blythswood yet appear forward in the canvass, without declaring his own determination as to offering his services to the District, or not—In my way hither from Glasgow last night, I understood *Mcdowal* [2] had posted west on Sunday—he posted back again yesterday—Ld Adv: had been expressing, at the Inns, the utmost anxiety to see him—I have just been informed, mirabile dictu, that Mcdowal is to declare himself candidate in room of Ld Adv.—This must be in the idea that he possesses a prevalent interest in the Burgh of Renfrew, & that Glasgow & Dumbarton are sure, which last no doubt is the case—However that be; certain it is, that a *majority* of the Renfrew Council have already declared *properly,* and as Speirs will now immediately open his canvass in *person,* I *expect,* more than hope victory there—Many of the Inhabitants found cause to repent their former unnatural & imprudent support of Ld Adv: in opposition to the Candidate of a family so capable to do essential services to *their* families as Speirs's,[3] and from the detail of circumstances of which I am fully apprized, unnecessary to trouble you with, I do not even think Mcdowals westindia purse, (the engine no doubt meant to be played against us) need alarm you; though it undoubtedly ought to quicken our attention to all the motions of the ennemy —adieu—

We go on triumphantly in Fife— [4]

NOTES

1. For the return of a member at the district poll.

2. William McDowall (?1749–1810), described by the *H of P* as "a non-practising lawyer, concerned mainly with the management of the family estates [in Renfrewshire and Wigtown] and West Indian enterprises." Ambitious for his political interest in Scotland and a supporter of Pitt, he was currently seeking a seat, having in 1786 surrendered his for Renfrewshire in consequence of a political agreement made at the general election of 1784. In August, 1789, he was to be returned for Ayrshire as a stop-gap until the general election for his close friend, Sir Adam Fergusson. At the general election in 1790 he will be returned by all four burghs for the Glasgow district.

3. Both McDowall and Speirs had heavy concentrations of property near Renfrew.

4. Henry Erskine was the Opposition candidate for Fife. This reference may be to a Regency address, however.

John Morthland *to* William Adam
11 *February* 1789

Address: William Adam Esqr / Lincoln's-Inn-Fields / MP London
Postmarked: FE 11 *and* FE 14 89
Endorsed: Morthland. / Edinr Feby 10th

Edinr 11th Feby
1789

⟨Re⟩ferring to my former, I have now only to mention that yesterday there was industriously shown about, a letter from the Treasurer of the Navy [1] to his son in Law, the Solicitor,[2] bearing as follows, "I have the pleasure to acquaint you that Doctor Warren [3] waited on the Prince of Wales (such a day) and told him, he, Dr W., thought it his duty to inform his Royal Highness, that from several symptoms, particularly, his observation of his Maj-

43

esty's *eye,* he had now solid grounds to believe his Majesty would obtain a speedy recovery"—I did not see the letter, but these words, or these with mere *insignificant* variations, have been reported to me by several persons *who* said *they saw* the letter. I need not add, after what I wrote formerly that it would be of no mean advantage to have it in our power to give the Treasurer the lie—

Did Dr W. or did he not, make the said visit & speech imputed to him?—

I am getting myself made an elder at present, in order to qualify for being elected a member of next General Assembly [4] to vote for your friend Prof. Dalzel [5]—My view is to get in for one of Sir John Anstruther's Burghs [6]—Will you, when you see our honest friend *John,* speak to him to mark me down—

Arse-y [7] has now declared for the *Burg* ⟨. . .⟩ so little Ilay must look out elsewhere—Speirs opens his house forth-with—& I hope the best—perseveranti dabitur—

NOTES

1. Henry Dundas, later Lord Melville (1742–1811).

2. Robert Dundas of Arniston (1758–1819), whose father was the half-brother of Henry Dundas, later Lord Melville. Robert had been solicitor-general for Scotland since 1784 and was one of Henry Dundas's principal agents in Scotland.

3. Dr. Richard Warren was one of the physicians in attendance on the king during his insanity. He had become associated with the Whig view of the seriousness of the king's illness and had always been reluctant to indicate any sign or hope of recovery.

4. Of the Church of Scotland.

5. Andrew Dalzel (1742–1806), professor of Greek in Edinburgh University. Later in this year he was to be elected principal clerk to the General Assembly, but only after a close contest and scrutiny.

6. Anstruther Easter Burghs.

7. This apparently refers to McDowall.

John Morthland *to* William Adam
13 *February* [1789]

Address: William Adam Esqr / MP / Lincoln's Inn Fields / London
    Postmarked: FE 13 *and* FE 16 89

Feby
Edr Friday 13th

Last night I made some important discovery. Col. Campbell[1] disgusted by the ill usage of the Ducal[2] Party in dropping him, after Ld Adv.[3] quitted the field, and substituting Arsey,[4] gives us his *hearty active* support—He will even (if I mistake not) vote with us in Renfrew *County*—but mum—Hamilton of Wishaw,[5] a very considerable heritor of Lanarkshire, and also a freeholder of Renfrewshire, moreover disgusted at *our Duke,* assured me last night he would go all lengths in supporting Mr Elphinston's interest in the Burghs—And had our Friend Mr *Shaw* Stewart[6] been at his hand when in the humour in which he spoke to me, his vote in *the county* would have been secured—He will join in calling a Lanark-shire meeting to address the Prince; &, with the influence I know he possesses, particularly over an important branch of the Clan *Hamilton,* I look upon him as a capital card—The accession of him & Campbell, in my mind, *ensure your friend's success*—However I should be glad to see him in person among us as soon as convenient—

Since the *Treasurer's letter,* we are told, it is all follow to think of a change of Ministry or dissolution of Parliament—

Pray let me know what to trust to in these reports—I wish in every thing that deeply interests myself & friends, to know the *blackest* & *worst* side—

NOTES

1. Of Blythswood.
2. Hamilton.
3. Ilay Campbell.
4. McDowall.
5. William Hamilton of Wishaw is an intriguing example of the possible effectiveness of Opposition organization out of doors. Adam, *Pol. State,* under Renfrewshire (pp. 280–281), notes that "at last election [he] supported Mr. M'Dowall, but has lately joined the friends of Opposition." Hill, the compiler, also comments on Hamilton under Lanarkshire (p. 219): "Good estate. Opposition principles. An Independant Friend." The Independent Friends was an Opposition political club organized in February, 1785, by Opposition leaders in Edinburgh precisely in order to instill and strengthen Opposition sentiments in men of Hamilton's description (William Robertson the younger to William Adam, 28 February 1785, Blair Adam MSS.).
6. John Shaw Stewart (1739–1812), M.P. Renfrewshire 1780–1783 and 1786–1796, possessed the leading interest in that county. He was a consistent supporter of Opposition.

William Robertson *to* William Adam
15 *February* 1789

William Robertson (1753–1835), advocate and eldest son of William Robertson, the historian, was one of the principal men of business in the Edinburgh coterie, apparently headed by Henry Erskine, which took the lead in initiating and organizing Opposition extraparliamentary activities in Scotland. It was this same circle, for example, which had organized both the Independent Friends and the propaganda against Pitt's Irish propositions in early 1785. Now it was preparing for a general election at the same time that it was organizing a movement for Regency addresses. Hill concluded in his survey (Adam, *Pol. State,* pp. 339, 342) that "the influence of the Countess of Sutherland and Earl Gower [1] [in Sutherlandshire] is almost insurmountable, and has been exerted in the creation of liferent votes which exceed in number those of the real Freeholders [a liferenter, or person given possession of a property for life, had the right to vote in Scottish law]. This circumstance, as well as others, has, however, had the effect of exciting discontent among a few; and perhaps something might be done in opposition to the Gower interest by starting a real proprietor, for instance Mr. Dempster,[2] against it; but such an attempt at next Election, it is thought, would be entirely fruitless." Hill adjudged 22 out of 34 votes in the county to the Sutherland-Gower interest.

My Dear Sir

When going through the Rolls of Freeholders in the different Counties, an idea occurred that a successful attempt might be made on the County of Sutherland, notwithstanding the powerful influence of the Sutherland family. This idea originated from some hints conveyed to us from a leading interest in the County. It is unnecessary to trouble you at present with any views of the interests in that County, to state to you the grounds on which our hopes are founded, or to enter into any detailed account of a scheme which is yet in embryo, & which was conceived only yesterday at a meeting with the Dean,[3] Lord Ankerville [4] McLeod Bannatyne [5] & me.

A difficulty however occurred for the solution of which we agreed to apply to you, & as all operations must be suspended till it is removed we beg to hear from you as soon as possible.

Although Lord Gower by his fathers connections goes alongst with Mr Pitt, yet he has been represented as being strongly attached to Mr Fox & his friends & as a man who would most cordially support them were he at liberty to act according to his own inclinations. If the fact is so, & if there is any prospect of his coming round, perhaps our friends would not wish any attack to be made upon him in his own County. If they are restrained by these motives the attempt must be abandoned, if they are not our operations must be begun immediately, & every thing will depend on the most profound secrecy.

The business of addressing [6] goes on well. Addresses have already been sent up from the Town Councils of

Burntisland, Dysart, Rutherglen, Lauder, Jedburgh, &
from the Burgesses & Inhabitants of Burntisland, Perth,
Kinghorn, Dysart & Dumbarton—I presume the Stirlingshire Address would be carried yesterday & in the course
of this week there will be many more. Will Sir James
Erskine [7] never write about the Fife election. I ever am

Edinr 15th. Feby:

1789:

William Adam Esqr

My Dear Sir
Yours most sincerely
WM ROBERTSON.

NOTES

1. Elizabeth, Countess of Sutherland (*b.* 1765), had succeeded
her father, the 18th Earl, when only a year old. In 1785 she had
married George Granville Leveson Gower, styled Lord Gower,
eldest surviving son of the 1st Marquess of Stafford. Stafford was
Privy Seal in Pitt's Ministry. Young Gower sat on the family
interest in Staffordshire and voted with Pitt on the Regency.

2. George Dempster (1732–1818), member for the Perth
Burghs 1761–1768 and 1769–1790, was a man of great integrity
and independent views, tending (though not without many exceptions) to be a critic of whatever government was in power and
voting with Opposition during the Regency. In 1786 he had purchased the estate of Skibo in Sutherlandshire, and Hill anticipated
that he would be placed on the roll of freeholders for that county
in 1790 (Adam, *Pol. State,* p. 342). He was, but did not vote
(Mackenzie, *Pol. State,* pp. 186–189).

3. Henry Erskine.

4. David Ross of Inverchasley, Lord Ankerville, is listed by Hill
as a voter in Sutherlandshire in the Sutherland–Gower interest
(Adam, *Pol. State,* p. 340). In his section on Ross-shire, where
Adam was to stand in 1790 on the interest of Francis Humberston
Mackenzie, Hill wrote that Ankerville, who "inclines to Opposition, is connected with the Lord Privy Seal [presumably of Scotland, James Stuart Mackenzie of Rosebaugh], Lord Mountstuart,
etc. . . . Not a very large estate. He has a good deal of personal
interest in this County, but it is thought will oppose Mr. Humberston M'Kenzie, from an aversion to his great interest founded
on his liferent votes" (*ibid.,* p. 294).

5. Bannatyne McLeod was described by Hill as a lawyer, sheriff
of Bute, a "friend of" and "influenced by" Lord Mountstuart, and
"a friend of the Dean's" (Adam, *Pol. State,* pp. 76, 172, 261–2).

6. For the Regency.

7. Sir James St. Clair Erskine (1762–1837), nephew and heir of Lord Loughborough, who governed his political conduct. Erskine had a considerable personal interest in Fife, and Loughborough was ambitious that Sir James represent the county.

William Adam *to* George Keith Elphinstone—[*c.* March *or* April 1789?]

Endorsed: Mr. Adams / Letter to / Captn. K. Elphint.
Corrected draft in the hand of Adam. The endorsement is in the hand of Adam's clerk. The reference to dissolution suggests March or early April, 1789. The letter was found in a bundle of letters of 1789, mostly from the Duke of Portland.

Dear Keith

I have conversed fully with the Duke of Portland & he desires me to communicate freely to you, in confidence, as follows.

If Parliament were to be dissolved immediately there would be no fund. But if it is put off there is a plan on foot likely to produce a very respectable One—If that plan does take place (which though not a certainty yet is next to one) His Grace will certainly consider as highly proper to give such a sum as you mention.

There is I think (in spite of the reports) no chance of an immediate dissolution: & I really think there is so fair a prospect of the fund, that I would advise you, with the prospect you have of success, by no means to desist. At the same time I do not wish to represent the fund as an absolute certainty, as I should perhaps in doing so be going beyond what the Duke of Portland would wish, as he never wishes to promise when he cannot positively ensure performance.

Yours ever
W. ADAM

49

George Augustus North *to* William Adam
3 *April* [1789]

Endorsed: Bath April 3d. 1789 / Mr North. / About a seat in / the Event of a Dissolution

George Augustus North (1757–1802), 1st son of Frederick, Lord North, and grandson of the 1st Earl of Guilford, was M.P. Harwich 1778–1784, Wootton Bassett 1784–1790, Petersfield June–December, 1790, and Banbury December, 1790 to 5 August, 1792, when he succeeded his father as 3rd Earl of Guilford. He was an intimate friend of William Adam.

Bath April 3.

Dear Adam

The report of Dissolution encreases so fast that I can not but believe it. I have written to St. John [1] to know his determination about Wotton Basset, but not to depend on one thing, Do seize upon a seat for me if you can find any to be sold tolerably cheap; Annuity all things considered I think would suit me better than the gross Sum— yet the Parsons Juice that you told me of was enormous. At all events let me know if this event takes place before I come to town, which will be on the 20th. Adieu believe me

Sincerely yours
G. A. NORTH

Tierney should be spoken to, not to start ⟨2⟩ candidates— [2]

NOTES

1. Henry St. John (1738–1818), 2nd surviving son of John, 2nd Viscount St. John. The St. Johns strongly influenced the return of one member at Wootton Bassett. Although the family had been closely tied to the Crown through place and pension, Henry and his brother John went into opposition with the fall of the Coalition.

2. George Tierney (1761–1830) had contested Wootton Bassett unsuccessfully in 1784 as a Pittite on the Hyde interest. By December, 1788, he was a Foxite and contesting a bye-election at Colchester. A double return was made, and he was not declared elected until 6 April 1789. The reference to his activities here is therefore not clear.

Laurence Hill *to* William Adam
6 *April* 1789

Endorsed: L. Hill. Edr. 6th Apl / 1789 / with a State of / Orkeney— / To be shewen to Sir / T. D. / To mention to him / Ross of Cromarty—[1]

Edinr. 6th. April 1789

Dear Sir

I wrote to you sometime ago and as I have received no answer I presume the request I made of presenting my compilation to the Duke of Portland was improper, so I have dropt all thoughts of going to London though I shall still go on with my work.—I am writing it out in alphabetical order but I have gone out of my way to send you the inclosed copy of the part respecting Orkney.

Without the gift of prophecy I fear I may foretell that that county will be lost—by a little activity it might have been kept.

If the enclosed is thought of any importance and that you should advise with Sir Thomas on the subject I earnestly request you will get a copy made by a Clerk of your own as I would not wish to have it known that the information came through me and yet I fear it will be suspected—Sir Thomas is a most respectable good man but he is surely no very active politician.[2]

My Information in Orkney was chiefly got from a very intelligent man from the north whom I met with by accident and who was no way connected with either party.—

I think there are other counties in Scotland that will be lost from want of care—Professional men when they are connected with party have their attention occupied with their business—and men of fortune will not give themselves the trouble to do the drudgery of opposition—

I am with esteem
Dear Sir
Your most obedient
faithful humble Servant
LAURENCE HILL

NOTES

1. Alexander Gray Ross of Cromarty. He had inherited a great estate in Cromartyshire from George Ross (1700–1786), M.P. When Hill drew up his "state," he thought Ross would be a candidate for Cromarty in opposition to the Government candidate, Alexander Brodie. Hill does not mention Ross in connection with Orkney, nor does he appear on the list of Orkney freeholders in 1790. See Adam, *Pol. State,* pp. 84–85; Mackenzie, *Pol. State,* pp. 140–142.

2. "Sir Thomas Dundas, whose respectable and independant character is above eulogium, has by far the most considerable estate and interest in this County [Orkney], and should naturally return the Member. A spirit of jealousy among the smaller proprietors has produced an opposition to him" (Adam, *Pol. State,* p. 243, introduction to Orkney).

George Augustus North *to* William Adam
10 *April* [1789]

Endorsed: Bath 10th Apl. 1789. / G. A. North— / Seat. Ld Gd.
will give / an Annuity.

Dear Adam

I am much obliged to you for the trouble you have
taken: It is now particularly necessary, as Lord Guilford
will pay an annuity, but has declined Wotton Basset as he
thought £3000 a sum to large to be conveniently advanced at once. Lord Robert [1] is to have Wotton Basset,
as that is entirely out [of] the question. Bob Drummond
says he has from the most perfect authority assurances
that the Parliament will not be dissolved in the course of
1789: If that is so We shall live till September 1790.
Adieu believe me ever yours

GEO AUG NORTH

Bath April 10.

NOTE

1. Lord Robert Spencer (1747–1831), 3rd son of Charles, 3rd
Duke of Marlborough. Lord Robert was an intimate social companion of Fox and since 1781 had followed Fox in his political
conduct, despite the Government sympathies of his family. Since
1771 he had been returned for Oxford city on his father's interest.
In 1790 Marlborough switched the Pittite Francis Burton from
New Woodstock to his maverick son's seat at Oxford, and Lord
Robert looked to the party for another opportunity. He was an
unusually forward supporter of Fox in Westminster, an odd fact
in view of Lord Robert's retiring disposition.

Sir Gilbert Elliot *to* Lady Elliot
11 *April* 1789

Source: Minto MSS, National Library of Scotland.

In 1786 Lord Delaval had been called to the upper House and had thus vacated his seat at Berwick. Both Sir Gilbert Elliot and John Hiley Addington (brother of Henry, later Lord Sidmouth) came forward as candidates. Although the latter enjoyed both the interest of Delaval and of Government, Pitt having even assured him that he would be at no expense, the election was carried by Elliot, who apparently enjoyed the support of John Vaughan, the other member for the borough. It was clear, however, that Elliot could not be returned again for the constituency; he wrote to his wife on 28 February 1789 (Minto MSS) that "Lord Delaval has already secured the seat for Capt. [Charles] Carpenter at the General Election," as indeed happened. Elliot's greatest hope—and an object toward which he had long been planning—was that he might find it feasible to stand at the general election for Roxboroughshire, his home county for which both he (1777–1784) and his father before him had been members. But Elliot felt he had no prospect for the county if Parliament were to be dissolved before mid-1790. Toward the middle of March, 1789, in the wake of the Regency Crisis, the most alarming and convincing rumors began to circulate that a dissolution was imminent. By that period Elliot had established himself as one of the leading men of business among the Whig opposition, and he apparently felt it natural to turn to his party for assistance in finding a seat. He also reminded his brother-in-law, Lord Malmesbury, of his former intimations that Elliot might be returned for Christchurch, a borough which had long been controlled by Malmesbury's elderly cousin, Edward Hooper (whose heir Malmesbury was). Malmesbury, the renowned diplomat, found it impossible to tell a straight story; and Elliot, who was already disgusted at what he believed to have been Malmesbury's equivocal and self-seeking conduct during the early stages of the Regency Crisis, quickly became convinced that his relation was playing a double game and was perhaps seeking once again to regain the favor of Government. Elliot was increasingly inclined, then, to turn to the party for a seat. He wrote to his wife on 19 March

(Minto MSS) that he would "immediately speak to the Duke of
Portland about a seat, but as I cannot contribute money towards it,
& as I know how few they have to dispose of without money I see a
strong possibility of my being left out once more, if the dissolution
should take place as soon as it is expected." By 21 March (*ibid.*)
he had "seen the D of Portland & talked over the Ch. Church
business with him as much as I could, & perhaps more than I ought
quite—I could not help letting out my distrust of Lord Malm[es-
bury]'s sincerity on the occasion—I let him know distinctly however that I had no prospect of a seat except by the Duke & his
friends. He is very friendly as possible & intends very sincerely to
take care of me, but what the difficulties may be cannot yet be
known." A resolution to Elliot's difficulties came in mid-April.

Park St. Saturday 11th. Ap: 1789

The extreme shortness of this letter must be made up by
a satisfactory piece of intelligence which it will give you.
I am now sure of a seat in the next Parliament without
expence. This is, however, all that I can tell you on the
subject, for it is all that I know myself—The D. of Portland sent for me to day, & told me that as there was no
longer a prospect of a dissolution taking place immediately, the subject he wished to speak to me about was perhaps not so important; but he had so much satisfaction in
it himself that he wished to communicate it to me as much
for his own pleasure as for relieving my mind from any
anxiety I might feel on the subject—He then told me that
there was a seat secure for me—But that he could not tell
me a word more; & that I must not ask him a word more
about it. He expressed in the kindest manner possible the
relief it had been to his mind, & the great satisfaction he
felt in accomplishing this object—He then added that
having thus provided for what was most essential, by securing my seat, he had next felt a great desire to turn this
circumstance to still better account—That his great wish
was to see me member for the County of Roxburgh,
which he knew was what I should prefer myself to any

other place, & was the sort of representation which he
thought became me best, & was also most suitable to the
other objects which he wished to see obtained for me—
That the seat which was secured for me might be given to
any body he pleased, & that it had struck him that Sir G.
Douglas [1] might be induced by the offer of a certain &
quiet seat, to relinquish the County & joyn me. That the
seat should be given either to him or to any other person
who could place me in the County of Roxburgh—& he desired to know whether I thought this plan practicable—
Certainly nothing was ever more thoroughly kind, or
considerate than this proposal. I told him that I thought
no such arrangement could take place *immediately,* on account of the warmth of the *Court* Politicks, which would
render the Duke of Roxburgh altogether intractable at
present; but that with a little time, for the *passionate*
part of the Politicks to subside, I thought there was a
prospect of success in that way. Either by Sir G. Douglas
—or even Mr Rutherfurd [2]—For if I can form such a
strength as to hold the ballance & turn the Election to
either of my opponents that I choose, which I hope will
be the case, I think that rather than lose the seat entirely
one of them may consult his own interest so far as to
accept of this offer, & support me in the County—That I
shall make it my business however to examine this question, & that I shall direct my County operations towards
the accomplishment of this plan—The Duke said he was
ready to act immediately, & that he should indeed have
settled the whole business himself before he had spoke to
me at all on the subject, if he had not been afraid to venture without consulting me as to the prudence of attempting it—But that the thing would *always* be open, & would
do just as well, so far as related to the other seat, hereafter as now, & that he should wait my instructions on the
subject—All This is like him & nobody else—I have not
time for another syllable—only that I think you had bet-

ter not say a word on the subject to *any body,* not even to Eleanor— [3] Till we consider what effect it might have in the County if it were known that I was provided else where—As for the other scheme of a compromise, that ought certainly to be perfectly secret, till the time comes for trying that expedient, & the admiral [4] could not know it without its being known to Mr Elliot,[5] & therefore to Mr Rutherfurd—God bless you all—

NOTES

1. Sir George Douglas, 2nd Bt. (1754–1821), M.P. Roxburghshire 1784–1806 on the interest of the Duke of Roxburgh, was a prominent and firm supporter of Pitt.

2. John Rutherfurd (c. 1748–1834) of Edgarstoun, who stood for the county in 1790 but lost to Douglas, was related to Sir Gilbert by marriage.

3. Sir Gilbert's sister, who in 1776 had married William Eden, a close friend of Elliot, but since 1786 a prominent Government man of business.

4. John Elliot, an uncle of Sir Gilbert.

5. Andrew Elliot (d. 1797), uncle of Sir Gilbert and formerly Governor of New York. The eldest sister of Andrew and John, another Eleanor, had married a Rutherfurd.

EPILOGUE

On 14 April Sir Gilbert was disabused of his suspicions of Lord Malmesbury, who on that day showed him a letter he had received from Hooper. "It gives him an account of the state he found the Borough in, which is very little less than totally lost to Mr Hooper & his family—Mr [George] Rose, secretary to the Treasury, has been carrying on an intrigue there for a considerable time & has succeeded so far that the Electors declare their resolution to choose him at the next election—They say at the same time that from respect to Mr Hooper they will again choose L[or]d Malm[esbury]'s friend, Mr [Hans] Sloane, & that if he will content himself with one & one, there will be no further attempt made at present to molest him—On looking over the list of Electors with L[or]d Malm[esbury] it appears clearly that his interest there is entirely defeated; & that there is a most decided majority ag[ains]t him, so that the wonder is that they consent to give him even one member. The effect of this is much worse than the loss of a member at present, for by the constitution of the Bo[rough] [Christchurch was a corporation borough] whoever has a majority once may keep it for ever & gain entire possession of the Bo[rough] *by proper management.* And there is little doubt of Mr Rose managing it properly. . . . This plot ag[ains]t Mr Hooper's interest in favour of the Treasury was begun in L[or]d North's time by Jack Robinson; & has been carrying on during the whole of Mr Pitt's administration notwithstanding his assurances to the contrary to L[or]d Malm[esbury] who had an explanation with him on the subject when he first accepted of the Hague [in 1784]" (Elliot to Lady Elliot, 14 April 1789, Minto MSS). On 24 April Elliot wrote a letter to his wife (Minto MSS; published in Countess of Minto, ed., *Life and Letters of Sir Gilbert Elliot* [London, 1874], I, 355–356) which not only relates the outcome of this prolonged negotiation but also provides an unusual insight into the qualities of Portland as a party leader. "I passed the whole evening yesterday, that is, from half after nine to almost one in the morning, with the Duke of Portland alone—We talked over, fully & confidentially all that relates to the subject of our correspondence, & I have found in every word fresh reason for loving his kind & affectionate heart, & for revering the true greatness & nobleness of his mind—It is needless to repeat the particulars of our conversation; but its whole tendency was to put my mind at rest, & to make me satisfied with myself, and to remove every notion of obligation to him—This is not like all the *Lords* with whom I have *nearer connexions,* nor is it indeed perfectly like any man but himself that I have ever seen—He expressly approved of my resolution as proper, & as necessary in the circumstances of my Family [grave financial difficulties were forcing Elliot to spend more time on his Scottish estates, which made him consider retiring from Parliament rather than ask for a party seat]—But *he pressed* on *me* the propriety of continuing in Parl[iamen]t (*not of attending*) & said repeatedly that he considered it as of importance to our cause & to our Party that I should be in the House of Commons, whether I should ever attend a single day or not, for 2, 3, or even four or five years to come—He said that he saw no difficulty & that the only thing to be done was to make *my own mind* easy on the *sub-*

ject—I asked him whether I should open the matter to Mr Fox & he advised me to do it—Telling me that of all men he was the most liberal & the most considerate of private interests & duties —I shall therefore explain my situation fully to Fox—Burke— [Sylvester] Douglas—& Sir George [Cornewall]—I have already to [William] Elliot [of Wells]—but I do not propose to carry the confidence further." Fox was of course leader in the House of Commons; Burke, Douglas, Cornewall, and Elliot of Wells were close personal and family connections. Elliot was still hopeful in July of coming to terms with the Duke of Roxburgh for the county (same to same, 14 July 1789, Minto MSS); but that negotiation never succeeded. In 1790 he was returned for Helston and, he was surprised and gratified to find, through the intervention of Lord Malmesbury (same to same, 15 May 1790, in Minto, *Life and Letters*, I, 362).

Sir William Augustus Cunynghame *to* William Adam—27 *April* 1789

Sir William Augustus Cunynghame (1747–1828), 4th Bt., had been member for Linlithgowshire since 1774. A close adherent of Lord Mountstuart and an outspoken defender of Scottish interests, he was returned in 1774 with the support of the Hopetoun interest. He supported the North Ministry, voted against Shelburne's peace preliminaries and consistently and actively supported the Coalition both before and after its fall. Henry Dundas had attempted to unseat him in 1784 in a heated contest, but without success. In 1790 Cunynghame was to lose his seat when the Pittite Earl of Hopetoun withdrew his support and put forward his brother, John Hope, as a candidate; nor was Cunynghame able to find another seat, despite the efforts of the party.

Livingstone Monday
27th. April 1789

Dear Adam

I am really anxious to hear, if you have been able to do any thing with respect to Mr. James Johnstone's Interest with his Brother,[1] in the Disposal of his Vote, & Interest in the County of Linlithgow at the next Election, which from the Desertion of Sir Rt. Dalyell,[2] is now become a Matter of great Consequence, as Mr. Johnstone of Straiton, has given the Life Rent Vote, which his Brother James refused to accept, to John Gray the Town Clerk of Edinr. You will recollect that Mr. J. Johnstone uses the New York Coffee House, & is supposed to have some Connexion in Bussiness with Gurnell, Hoare, & Harrisons House; I dread very much Mr. Baron[3] coming from Stockholm to Vote against me, I find that he is a Relation of Mr. Listons[4] who is our Minister there, a Word from Sir Gilbert Elliot to Liston, would at least keep Mr. Baron in Sweden, if it did not make him vote for me; I shall be happy to hear that Mrs. Adam & all your Family are well; No News here of any kind, I find Dundas, & his Son in Law the Sollicitor,[5] moving Heaven & Earth against me, which I shall resist to the utmost of my power, and by the Assistance of my Friends hope to prevail. With much real regard I ever am Yours Sincerely ⟨While⟩

W A Cunynghame

Wm. Adam Esqr.

NOTES

1. Alexander Johnston of Straiton.

2. Sir Robert Dalyell of Binns.

3. Alexander Baron of Preston, of whom Hill notes: "A small estate in this County. Succeeded to an estate in Sweden, where he resides. A relation of Dundas of Dundas's" (Adam, *Pol. State*, p. 229).

4. Sir Robert Liston (1742–1836) was envoy extraordinary at Stockholm 1788–1793 and a former tutor and intimate friend of Sir Gilbert Elliot and his brother Hugh.

5. Robert Dundas of Arniston.

Laurence Hill *to* William Adam
29 *May* 1789

Edin 29 May 1789

Dear Sir—

I wrote to you some posts ago on the subject of Dr Blairs commission to be Chaplain to the Prince of Wales about which I see the Dean of Faculty [1] grows daily more & more anxious that it should not be delivered and I fear I cannot with propriety delay much longer to deliver it unless I have orders—I am averse to trouble Capt. Elphinstone about it on account of his state of health and I hope you will therefore have the goodness to excuse me for giving you this trouble though I am sensible that I have not a good title to plague you at all about this matter—If Capt. Elphinstone approves of it the Commission may ly in my hands till he comes to this country when he can settle the matter with the Dean of Faculty himself— [2]

Today I was receiving some money on another account from Mr Drummond of Perths [3] Agent when he requested I would receive for you and remit one years interest on Mr. Drummonds bond—I accordingly enclose a bill of Forbes & Hays at par for £75. and you will send down a receipt to be given to Mr Drummonds Agent.

I am ashamed at not having sent you sooner the two small vols. of my state—The hurry of the term & some other causes prevented it—but I think I may pledge myself to have it in your hands in fourteen days at farthest.—I wish to compare it with the scroll myself & must set apart a day for the purpose.

I have the honor to be with much esteem My Dear Sir
Your most obedient Servant
LAURENCE HILL

NOTES

1. Henry Erskine.
2. Elphinstone's involvement was presumably as Scottish secretary to the Prince. Hill's connection with Erskine, and whether this patronage is connected with electoral activity, is not clear. It is barely possible that Hill has been drawn into the broad activities of the Edinburgh coterie, and that he has coordinated his efforts on the survey with those described by Robertson in his letter of 15 February, *supra*.
3. James Drummond of Perth was described by Hill as having "a very large estate, and considerable interest [in Perthshire]. He got his estate from the present Administration, in consequence of the Act disannexing the forfeited estates in Scotland from the Crown. He is moderate in party, but from gratitude attached to Mr. Pitt and Dundas. He married a sister of Lord Elphinstone's, by whom he has an only daughter. Captain Keith Elphinstone and Mr. William Adam are his brothers-in-law" (Adam, *Pol. State*, pp. 256–257). He voted for the Government candidate in 1790 (Mackenzie, *Pol. State*, p. 156). The reference here seems to be to a private financial transaction.

Duke of Portland *to* William Adam
24 *July* 1789

Friday night 24 July 1789

Dear Adam

Cunynghame is come up & goes tomorrow to Brighton to secure the priority of the D. of Y-s application to Ld Torphichen [1] who is now on his road to town at the instance of Dundas & Pitt—Cunynghame deserves every exertion that can be made for Him, & I trust will meet with the success to which he has so justly intitled himself.

I send You the inclosed from Macbride, & wish You could find time to speak again to Erskine that I may be enabled to give M- such an answer as may put an end to this *boat* about Fowey, which I am persuaded can end in no good.[2] When You call at Tunbridge desire Ld North to take an early opportunity of exerting his influence with Ld Dartmouth Mr ⟨Chertis⟩ & Mr Wright for their interest in Bucks for Ld Verney,[3] & don't forget to inquire of Him the purport of the Bp of Winton's answer respecting Shebbeare.[4]

[bottom portion of page torn off—following is at top of verso]

As I fear I shall not see You before the end of the Circuit[5] let me remind You of ⟨Wilthe⟩ & the supervisorship of Tin.[6] & of the Chaplainship for Skinner's friend Dr: Wilgress.[7]

If You should pass ever an evening in town unengaged previous to the conclusion of the Circuit let me know it & I will meet You.

Your's ever

P

NOTES

1. James Sandilands, 9th Baron Torphichen (1759–1815). Hill described him as an army officer with a small estate, who "can make several votes" in Linlithgowshire and will support Hope, the Government candidate (Adam, *Pol. State,* p. 227). The influence of the Duke of York in this case was undoubtedly military.

2. Capt. John Macbride (*d.* 1800), a doughty naval officer of mercurial temper, had successfully contested one seat at Plymouth in 1784 against the Government interest and as a member of the Commons had supported the Opposition. It would appear here that he had become involved in attempts to extend the Prince's political influence in the Duchy of Cornwall, or at least in Fowey. The franchise in Fowey was vested in tenants of the Prince (who was lord of the manor) capable of being port-reeves and in inhabitants paying scot and lot. Political interest in the borough, however, was principally distributed between the Rashleigh and Edgcumbe families, both of which tended to be Pittite. At the general election of 1790 some friends of Opposition were to make an assault on the interests of these two families in the borough by means of a manipulation of the Prince's Duchy patronage. Two Opposition candi-

dates, Sir Ralph Payne and Molyneux, Baron Shuldham (?1717–1798), were put forward. They were successful at the poll in an exceedingly close contest, but their opponents were later seated on petition. For information on this contest and on the further manipulation of Duchy patronage in Fowey and elsewhere, see A. Aspinall, ed., *The Correspondence of George, Prince of Wales 1770–1812* (New York, 1963–1964), vols. I and II. Thomas Erskine was attorney-general to the Prince of Wales.

    3. William Legge, 2nd Earl of Dartmouth (1731–1801), had been Secretary of State under Lord North. Chertis and Wright are unidentified. Ralph, 2nd Earl Verney (1714–1791), the early patron of the Burkes and connection of the Rockinghams, had in his lifetime squandered a fortune and dissipated a very considerable political interest. After having been a member for Buckinghamshire since 1768, he was narrowly defeated in 1784 by 24 votes. Seriously in debt, he was forced to spend the next six years on the continent to avoid prosecution. By 1790 he was able to return to England and to stand once again for Buckinghamshire. He was returned unopposed at the general election.

    4. Brownlow North (1741–1820), Bishop of Winchester (Winton), was the elder half-brother of Frederick, Lord North, to whom he owed his rapid preferment. Shebbeare is not identified, nor is the patronage (presumably ecclesiastical) which is apparently involved.

    5. Adam's legal circuit through the home counties.

    6. The supervisorship is a Duchy of Cornwall office.

    7. Rev. Dr. John Wilgress, D.D. Skinner has not been identified. The chaplainship was evidently on the Prince's establishment.

John Macbride *to* Duke of Portland
19 *July* 1789

Endorsed by Portland: Portsmouth 19 July 1789 / Capt: Macbride / Rx 20
Enclosed in Portland to Adam, 24 July 1789.

Portsmouth 19th *July 1789*

I have just received the Enclosed from my Friend at Fowey which I think necessary to Enclose for your

Grace's information. Surely my Lord Something ought to be done upon the Occasion if the Borrough can be recovered it is of Importance. I shall await your Grace's answer before I reply to the letter—There are Seven Sail of the Line assembled here, it is Said in order to Maneuvre. I think it looks Very like a Spithead fight. I am my Lord Duke with great regard & respect

your Graces most faithfull
Humble Servant

Duke of Portland &c   JNO. MACBRIDE

Thomas Dormer *and* Joseph Austen *to* Capt. John Macbride—13 *July* 1789

Fowey the 13 July 1789

Dear Sir/

We think it necessary to inform you of our Proceedings relative to *certain affairs* in the most early manner from the friendly and decided part you have hitherto taken in them—and are to hope they will meet your Approbation.

From Circumstances lately occuring which we shall explain more at large when we shall have the honor to meet you, as well as the following Reasons, we have thought fit to recommend Mr. Harvey[1] to be appointed Deputy Steward to this Manor instead of our good Friend Mr. Tonkin[2] who can more eminently serve the Interest by claiming his right as Dutchy Tenent by which we shall gain a Majority in the Homage in the Dutchy Court, and likewise Mr. Tonkin will become a fit Person to be elected Port-Reeve, who is the returning Officer—At the same time we beg leave to observe the Stewardships in their present State are unattended with Emolument, un-

less a Contest shoud arise from this Borough, in that case
we have so settled matters that Mr. Harvey is to share
profits with your friend Mr. Tonkin.

> We are
> Dear Sir/ with the sincerest Regard
> your much obliged & very
> Humble Servants
> THOMAS DORMER
> JOSEPH AUSTEN [3]

C. Macbride.

NOTES

1. John Harvey was a mason by trade (*Universal British Directory*, III, 129).

2. Peter Tonkin, an attorney, alderman, and member of the corporation of Plymouth, was Macbride's agent during the general election (*cf. Universal British Directory*, IV, 264, 265).

3. See Aspinall, ed., *Corresp. of Prince of Wales*, II, 214. Thomas Dormer was listed among the local gentry by the *Universal British Directory*, III, 128.

Sylvester Douglas *to* William Adam
31 *July* [1789]

Address: William Adam Esq / Lincoln's Inn / Fields—
Endorsed: S. Douglas / 30th July 89
The thirty-first of July, 1789, fell on a Friday.

Sylvester Douglas (1743–1823), later created Baron Glenbervie, was at this time a practicing barrister with close connections in Whig society. On 26 September 1789 he was to marry Catherine Anne North, eldest daughter of Frederick, Lord North. His "arrears" were to be paid from the subscription which had been instituted in the summer of 1788 to cover the expenses of Lord John Townshend, the party's candidate in the great bye-election for Westminster. It would appear that he had advanced money during the contest, probably as an agent of the party, and on the understanding that it would be reimbursed.

My Dear Adam—

I am just going to set out for Monmouth—I presume you are now at Tunbridge, & if you are Miss North will have told you my history before you receive this letter which I only write to request most earnestly that you will, as far as you can, without inconvenience to yourself or impropriety, hasten the payment of my arrears in the Westminster election—It makes you know part (near 700£) of the money I am to pay to you & the other two trustees in our marriage settlement, & I shall feel extremely mortified if I have it not forthcoming in the beginning of September.

Pray write to me & inform me that the close of your Circuit has been profitable in the present and as promising for the future as its commencement—Ever most affectionately

yours
S. DOUGLAS

Friday. 31 July

EPILOGUE

On 4 August 1789 Douglas again wrote to Adam, this time from Herefordshire (Blair Adam MSS): "I dined & slept at Lord John's [Townshend] on my way to join the Circuit, & found from him that the scheme of collection rests still a scheme. This has a little augmented my sollicitude, which however I of course I [sic] did not discover to him—Nor will you let him perceive that I have mentioned the subject to you." Again on 15 August he wrote from his circuit at Haverford West (Blair Adam MSS): "I have just received your letter & thank you most cordially for the pains you have taken & promise to take on my account. I am very unhappy about the business, but will hope that it will still be settled more speedily than you apprehend."

Thomas Kennedy *to* William Adam
5 *August* 1789

Endorsed: T. Kennedy / 5th Augt 89

Thomas Kennedy of Dunure (*d.*1819) had in 1779 married Jean Adam, eldest daughter of John of Maryburgh and sister of William.

Greenan 5th Aug: 1789

Dear Adam

Macdowall carried his election on the 3d by a majority of 21 votes when we came to call the roll for the Member.

We put the Oath of Trust to most of Lord Eglintounes & Sir Adam Fergussons Voters who all took it, which put an end to our hopes as we knew for certain for some time past that if these gentry came well up and took the oath that they must greatly out number us.

Lord Dumfries's interest almost totally failed and part of Lord Glencairn's; Sir John Whitefoords was very effective & Lord Cassillis's friends mostly real were almost all present. If the present opposition keep together and do what is in their power cordially it is certainly possible still to beat Sir Adam. However unless they exert themselves it [is] useless I think to move at all. I have declared this most explicitly to some of the principals and mean to call upon them to declare without delay. What I have said as to the possibility of beating Sir Adam can only be true, provided the Parliament is not dissolved for more than a year after this time.[1]

At the time when I made applications to you for Mr Andrew Blane,[2] when I saw he had little chance of succeeding as to the object he had then in view even if there had been a change of Ministers, I advised him to ask for something else or for a promise. He did not desire to press that then, but from the answer he made and from what has happened since he expects from Lord Cassillis and me that we should do whatever is in our power to obtain from the Duke of Portland a promise that in case of his coming into power he would take an early opportunity of giving something to Mr B. fit for him to accept. Lord Cassillis has promised to write to you upon this subject desiring that you may lay it before the Duke of Portland. However as his Lordship is rather uncertain as to performance in such matters, I should be very glad if you would do it as soon as you have a proper opportunity even if you have no letter from him, and at the same time as Lord C. ought & really intends to make the application I think it may be done in his name.

This letter is carried by Doctor Blane [3] who came down to vote having missed a letter that was written to him to let him know he was tied off.[4] I have not seen him but was informed by his Brother he was to set out for London immediately & I thought it better to write by him than by the Post.

We are tolerably well here and send our Love to Mrs Adam and all your Infants, the eldest of them I am afraid will not be pleased with that name. Believe me always

Yours &c
T.K.

NOTES

1. Parliament was to be dissolved 12 June 1790.

2. Andrew Blane, Writer to the Signet, brother to Thomas and Dr. Gilbert Blane, all of them voters in Ayrshire and supporters of Cathcart (Adam, *Pol. State,* pp. 37, 40–41).

3. Dr. Gilbert Blane was physician to the Prince of Wales.

4. The more usual term is "paired off"; *i.e.,* formal arrangement had been made for both Blane and one other voter of known opposite sentiments whereby each was bound not to vote, thereby cancelling the effect of their absences. In the eighteenth century this

was considered a perfectly acceptable substitute for voting when attendance was impossible or might impose unusual difficulties, although it was realized that a man's presence carried weight apart from his vote.

Duke of Portland *to* William Adam
7 *August* 1789

London Friday Even: 7 August 1789

My Dear Adam

I infer from Your's that the D. of Y. was not able to make any impression on Ld Torphichen, & I am heartily sorry for it. But yet I will not despair as Cunynghames activity & merits ought to command the success which is so justily their due—You left the business respecting the D of Q. in as safe hands as it could be placed, but it would still have been better for some person to have been empowered by the P- to negotiate with the Duke & I should have thought, ignorant as I am of the reasons of Fox's disinclination to undertake that commission, that he was the fittest for that purpose.[1] Pray let me see You before You take any steps respecting Fowey. I must be in town again on Thursday or Friday next when I hope to meet You, & as nothing seems to pass & You will be glad to pass some days at home after the business You have been engaged in, I will not desire You to come over to Bulstrode [2] till We have met here in town.

How do You explain Cathcarts dismission from the Post Office. I have sent to Cheap about Maitlands business & expect to see Him tomorrow morning.[3]

sincerely Your's ever
PORTLAND

NOTES

1. William Douglas, 4th Duke of Queensberry (*d.* 1810), had the "commanding interest" in Dumfriesshire and the "controuling interest" in Peeblesshire (Adam, *Pol. State,* pp. 97, 250). At the general election Sir Robert Laurie, who had occasionally supported Opposition in the Parliament of 1784, was to be returned again for Dumfriesshire. William Montgomery, the eldest son of James Montgomery, Lord Chief Baron of Exchequer, was to be returned for Peeblesshire. In 1784 Queensberry and the Chief Baron had agreed upon the return of David Murray, a Pittite, until the young Montgomery was available. Hill noted in early 1789 that the two families had already agreed that William was to come in at the general election, but he was not certain whether William would follow the line of the Queensberry and Townshend connections of his family or incline toward Government (Adam, *Pol. State,* pp. 250, 254). William Montgomery does not appear in the Opposition minority lists of 12 April 1791 or 1 March 1792.

2. The Buckinghamshire country seat of the Duke of Portland.

3. By at least 1774 the control of Malmesbury had passed into the hands of Edmund Wilkins, a Malmesbury apothecary and former agent of Lord Suffolk. Wilkins was in the habit of selling his two seats; one in 1774 and two in 1780 had gone to Government. In 1784 he had returned two Opposition candidates, Lords Melbourne and Maitland. On 17 August 1789, his father having died, Maitland succeeded as 8th Earl of Lauderdale and automatically vacated his seat. In 1790 he was to be returned to the House of Lords as a representative peer. Meanwhile the Opposition scurried to find a successor at Malmesbury, curiously beginning their search more than two weeks before the death of the 7th Earl. On 2 August 1789 Fox wrote to Portland (Add. MSS. 47561, f. 113) : "An application to Cheap is the only right measure about Malmsbury [sic] as I know nothing of the terms upon which Maitland came in." In the event Wilkins returned a candidate recommended by Pitt at the bye-election of February, 1790, while at the general election he returned the same candidate, Paul Benfield, along with Benjamin Bond Hopkins, who during the previous Parliament had proven himself a Pittite. Cheap has not been identified.

Charles James Fox *to* William Adam
9 *August* [1789]

Address: William Adam Esqr. / Richmond Park
Endorsed: Mr Fox / Augt 9th 89
Adam had a cottage in Richmond Park, where he lived when business did not keep him in London.

The right of election in the combined boroughs of Weymouth and Melcombe Regis was vested in the freeholders, who numbered about 300. The constituency returned four members. The sole patron of the boroughs since 1779 had been Gabriel Steward. In 1790 Steward was to sell his property and interest in the boroughs to Sir William Pulteney for a sum which the *H of P* (article on Steward) stipulates at £30,000 but which T.H.B. Oldfield (*An Entire and Complete History . . . of the Boroughs of Great Britain* [London, 2nd ed., 1794], I, 189) cites at £63,000 (the figure is not mentioned in other editions of Oldfield). Pulteney was a prominent and rather independent member who had generally praised and supported Pitt in the Parliament of 1784. At the general election he returned four candidates for Weymouth who had not held seats during the previous Parliament and who do not appear on the Opposition lists for the sessions of 1791 and 1792. Two staunch Oppositionists who had been sitting for the constituency, Welbore Ellis and John Purling, were forced to look for other seats, Purling without success and Ellis only in 1791.

Dear Adam

I wish very much you would make some inquiries about Weymouth. If Steward is inclined to sell for so small a sum as you mentioned and there is any reasonable ground for thinking the thing safe I know a very good Man who would purchase it immediately. Pray answer this directing to me at Brighton.

yours ever
C. J. Fox

St. Anne's Hill
9. August.

John Anstruther *to* William Adam
[27 *August* 1789]

Address: Willm. Adam Esq / Richmond Park / Surry
Postmarked: AU 28 89 / MARGATE
Endorsed: J. Anstruther / Margate / 27. Augt. 1789

John Anstruther (1753–1811) had been returned on the family interest for his father's constituency, Anstruther Easter Burghs, in January 1783. He had been a vocal and prominent supporter of Opposition in the Parliament of 1784. By early 1789 he had broken with his father politically and was thrown upon his own resources in seeking a new seat at the general election (Adam, *Pol. State*, p. 125). After making several attempts over a period of months, the party finally secured Anstruther a seat at Cockermouth, one of Lord Lonsdale's boroughs. The approach to Lonsdale was made through Alexander Wedderburn, 1st Baron Loughborough (1733–1805), which may provide the context for the postscript (but Loughborough had also handled the negotiations of 1784 in returning his nephew, Sir James Erskine, for Carlisle's borough).

Dear Adam

In Consequence of what you was so good as to say to Fox at Brighton I wrote to Pelham [1] upon the subject and am sorry to find from his answer that Old Q [2] says he will bring in two friends but will take no recommendation. I am sorry for it as it ends my Views in that Quarter and probably in any other so that I suspect I shall be fated to be one of the few Martyrs of the Year 1790. Having Escaped the Martyrdom of 1784 I might have thought my self safe but in spite of all I am afraid I shall like most other Martyrs wear the Crown against my will.

I mention Pelhams answer to you least any thing should occur in the summer or if you see Tom that you may Enquire how far it may or may not be possible to work on Old Q.—It has occurred to me that Carlisle [3] must have somebody for Morpeth as his son will not be of age—and I presume he will not sell—Do you know if he has any Views to any one? If so write to me about it.

We had Ld Tichfield here for two days. I picked him up miserable waiting for a packet he looked into the Books saw the name of Adams which he took for you being told he was in Parliament went and Called and to his astonishment found a Man whose face he never saw, when he found my name he was afraid to Venture a Second Mistake and it was by accident I met him in the street.

The Great Mr Hastings is here in Splendid Poverty and the Mountstuarts are near almost all the rest are hoc ⟨Genies⟩ Omne. The Shepherds tired of us and are gone to Ramsgate.

Mrs A is much better for her dipping and will I hope get through the winter without Rheumatism. She begs her Love to you Mrs Adam & the Elphinstones

& believe me Yours Ever

J ANSTRUTHER

Pray do you know if
Loughborough be gone

NOTES

1. Thomas Pelham of Stanmer (1756–1826), a close friend of many leading Opposition politicians and supporter of the party as member for Sussex.

2. The Duke of Queensberry.

3. Frederick Howard, 5th Earl of Carlisle (1748–1825), was the patron of Morpeth, where he had the return of two members. In 1784 he had returned two staunch Oppositionists, Sir James Erskine and Peter Delmé. Delmé died 15 August 1789, and it is this vacancy about which Anstruther enquires. At the bye-election in September Carlisle returned Francis Gregg, a close friend to whom the family owed obligations; Gregg was to occupy the seat until Carlisle's son might come of age. He voted with Opposition 1791–1792.

Lord John Townshend *to* William Adam
[*ante* 30 *August* 1789]

Endorsed: Lord J. Townshend / Westminster Subscription
This letter must be dated before that from Lord Robert Spencer to Adam
of 30 August 1789 (*infra*).

The subject of this letter is the subscription for Townshend's expenses in the Westminster bye-election of 1788. The subscription had been instituted immediately following the election, but the early response had been inadequate to the huge expenses incurred. Lord John Townshend (1757–1833), 2nd son of George, 1st Marquess Townshend, was a lord of the Admiralty under the second Rockingham and Coalition governments. An intimate friend of Fox from his youth, he had been "martyred" for his political attachments at the general election of 1784. But even without a seat he continued to be active as an Opposition man of business and political writer, as well as a popular member of Whig society.

Feltham Place

Dear Adam

I enclose you the letter which I submitted to the D. of Portland some days ago. I cannot help thinking that this plan, or something like it, is the only chance we have left. My chief doubt is with respect to the Postscript. I fear if it is so worded that most of our friends will subscribe only 100£. I think it would be the better way to specify the particular sums which certain persons have subscribed, & selecting these according to the person to whom you are applying. For instance a letter to Ld Cholmondeley [1] might state that such & such persons have subscribed *500*–a letter to Ld Powis [2] or Ld Malmesbury [3] that such & such had given *200*–to Sir J. St. Aubyn [4] or Sir H. Bridgeman [5] that such & such subscribed *100*. To the *last* class (for I hope we shall go no lower than fifties) that such & such have subscribed 50£.

75

However you will consider all this with the Duke & Ld Robert.[6] Settle it as you like, but pray let *something* be settled. & when the form of the letter is agreed on (which is the least material part) do pray take some steps for an immediate application to those whom we propose to be of the Committee & settle directly through whom the applications are to be made.

Ld Robt must urge Ld Fredk.[7] Dudly North will write to Pelham[8] & Sir Gerd Vanneck.[9] The Duke to Coke[10]—Any of us can speak to Ld Wm Russel.[11] Who shall ask Ld Clive[12] & M. Angelo[13] you must settle at Bulstrode—But pray let it be done. For if you miss this opportunity of arranging the business at Bulstrode, we shall do nothing before winter.

Pray let me hear from you when you return. Believe me

yours Ever
Most sincerely &c
J : T–

I think Ld Robt should certainly sign the letters, if you don't.

NOTES

1. George James, 4th Earl of Cholmondeley (1749–1827).

2. George Edward Henry Arthur Herbert, 2nd Earl of Powis (1755–1801).

3. James Harris, 1st Earl of Malmesbury (1746–1820).

4. Sir John St. Aubyn, 5th Bt. (1758–1839).

5. Sir Henry Bridgeman, 5th Bt., later 1st Baron Bradford (1725–1800).

6. Lord Robert Spencer.

7. Lord Frederick Cavendish (1729–1803), 3rd son of the 3rd Duke of Devonshire, uncle of the "unpolitical" 5th Duke, and brother of Lord George Augustus and Lord John Cavendish.

8. Charles Anderson Pelham (1749–1823), later 1st Baron Yarborough. Reported in 1780 to be "one of the richest commoners in England," he had been returned unopposed as member for Lin-

colnshire since 1774. He had opposed the North and Shelburne administrations and had consistently and actively supported Opposition since 1784.

9. Sir Gerard William Vanneck, 2nd Bt. (?1743–1791), one of the most wealthy of London merchants, had been member for the family seat at Dunwich since 1768, an opponent of the Grafton and North administrations and a consistent though silent supporter of Opposition since 1784.

10. Thomas William Coke (1754–1842) of Holkham, Norfolk, renowned even in his own day for agricultural experimentation. A warm admirer and personal friend of Fox, he had been one of "Fox's Martyrs" and did not sit during the Parliament of 1784. Returned again for Norfolk in 1790, he retained that seat almost without interruption for the next forty years.

11. Lord William Russell (1767–1840), 3rd son of Francis, Marquess of Tavistock, and younger brother of Francis, 5th Duke of Bedford. The Russells, of course, were one of the great Whig families, as were the Cavendishes, immensely wealthy and with political interests centered in the home counties. Lord William, having just come of age, had been returned unopposed for Surrey on 19 January 1789.

12. Edward, 2nd Baron Clive (Irish) (1754–1839), brother-in-law and eventual heir to the title of the 2nd Earl of Powis, who was also his political ally in Shropshire. A connection of Alexander Wedderburn, he supported the North administration and followed the Coalition into opposition.

13. Michael Angelo Taylor (?1757–1834) has first entered the House as a member for Poole in 1784. At first he actively and vocally supported Pitt, who had assisted him in securing his seat at the election, and was a government teller on Richmond's fortifications bill in February, 1786. By the following May, however, he was being drawn into Opposition circles through his support of the impeachment against Warren Hastings, for which he became a manager. By 1789 he was entirely Foxite and continued to be so through the period of the French Revolution.

Circular Letter for the Westminster Subscription

Endorsed: Proposed Circular Letter / for the Westminster Subscription
This is a copy of the letter submitted in Townshend's letter to Adam of *ante* 30 August 1789. The letter and the endorsement are in Adam's hand. Both Townshend's letter and this copy of his enclosure were found in the same bundle of Adam's parliamentary papers.

I take the liberty of acquainting you that the following Gentlemen have at the desire of several others of our common friends, formed themselves into a Committee for the purpose of collecting subscriptions; in order to defray certain accumulated expences, which from a variety of concurrent circumstances, have unavoidably accrued: & which, after many heavy ones already paid, remain unliquidated. The Gentlemen who compose this Committee are

Ld. Fredk: Cavendish
Ld. Wm: Russel
Ld. Robt: Spencer
The Earl of Lauderdale
Ld. Clive
Sir Ger: Vanneck
M. A. Taylor Esqr [crossed out]
T. W. Coke Esqr.
Dudly North Esqr [1]
Cha: And: Pelham Esqr
X Wm Adam Esqr [crossed out with "X" in front]

I am also requested to inform you that the debts to be discharged amount to no less a Sum than twelve thousand Pounds. In order to raise this Sum, we find ourselves under the necessity not only to recur to those upon whom former expences have already fallen very severely, but to extend our applications to a larger circle of our friends. Under these circumstances, where the honour of the party is so materially at stake, the Committee desire me to express their hope that they shall not too much trespass upon you by taking the liberty to solicit your assistance on the present occasion.

You will permit me to entreat as early an answer as you can conveniently favour me with.

I have the honour to be &c.

P:S:

The Committee have further desired me to inform you that upon the occasion of the last subscription (except in the instance of three or four individuals, who subscribed some thousands) the sums contributed by our friends in general varied from 100 to 300 £—

NOTE

1. Dudley Long North (1748–1829) was one of the principal and most valued men of business among the Opposition, though a speech impediment prevented his contributing to debate in the House. A connection of the Cavendishes, he was currently sitting for Great Grimsby on the interest of Charles Anderson Pelham.

Lord Robert Spencer *to* William Adam [30 *August* 1789?]

Address: William Adam Esqr. / Richmond Park
Endorsed: Lord Robt Spencer / Sepr 1789. / Wesr Subscrip.
Spencer wrote from Petworth with a postmark of 3 September 1789, which fell on a Tuesday; thus this letter must be dated Sunday, 30 August 1789.

Dear Adam,

I have seen Lord Frederick,[1] who consents to be of the Committee, but he rather thinks it would be better not to specify the sum wanted, and I am inclined to agree with him as the postscript will give people a hint of the kind of sum they are expected to subscribe: however it is not very material. You forgot to add Sir James St Clair.[2]

I have just been recommending my Cook to the D of

Clarence—pray back my recommendation if you have an opportunity. He cannot have a better Cook—I only part with him for the sake of taking Delme's, who is an old acquaintance & who will also be a kind of Maitre d'Hotel, which will be a great convenience to me. I'll write to you from Petworth [3] when I have seen Ld John.[4]

Yours ever sincerely
R SPENCER

Richmond
Sunday

NOTES

1. Lord Frederick Cavendish.
2. Sir James St. Clair Erskine. It is not clear whether his name was to be added to the committee or to a list of persons to whom applications were to be made.
3. Petworth, in Sussex, was the chief seat of the Wyndhams, Earls of Egremont.
4. Lord John Townshend.

Duke of Portland *to* William Adam
31 *August* 1789

Bulstrode Monday Even 31 August 1789

My Dear Adam

I have this moment received a Letter from our friend Philipps of Carmarthen informing me of his having just learnt Sir Wm: Mansel's intention of opposing Him at the general Election, & desiring me to apply amongst others to Mr: Meredith Price of Lincolns Inn for his vote & interest in his Philipps's behalf. As I have not the least acquaintance with or knowledge of Mr Price I am obliged to give You this trouble as I am persuaded You will think Philipps intitled to every exertion We can make in his favor.[1]

Have You ever had any conversation with Baldwin relative to Leicester & Worcester since our meeting at B. House? [2]

Lushington writes me word that he has given his voyage to Ld Fitzwilliams recommendation, & seems surprized after Jacob Wilkinson's conversation with me upon the subject (the substance of which I related to You) that he had not heard from Ld F. or me upon it. [3]

I wish the state of Hythe could be represented to Ld North, as it may be very material before Evelyn goes there again which Shove tells me he will be obliged to do very shortly. [4]

Your's Ever

P

[The following notes appear on verso in the hand of Adam and are crossed out as indicated:]

Duke of Portland
    (Hill)—
Anstruther [crossed out]
Gibbs—
Jackson—
Shove— [crossed out]
Pelham [crossed out]
Ld Lauderdale [crossed out]
D. North [crossed out]
Ld Clive [crossed out]
Douglas [crossed out]
Ld Robert (no list from Td—) ["Robert" crossed out]
Cunningham [crossed out]
Kennedy— [crossed out]
K. Elphinstone [crossed out]
⟨Murry⟩ [crossed out—the name could be "Merry"]
Cotsford.
    W. Adam

NOTES

1. John George Philipps (?1761–1816) of Cwmgwili, who had inherited the dominant political interest in Carmarthen from his father, had been returned unopposed for the borough in 1784 and had supported Opposition during the ensuing Parliament. Sir William Mansel, 9th Bt. (1739–1804), an influential Carmarthenshire squire, had been returned unopposed for the county in 1784 as a follower of Pitt. His attendance for important divisions in the House was most infrequent, however, and it has been suggested (*H of P*) that for this reason Government withdrew its support from him during the general election of 1790. By August, 1789, he was canvassing Carmarthen borough, as can be seen here. In the event Mansel did not stand a contest and Philipps was again returned.

2. This is surely William Baldwin (*c.* 1737–1813), a London attorney who at this time was a principal negotiator in settling the debts of the Prince of Wales and who was a leading Whig manager in Westminster elections. In 1795 he was brought into Parliament by Lord Fitzwilliam as member for Malton, replacing the recently deceased son of Edmund Burke. It would appear here that a meeting (probably comprising only Adam and Portland) at Burlington House in Piccadilly, the town residence of Portland, had suggested he might find an opportunity for a seat at Leicester or Worcester, though there is no clear evidence that he so much as canvassed a constituency in 1790. Alternatively, Baldwin may merely be seeking a position as an election agent, a not infrequent activity for men in his profession.

3. Stephen Lushington was at this time a director of the East India Company, and the subject here is a writership or some such company patronage at the disposal of Lushington which would enable a man to seek his fortune with the company in the East. Such patronage had great reputation and was eagerly sought. Jacob Wilkinson (*c.* 1716–1791), a wealthy London merchant, was a former director and Rockingham supporter within the company.

4. William Evelyn (?1734–1813) had been member for Hythe since 1768. Both he and Sir Charles Farnaby Radcliffe, his fellow member for the borough since 1774, had supported North's administration and opposed Shelburne's peace preliminaries. But after 1783 Farnaby Radcliffe continued to support Government while Evelyn went into opposition. Government had continued to support Evelyn in his candidacy in 1784, but probably more out of opposition to the bid for interest which the radical John Sawbridge had been making in the borough since 1774 than from particular preference for Evelyn. Earlier in the century the Lord Warden of the

Cinque Ports had exercised a considerable political influence in the borough, but since 1774 the influence of that office had diminished. Lord North had held that office since 1778. In 1790 Evelyn and Farnaby Radcliffe were once again returned. A. H. Shove was a barrister of Lincoln's Inn and a founding member of the Whig Club (*Whig Club*, 1792 ed.).

Richard Troward *to* William Adam
31 *August* 1789

Endorsed: Mr. Troward / 30th. Augt. 89 / Hertford

The *H of P* describes Hertford as "an independent borough, generally reckoned one of the most uncorrupt in the kingdom. . . . The representatives were nearly all drawn from local gentry." Although there were a few leading families, "almost any substantial Hertfordshire country gentleman would have had a chance." William Baker (1743–1824) came of a wealthy mercantile family with estates in Hertfordshire. His father had been a prominent M.P., a political connection of Newcastle and later of Rockingham. The younger Baker had himself been a connection of Rockingham, whose assistance he had sought in obtaining a seat in 1774 and whose instrument he had been to some extent in metropolitan politics. In 1780 Baker had successfully contested Hertford on his own interest. In 1783–1784 he actively supported the Coalition, was defeated at the general election, and was forced to remain out of Parliament until the general election of 1790, when he was returned for Hertfordshire in a major Opposition triumph. Baker also contested Hertford, but John Calvert, whose record in the preceding Parliament had been in support of Pitt, was once again returned for the borough, along with Nathaniel Dimsdale, whose father had occupied that seat since 1780 and who had also generally supported Government. William Hale (*d.*1793) of King's Walden, Herts, referred to here, was the descendant of Paggen Hale, who had been member for the county (1747–1755) rather than the borough. Hale was connected by marriage with Sir Charles Farnaby Radcliffe and Lord Grimston, both families being oriented toward a support of Government (John Burke, *A Genealogical and Heraldic History of the Commoners of Great Britain and Ireland* [London, 1st ed., 1833], III, 14). In 1790 he unsuccessfully contested the county.

Dear Adam,

The leading men of Hertford some time ago had a meeting upon the subject of Members for the next Parliament and the Deligation given their Chairman (which extends to one Seat only) has been by him communicated to me and he expects a recommendation from me—What further I have to say I don't know how to write, and as I presume you are frequently in town pray let me see you on the subject that we may determine what to do.

> Dear Adam
> Yours truly
> Rd. Troward
> N.P. 31st. Aug 1789.

I should think you & I might lock ourselves up in Pall Mall [1] for a few forenoons to a good purpose—I can attend you at any time.

[the following is at the head and upside down:]

P.S. Since writing this the inclosed came—Hale is the Chairman of the party whose ancestors used to represent the Borough.

NOTE
1. This may refer to the apartments above Becket's.

Duke of Portland *to* William Adam
3 *September* 1789

Bulstrode Thursday morn: 3 Septr: 1789

Dear Adam

I am much obliged to You for Your Letter to Mr Kennedy it is exactly what I could have wished to have

been said to Ld Cassillis, & certainly as frank as prudence
& fairness will admit of being said to any one in the
present state of Our Political Warfare. I have forwarded
it under my frank & Seal as I have that to Shove which I
rather fear they will think rather cold. I will write to
Baldwin by this nights post—a *Loser hand* than Hale
does not exist—I know he has been hawking about his
pretended interest in Hertford to every body that he
thought would bite. He wrote me a letter during the
Regency business for the purpose of introducing himself
which occasioned me to inquire about him of Our Friends
& from them I give You my description of Him. Since
that business & I believe about a month or six weeks ago I
had another Letter from Him containing the same offer
he has made through Troward but full of impertinence &
injustice to Baker to which I returned a very short answer, & can not therefore give or be supposed to give any
sanction to Hale or any proposition which originated
with Him—I am sure with such a man as Baker at their
door *who will represent* them if they chuse it there can be
no hurry for acceding to the proposition, & I believe the
only view in pressing it is to open Houses & to put money
into Mr. Hale's pocket. From this You see I cant forward the Letter to Cunninghame.[1] & I think it had better
be deferred till some inquiry can be made respecting the
names in Trowards Letter which I will send this evening
to Byng [2]—My hopes of our new Ally [3] were never very
sanguine, but yet I think the P–[4] might have managed
him to a better purpose.

sincerely Your's ever
P

NOTES

1. Sir William Augustus Cunynghame, who was now despairing
of success in Linlithgowshire.

2. Either the elder George Byng, a staunch old Rockinghamite
who did not die until 27 October 1789, or his son, the younger

George Byng (1764–1847), member for Middlesex 1790–1847, who was soon to become a leading Foxite.
3. Duke of Queensberry.
4. Prince of Wales.

Duke of Portland *to* William Adam
3 *September* 1789

Address: To / William Adam Esqre. / Lincolns Inn Fields / London

Sir William Molesworth (1758–1798), 6th Bt., of Pencarrow, Cornwall, had been returned without opposition as member for Cornwall at both the bye-election and general election in 1784. He was a highly independent member of the House. At first he tended to support Government, and seconded the Address in May, 1784; but as the Parliament wore on he tended more frequently to support Opposition, voting with them on the Richmond fortifications bill and the Regency. By the late summer of 1789 the Government had decided to support an opposition to Molesworth at the general election. Francis Gregor (*c.*1760–1815), of Trewarthenick, Cornwall, was successfully returned against the Opposition candidate. Sir Francis Basset (1757–1835), 1st Bt., of Tehidy, Cornwall, M.P. Penryn 1780–1796, was one of the most powerful political figures in the southwest of England. A naturally aggressive man with intensely but sporadically felt ambitions, highly jealous of his interests and with a mercurial temper, he had put forward ten candidates and contested five Cornish boroughs in the general election of 1784. He returned four members and was moderately successful in four out of five of the constituencies. In Parliament Basset had supported North's administration and later followed the Coalition into opposition.

Bulstrode Thursday Even : 3 Septr : 1789

Dear Adam

I have just received a Letter from Sir F. Basset acquainting me that an opposition is to be made, at the

86

instance & under the patronage of Administration, to Sir Wm: Molesworth at the next general Election; the name of the person (as well as I can make it out in Sir Fra:'s character) is Gregor, & he states him to be as formidable an opponent as could have been fixed upon. He desires me to write to the Dukes of Bolton Bedford & Nland & the E. of Bucks. & wishes for an application to Ld Carteret, which I think I can procure through Ld Foley without committing myself.[1] Sir Fras: is much hurt at the Report of Kerney's being appointed to the Stewardship of Fowey as Kimber held that office at his (Sir F's) recommendation, & he wishes very naturally that the appointment of Kerney might be Stopped. If it should not be completed, I therefore have now an additional reason for wishing it to be reconsidered at least.[2]

Your's ever

P

NOTES

1. Bolton had not voted on the Regency. Bedford, Northumberland, and Buckinghamshire had voted with Opposition. Carteret had voted with Pitt, Foley with Opposition (John Stockdale, *Debates in the House of Lords on the Subject of a Regency,* pp. 190–192).

2. The *H of P,* III, 397, identifies a J. Kimber in 1777 as the "steward of Philip Rashleigh," the highly independent member for Fowey whose family interest in the borough Basset temporarily disturbed in 1784. In 1797 a John Kimber, an attorney, was an alderman and Town Clerk of Fowey (*Universal British Directory,* III, 129).

Lord Robert Spencer *to* William Adam
[3 *September* 1789]

Address: Willm Adam Esqr / Richmond Park / Surrey
Postmarked: SE 3 89 / PETWORTH
Endorsed: Lord Robt Spencer— / Sepr 89. Westr. Sub—

Petworth

Dear Adam

Townshend [1] agrees with Lord Fred.[2] & me about leaving out the sum total wanted: The Postscript must also be left out to those who have already subscribed: When I see the list I can mark those pretty exactly: Townshend will send it to you—the list I mean—as soon as he gets back—He says he shall stay at his own house or thereabouts for some time—I think therefore you had better not attend to the engagement for friday in next week—Adieu

Yours ever
R SPENCER

NOTES
1. Lord John Townshend.
2. Lord Frederick Cavendish.

Sir William Augustus Cunynghame *to* William Adam—3 *September* 1789

Address: Wm. Adam Esqr. / Lincolns Inn Fields / M.P. London
Postmarked: SE 8 89
Endorsed: Sir W. A. Cuninghame / 3d Sepr 1789 / Scotch Politics
Either the postmark is that of London, which would indicate date of receipt; or Cunynghame delayed mailing the letter.

Livingstone Thursday
3d Septr. 1789

My Dear Adam

I should sooner have thanked you, for your Friendship in exerting yourself so much with the Prince, & Duke of York, about Old Q,[1] had I not waited to endeavour to find out, what were the Motives, that induced Ld. Torphichen to pay so little attention to the Duke of Yorks Letter, and to be so decidedly a Government Man, the Exact & Specific Promises, which they have made him I known [sic] not, but it was all done by Rose,[2] without the least Knowledge of Dundas, and the Connexion commenced between Rose & the Torphichen Family in February last, by his procuring a Ship in the County Trade in India, for the Son of Captain Sandilands who was in the Regiment with us, this he did at the desire of Ld. Marchmont,[3] who paid the Expence of Riging out this Youth. Ld. Torphichen finding Roses Power entered into Terms with him, & in order to make himself of Consequence, split his Superiorities [4] in this County, for he has no Estate in it; upon this being done, Rose wrote him to come to London, but no Bargain was concluded with Rose nor had Ld. Torphichen even seen him untill Two days after I delivered the Duke of York's Letter to him, & the Bargain will only be fulfilled, in case the Parliament lasts long enough to make his Votes effectual; which if it does, I am really affraid, that my Hopes of Success in this County are over for the present, but as nothing short of such great exertions of Government, could have beat me, of Course I, & my Family, will have it, when ever any change takes place; In the meantime, I shall exert myself, & spare neither my Purse or Person in the Cause, had all our Friends in this Country done the same, we should have made a better figure in Scotland at next Election, than I expect we shall do; for my Own part I see no

Chance I have except from Q, & was he to change his Opinions I should certainly give him up the Seat, in whatever Period of the Parliament it was; although I should not hold myself indebted to him for it, but to the Prince & the Party. Renfrew [5] & Stirling [6] is certainly ours, Aberdeen [7] & Roxburgh [8] I have little hopes of, Raith [9] will carry his Towns, as I hope Elphinstone [10] will, to whom and Family, & to Mrs. Adam pray remember Lady C. & me in the kindest manner. I am much affraid of Fife,[11] & dread Orkney,[12] Sir Thos Dundas has made no Compromise with Honyman, which I so much wished, & Honyman is at last gone to Orkney, I imagine to assist the opposite Interest. Sir J. Sinclair [13] & the Northern Burrows,[14] are both thought to be in a good Way; Sandy Brodie is to be their Candidate for Cromarty.[15] I recollect my Dear Friend, nothing further to trouble you with at present, excuse this long Scrawl, favor me with a few Lines, when you are at Leisure and believe me ever yours Sincerely ⟨While⟩

W A CUNYNGHAME

P.S.
Colonel A. Stewart [16] will be staunch with us, if they give a Regiment over him to Colonel Chas. Stuart [17] or Ld. Ballcarrass [sic].[18] Otherwise he is wavering. Ld. Abercorn [19] is thought dying.

NOTES

1. Queensberry.

2. George Rose (1744–1818), John Robinson's successor as secretary to the Treasury, was the Government's manager for general elections and patronage in England as Dundas was in Scotland.

3. Hugh, 3rd Earl of Marchmont (1708–1794).

4. For a concise explanation of the complex electoral structure and procedure of Scotland, see especially *H of P,* I, 38 ff.

5. John Shaw Stewart was returned for Renfrewshire by 22 votes to 21 against Alexander Cuninghame of Craigends (Mackenzie, *Pol. State,* pp. 165–167).

6. The reference is undoubtedly to Stirlingshire, where Sir Thomas Dundas was returned by 28 votes to 22 against Sir Alexander Campbell of Ardkinlass (Mackenzie, *Pol. State,* pp. 183–185).

7. George Skene of Skene (1749–1825) had come in for Aberdeenshire at the bye-election of 1785 on his own interest and that of Lord Fife, his relation, but on the understanding that he would support Government. In the House he took a rather independent line, and he joined the Independent Friends, the club founded by the Opposition leaders in Edinburgh. By September, 1788, Fife was so dissatisfied with Skene as to withdraw his support and to enter an alliance with Dundas and others for the return of James Ferguson of Pitfour (1735–1820), a close friend of Dundas who had unsuccessfully contested the county against Skene in 1785. Skene began his campaign in the autumn of 1788, voted with Opposition during the Regency Crisis, and was forced to withdraw from the contest in Aberdeenshire before it went to the poll. Skene remained out of Parliament until 1806. See *H of P;* Adam, *Pol. State,* p. 5; Mackenzie, *Pol. State,* p. 48.

8. Opposition undoubtedly preferred John Rutherfurd to Sir George Douglas, the latter being the candidate of the Dukes of Buccleugh and Roxburgh and a firm supporter of Government. Douglas was returned 30 votes to 25 (Mackenzie, *Pol. State,* pp. 174–177).

9. William Fergusson of Raith: "Married a sister of the Countess of Dumfries. Opulent. Much attached to Opposition. A family. Present Candidate for the Burghs in Fife," *i.e.,* the Dysart Burghs (Adam, *Pol. State,* p. 141). In September, 1788, Henry Dundas had persuaded Robert Lindsay, brother of the Earl of Balcarres, to stand in the place of the incumbent, Sir Charles Preston, a wavering Pittite. Lindsay withdrew within the year due to the expense; he was replaced by Charles Hope of Waughton, son of the Earl of Hopetoun (Furber, *Dundas,* pp. 222–223). The Opposition seems to have had its troubles as well, for it was John Craufurd of Auchinames rather than Ferguson who stood a poll in 1790. Craufurd carried Dysart and Burntisland, but Hope carried Kirkcaldie and Kinghorn, the returning burgh, thus winning the election (Mackenzie, *Pol. State,* p. 233).

10. G. K. Elphinstone.

11. Hill noted Henry Erskine as Opposition candidate for Fife in early 1789 (Adam, *Pol. State,* p. 143). As late as 30 March 1790 the Duke of Portland wrote to Erskine congratulating him on "the prospect you give us of your success in Fifeshire" and apparently agreeing to assist him in his contest, though by what means is

not specified (Alex. Fergusson, *Henry Erskine* [Edinburgh, 1882], p. 321, who mistakenly records his candidacy to have been for the Dysart Burghs). At the general election Erskine apparently declined a poll, for William Wemyss, a firm Pittite, was unanimously returned (Mackenzie, *Pol. State,* p. 97).

12. Hill had warned in early 1789 that "a spirit of jealousy among the smaller proprietors has produced an opposition to him [Dundas]. Among these the most considerable is Mr. Honeyman of Graemesay, who has now divested himself of his estate (reserving his vote) in favor of William Honeyman the Lawyer, his eldest son, who was made Sheriff of Lanarkshire through the interest of Mr. [Henry] Dundas, and is son-in-law to the Lord Justice-Clerk, preferred to that office by the same interest. . . . This is the best estate in Orkney next to Sir Thomas's" (Adam, *Pol. State,* pp. 243–245). In the event Sir Thomas Dundas's candidate, his cousin Thomas Dundas of Fingask, was defeated 13 votes to 19 by John Balfour, who was a nabob just returned from India and was supported by the Honymans (Adam, *Pol. State,* p. 246; Mackenzie, *Pol. State,* pp. 142–144). Balfour does not appear on minority division lists 1791–1792. Furber notes that Sir Thomas's family "did not regain its power in the far North until 1807 or later" (Furber, *Dundas,* p. 248).

13. Sir John Sinclair (1754–1835) of Ulbster had the dominant interest in Caithness, was first returned for that county in 1780 and subsequently at every election in which that county returned a member until 1812 (Caithness alternated with Buteshire in returning a member at general elections). He was essentially an independent man, but in the early 1780's he began to associate himself with Pitt through a common interest in financial and commercial policy. He at first tended to vote with Government in the Parliament of 1784, in which he sat as member for Lostwithiel on the Government interest. But by 1788, finding himself less intimate with Pitt than he would have liked, he was beginning to revert to independence, and voted with Opposition on the Regency questions. At the general election of 1790 he was unanimously returned for Caithness and continued to vote with Opposition on party questions 1791–1792. *H of P;* Adam, *Pol. State,* p. 77; Mackenzie, *Pol. State,* p. 74; Debrett, XXIX, 157; *ibid.,* XXXI, 400. Henry Dundas contemplated an attack on Caithness in 1790, but apparently it never came off (Furber, *Dundas,* pp. 226–227).

14. On the Northern or Tain Burghs, see the correspondence of F. H. Mackenzie and D. Macleod of Geanies, below.

15. Alexander Brodie (1748–1812), M.P. Nairnshire 1785–

1790, Elgin Burghs 1790–1802, a wealthy nabob and brother of Brodie of Brodie. A firm supporter of Government in the House, he was in turn strongly supported by Dundas in rather extensive electoral activities in the north of Scotland. But even with Government support he was narrowly defeated in Cromartyshire in 1790 by 4 votes to 3, the deciding vote being cast by the praeses or chairman of the election meeting. The successful candidate, Duncan Davidson of Tulloch, a wealthy West Indian, does not appear in the Opposition minority lists for 1791–1792. *H of P;* Adam, *Pol. State,* pp. 84–88; Mackenzie, *Pol. State,* 75; Furber, *Dundas,* pp. 229–231.

16. Alexander Stewart (*c.* 1739–1794), M.P. Kirkcudbright Stewartry 1786–1794, had long been seeking preferment from the Government, but without success. He finally came to vote with Opposition during the Regency, but Hill reported in early 1789 that he was "not steady in Opposition" and that it was "uncertain how he will go" (Adam, *Pol. State,* pp. 34, 208). In June, 1789, he was flatly told by Dundas that any chance of preferment had been obviated by his Regency votes (*H of P*). He does not appear on the Opposition minority lists for 1791–1792.

17. Charles Stuart (1753–1801), 4th surviving and favorite son of John, 3rd Earl of Bute, and younger brother of Lord Mountstuart. M.P. Bossiney 1776–1790, Ayr Burghs 1790–1794, Poole 1796–1801. Stuart tended to waver in his parliamentary conduct (when he was present) between the staunchly Government politics of his father and the opposite political sentiments of his two brothers and his own social circle, finally voting with Pitt on the Regency. He had been seeking preferment since the closing years of the American War and was highly dissatisfied with his treatment by Government.

18. Alexander Lindsay, 6th Earl of Balcarres (1752–1825), supported Henry Dundas in Scottish politics (Furber, *Dundas,* pp. 225, 233–234).

19. James Hamilton, 8th Earl of Abercorn, died 9 October 1789 while enroute to London. He possessed a small interest in Renfrewshire (Adam, *Pol. State,* pp. 281 ff).

D. C. Fabian *to* Duke of Portland
5 *September* 1789

Endorsed by Portland: Half moon Street 5 Septr: 1789 / Mr: Fabian / Rx 6 / Is the writer or his application / worthy of attention. / The cause of my sending Venison to / the Bull's head in Stratton Street / was one of the Stewards having been / an old Servant of mine.

One of the most interesting and significant organizational devices to emerge from the Westminster bye-election of 1788 was the permanently established (or so it was intended) parish political club. French Laurence described one such club to Edmund Burke in a letter of 16 August 1788 (*The Correspondence of Edmund Burke,* ed. Holden Furber [Chicago: University of Chicago Press, 1965], V, 410): "I was again obliged to postpone my visit [to Burke at Beconsfield] in consequence of the arrival of half a buck for the St Anne's committee; and I am, I believe, the only person in Town to meet such of the Parishioners, as we have thought proper to invite; and to settle with them, what is absolutely necessary to our future success in the Parish, a Parochial Club to assemble once a month during every session of Parliament. We are to have our Venison on Monday at 6s a head, wine included. I know, that it would be of infinite importance to our future objects if you could make it convenient to attend." The meeting was to be held at the King's Arms, Compton Street, which had been the Townshend parish headquarters during the bye-election (*The Times,* 16 July 1788). These parish clubs were obviously designed for men whose social rank was below the membership of the Westminster Whig Club, of which neither Fabian nor Thomas Rose were members (*Whig Club,* 1792 ed.). But the Whig Club, which had emerged from the Westminster election of 1784, also met once a month during the parliamentary session, and the annual dues of the senior club ran to only £2.12.6 which, given some seven to eight meetings a year, was surprisingly close to the six shilling dinner of the St. Anne's club. The Middlesex Freeholders Club, which was socially comparable to the Westminster Whig Club, also sold its tickets at 6s (*e.g., Morning Chronicle,* 3 February 1791). The supporters of Government interests founded similar parish and freeholders clubs in this period, but their clubs seem never to have been the first in the field and they seem generally not to have prospered so well or to have survived so long as the Opposition clubs. A lack of evidence makes it impossible to determine how long these particular parish clubs in Westminster remained active.

Half Moon Street Septr. 5th. 1789

My Lord Duke

Being desirous of giving every information to your Grace that may tend to Cement unanimity in a cause in which I have the honor to be engaged, I trust your Grace will not deem it impertinent in me in relating the following circumstance.

Soon after the last Election for Westminster [1] it was thought necessary, that a Club should be established among the Tradesmen in the Parish of St. George Hanover Square—Mr Thomas Rose of Davies Street Grocer exerted himself with such Success so as to be able to form a very respectable Society who meet once a Month at the Braunds head Bond Street [2] for the purpose of Communicating any information that may be beneficial to the Interest of Mr. Fox in the next Westminster Election.

Independent of this Club there are several others in Grosvenor Mews, Davies Street, and Bruton Mews, where Mr Rose constantly attend, and a few nights since at one of these meeting a Member declared "that the Duke of Portland had sent a whole Buck to the Bulls head in Stratton Street, but that no Venison had found its way there; notwithstanding the Promises of Ld. Robert Spencer and Col Byron [3] of sending some—"

I beg leave to hint to your Grace that a Dinner will be held in the course of next week at one of those houses and if some Venison was sent it would be the means of removing that kind of Jealousy that prevail among the Tradesmen who frequent these houses, under an Idea that they are neglected—With respect to myself I beg leave to

refer Your Grace to Mr Fox, Mr Byng, Ld Robert Spencer, Ld John Townshend, Col Byron &c

I have the honor to be
Your Graces most obedient &
Devoted humble Servant
D. C. FABIAN

NOTES

1. The bye-election of 1788.
2. The committee rooms for the Townshend party in St.
George's, Hanover Square, during the bye-election had also been at
the Braund's Head, Bond Street (*The Times,* 22 July 1788). The
four other locations mentioned below did not enjoy that type of
distinction.
3. Thomas Byron, of Portugal Street, Grosvenor Square, was a
charter member of the Westminster Whig Club (*Whig Club,*
1788 ed.) and was the chairman of the Townshend parish committee in St. George's, Hanover Square, during the bye-election of
1788 (*The Times,* 16 July 1788).

Duke of Portland *to* William Adam
9 *September* 1789

Address: To / William Adam Esqre: / Lincolns Inn Fields / London

Bulstrode Wednesday Even: 9 Septr: 1789
My Dear Adam

I am much obliged to You for Your three last Letters.
With respect to Cornwall I had ventured before the receipt of Your's of Saturday to alter the applications I had
made the preceding day in favor of Sir W: M.[1] & insert
the name of Sir J. St Aubyn so that no time was lost &
they were dispatched by that nights post. & this morning I
received a very favorable answer from the Dss: of Bolton who is the only one of my correspondents on that sub-

ject from whom I have yet heard.[2] Meredith Price has written me the handsomest letter possible in regard to our friend Philipps.[3] & I endeavoured above a week ago to make Your friend Mr Hill [4] as sensible as I could of the very high opinion I entertained of his Services & Ability in support of the Cause. Douglas [5] who left us this morning will inform You of the strange confusion of interests which prevails in the County [6] & Borough of Carmarthen. I am very sorry to find from Him that Philipps's success is uncertain, & that unless Campbell [7] himself could be prevailed upon to stand for Pembrokeshire that the Representation of that County must remain in its present state—I can't guess how Keene [8] could know that my information respecting W.[9] came from You, I asked him whether he thought Ld H.[10] would be likely to treat for it in case it should be at liberty, but I did not mention Your name to Him. & am persuaded that the two persons only mean *one*. I had a Letter of inquiry from him yesterday, & in that he tells me that he has had a great deal of conversation with W. Ellis [11] upon the subject & that Ld H. is inclined *& ready* to purchase. Do You know whether Ld Porchester [12] makes any stay in town. Yours' ever

P

NOTES

1. Sir William Molesworth.

2. Molesworth withdrew with some indignation from the contest in Cornwall at the first sign of an opposition by Government. Sir Francis Basset then brought forward his first cousin and political dependent, Sir John St. Aubyn. St. Aubyn lost and was not again returned to Parliament until 1807. Gregor was returned at the general election and continued to hold the seat until 1806.

3. John George Philipps, candidate for Carmarthen borough.

4. Laurence Hill.

5. Sylvester Douglas, who had just completed his Welsh circuit.

6. In 1790 the county returned George Talbot Rice (1765–1852). Control of the county had for many years alternated

97

between his family and that of their rivals, the Vaughans of Golden Grove. Rice does not appear in Opposition minority lists during the Parliament of 1790.

7. John Campbell (1755–1821) of Calder, Nairn; Stackpole Court, Pemb.; and Llanvread, Card. M.P. Nairnshire 1777–1780, Cardigan Boroughs 1780–1796. Reared in England and Wales rather than Scotland, Campbell was commonly believed to be ambitious to stand for Pembrokeshire. He had been a staunch supporter of North's administration; and, after a wavering beginning, had finally come into steady support of Opposition in the Parliament of 1784.

8. Whitshed Keene (c. 1731–1822), M.P. Wareham 1768–1774, Ludgershall 1774, Montgomery 1774–1818, a Northite within the Whig Opposition during the 1784 Parliament.

9. Weymouth.

10. Francis Conway (c. 1719–1794), 1st Earl (later 1st Marquess) of Hertford, was the political patron of Whitshed Keene. He already had the nomination of two members at Orford. Six of his seven sons sat in Parliament during this period, but at the date of this letter only five were provided with seats. The *H of P* (article on Francis Seymour Conway) neatly sums him up politically: "his principal aims in politics were to provide for his children and obtain a marquessate." But he and his sons followed Lord North into opposition and opposed Pitt during the Parliament of 1784.

11. Welbore Ellis (1713–1802) had been continuously a member of Parliament since 1741, and during two periods, 1747–1761 and 1774–1790, he was a member for Weymouth and Melcombe Regis. An old and constant supporter of Government, he had nevertheless followed Lord North into opposition in 1784.

12. Henry Herbert, 1st Baron Porchester (1741–1811).

Duke of Portland *to* William Adam
16 *September* 1789

Endorsed: Duke of Portland— / Sepr 16th 1789. / Ld R. S's seat— Jarvis's / Money— Winchelsea ⟨by⟩ F—

Bulstrode Wednesday 16 Septr: 1789

My Dear Adam

I return You many thanks for Your's from Epsom which I received this morning—I dont know how Ld R.[1] can be accommodated in the way he wishes perhaps it may not be impossible to manage for Him the alternative he proposes. At least we must try. If the County should remain quiet there will be no room for him at B.[2] nor ought we to hope for an opening at L—[3] so that M—port[4] is the only accessible place which occurs to me at present. I could wish to defer advancing any money till about the middle of next month, & if the explosion could be stopped till then, I think it might be prevented ever breaking out—[5] I wish Charles would settle with Nesbitt, & that he had not been nervous when You saw Him as You say he had no reason for it[6] —Pray remember me most kindly to G. O.[7]

Your's ever

P

I intended to have been in town on Friday but must defer it till next week when I should be very glad to meet You there

NOTES

1. Lord Robert Spencer.

2. The reference is to Bletchingley in Surrey. Sir Robert Clayton, a Portlandite and at that time member for Bletchingley, was the sole patron of the borough. He had inherited large estates in Surrey and had been returned for the county in November, 1783, only to be defeated at the general election. Presumably he was ambitious to resume his seat for the county, or was thought to be so. It was probably also known that he would not again return his cousin, John Kenrick, for the second seat at Bletchingley; he and Kenrick had been publicly feuding in the courts.

3. Undoubtedly Lymington, which was solely in the interest of the Burrard family. The Burrards had a long history of support for the government of the day, but the nephew and heir and present member for Lymington was known to be discontented over

army promotion. In the event he continued to support Government, as did all members for the borough in the Parliament of 1790.

4. Milborne Port. Thomas Hutchings Medlycott (c. 1728–1795) had inherited an interest in the borough with the return of one seat. In 1779 he had purchased the remaining principal interest in the borough in a shady transaction financed by Lord North with government funds on the condition that Medlycott henceforward return one member nominated by the Government. He did so in 1780, and in 1781 he vacated his own seat in the borough in favor of a Government candidate. He returned the same members in 1784, but apparently not without expense. At a bye-election in 1787 Medlycott had returned William Popham, a nabob, who split his votes during the Regency between Pitt and Opposition. This may have led Portland and Adam to hope Medlycott might be prepared to return an Opposition candidate at the general election. But the members for his borough supported Government in the Parliament of 1790.

5. The reference is to the payment of Jarvis for expenses connected with country newspapers and the general election.

6. John Nesbitt (?1745–1817), a Foxite and connection of the Prince of Wales, had inherited the nomination of two seats at Winchelsea along with a large but encumbered fortune. By 1789 he was on the verge of bankruptcy and was seeking to dispose of his property in the borough. Just before the general election he sold it for £15,000 to Lord Darlington and Richard Barwell. At the general election Barwell, a nabob, returned himself for the borough and continued his support of Pitt. Darlington returned his son, Lord Barnard, who appeared in neither of the Opposition minority lists before he was called to the upper house in 1792.

7. Possibly George, 4th Baron (later Earl) Onslow (1731–1814), whose estate at Imber Court was rather near Epsom in Surrey.

Lord Robert Spencer *to* William Adam
27 *September* [1789]

Endorsed: Lord Robt Spenser / 27. Sepr 1789.

Dear Adam

Charles [1] has written to Nesbit. I suppose he will get an answer in a day or two, if he is in or near town—I had applied to General St John [2] but the proposal I made was conditional and I wished him to write to the D of Portland upon the subject: He is under some little difficulty with regard to Bob Conway,[3] but I don't understand that he has had any overture made him by Ld Hertford.

I know Fabian very well—He is an active fellow & tolerably intelligent, but I should be very cautious of giving him too much encouragement, since he made use of Ld Fitzwilliam's name in canvassing for the Clerkship of the Vestry of St George's—Perhaps though he may not have been to blame, for I have never heard his defence. I think too that by sending venison to some clubs the Duke might offend others. We have seen Mingay—He says, if the D of Grafton keeps his engagements, Birch & Buxton are to come in quietly, if not he means to stand himself.[4] Adieu

Yours most sincerely
R Spencer

Thetford
27. Sepr—

Charles thinks that Nesbit is engaged, but can't recollect to whom.

NOTES

1. Fox.
2. Henry St. John, who was managing Wootton Bassett for his brother Lord Bolingbroke.
3. Robert Seymour Conway (1748–1831) was the 3rd son of Francis, 1st Earl of Hertford. He had purchased a seat at Wootton Bassett from the St. Johns in 1784. He was not returned in 1790, and re-entered Parliament only in 1794 when a family seat at Orford was vacated by his brother, who was raised to the House of Lords.
4. Augustus Henry Fitzroy, 3rd Duke of Grafton (1735–1799), had the nomination of two members at Thetford during this period. James Mingay (1752–1812) was to be returned for Thetford in 1806, apparently on the Grafton interest, only to be turned out on petition following the general election of 1807 by Thomas Creevey, the radical politician, who had opposed Mingay on the interest of Lord Petre. At the general election of 1790

Grafton returned Robert John Buxton (1753–1839), 1st Bt., of Rushford, Norfolk, and Joseph Randyll Burch (*c.* 1757–1826) of Great Cressingham, Norfolk. Burch became a member of the Whig Club on 10 November 1789 (*Whig Club,* 1792 ed.). Buxton does not appear in the Opposition minority lists for the Parliament of 1790, while Burch has nearly a perfect voting record with Opposition. The Duke of Grafton pursued a rather independent line during these years, though he most frequently supported Pitt. It was not until the summer of 1793 that he went into decided opposition (C. J. Fox to William Adam, 18 September 1793, Add. MSS. 47569, ff. 14–15).

Duke of Portland *to* William Adam
7 *October* 1789

Bulstrode Wensday 7 Octr: 1789

Dear Adam

A bad cold & a worse head ach prevented my fulfilling my intention of being in town today, or writing to You by the Dss: who went up this morning for the drawing Room—I gave her a message for You respecting Saturday, as it will be very inconvenient for me to be absent from hence on that day & can not be necessary unless new & *credible* alarms arise respecting Dissolution which would render it very desireable & important to have a very early conversation with Fox upon that subject. In which case I will certainly come up. But as it occurs to me that You may have an opportunity of seeing the Prince tomorrow I wish the appointment of Dr John Wilgress to a Chaplainship which H.R.H. *forced* upon Skinner could be ordered to be made out—that the Supervisorship of Tin so long sollicited by Sir F. Basset for *Isaac Head* of Hilleston [1] could be arranged, & that H.R.H. could be put upon his guard respecting any applications that may be made to Him relative to the Sheriffdom of Cornwall which under the present circumstances of the Contest is of particular consequence—Many thanks to Elphinstone [2] for his kind intentions to comply with my request in favor of Hudson the Butcher, the state of the case is a very satisfactory answer at present & whenever the D. of C—[3] leaves St. James's a part of the Butcher business, I dare say will perfectly content him—I don't know that Your Letter had it arrived in time could have made any difference in E–s determination. I am certainly very sorry for it, but I don't know that I could have advised otherwise—I shall be glad to know the effect of my last short note—& wish as soon as You can learn any thing of *Lavender* to be informed of it.[4] Your's ever

P

NOTES

1. Isaac Head was a resident of Helston in Cornwall; the Supervisorship of Tin was an office in the Duchy of Cornwall. Basset was in competition for the appointment with the Duke of Leeds, who at this time was Secretary of State for Foreign Affairs. Head seems not to have been appointed. See A. Aspinall, ed., *The Correspondence of George, Prince of Wales 1770–1812* (New York, 1964), II, 16.

2. Probably G. K. Elphinstone.

3. Duke of Clarence.

4. Lavender was the man through whom a seat at Evesham was to be secured. Contests in Evesham were frequent, hard fought, and expensive. The *Universal British Directory* (III, 55–57) lists "Joseph Lavender" twice, once as an attorney, once as a partner in an Evesham banking house connected with Sir James Saunderson & Co. in London.

Duke of Portland *to* William Adam
13 *October* 1789

Address: To / William Adam Esqre: / Lincolns Inn Fields

Bulstrode Tuesday night 13 Octr: 1789

Dear Adam

I am rather glad You had not an opportunity of speaking to Fox on Grenville's [1] subject. I have written to Ld Fitz: [2] to give me *discretionary* powers to press him, & if I obtain them, I think I shall be able with the Letter I have received today from Ld Porchester to prevail upon Him to make a trial where neither expense nor disgrace can be incurred, & very possibly ground laid for success on a future & not distant Vacancy. [3] I am rather anxious for the Report of Lavender as I am pressed by Him & dont like to open it to Baker [4] till I know the value of my authority. sincerely

Your's &c

P

NOTES

1. Thomas Grenville (1755–1846), 2nd son of George Grenville, the prime minister, and brother of the Marquess of Buckingham and W. W. Grenville. Thomas was an intimate of Whig society, and his political loyalty and sympathies lay decidedly with his friends and not with his ministerial family. In 1779 he had succeeded to his brother's seat for the county of Buckinghamshire, but in 1784 he had lost that seat after having taken a forward part against his family and with the Coalition and having followed the latter into opposition. He did not sit during the Parliament of 1784. At the general election he was to be returned by P. C. Crespigny for Aldeburgh.

2. Lord Fitzwilliam.

3. The constituency referred to is Bath. In the event Bath returned two stout young Government supporters, Lords Bayham and Weymouth.

4. William Baker.

Duke of Portland *to* William Adam
14 *October* 1789

Address: To / William Adam Esqre: / Lincolns Inn Fields / London

This undoubtedly refers to the payments to Jarvis for expenses connected with country newspapers.

Bulstrode Wednesday Even 14 Octr: 1789

Dear Adam

If it is *very necessary* I will send You the order You remind me of by the return of post, but if I don't receive Your commands to that purpose, You may depend upon it the middle of next week.

Your's ever
P

Duke of Portland *to* William Adam
19 *October* 1789

Endorsed: D. of P. 19th Octr 89 / annexing a Drt of £200 I
received / from Ld Robt Spenser / was advanced to
pay / Jarvis to pay the Country / Papers—
The bottom portion of the single sheet has been torn away.

Bulstrode Monday 19 Octr: 1789

Dear Adam

Hereunder I send You an order for the sum required— I don't think Ld Sheffield has so much reason to be in good spirits as he appeared to have from the state of the Canvas he sent me, for he had only 95 positive promises out of 212 whom he canvassed, & there are besides 263 whom he did not see.[1] I have written to Ld

Cadogan for him to apply to His Son who is a great Leader among the Methodists [2]—I am glad to hear so good an account of Ld Breadalbane's Brother as well upon my friend Ld Kinnoulls as his own account.[3] I will write to Cornwall. Have You heard nothing more of Weymouth—Taunton,[4] or Tregony? [5]

Your's ever
P

NOTES

1. John Baker Holroyd (1735–1821), 1st Baron (later 1st Earl of) Sheffield. Sheffield was a Northite, a knowledgeable and respected authority on matters of trade and finance, who had followed the Coalition into opposition. No longer enjoying the support of Government, he lost his seat at Coventry in 1784 and did not sit during the ensuing Parliament. In 1790 he successfully contested Bristol. The constituency referred to here cannot be Coventry or Bristol, however.

2. William Bromley Cadogan (1751–1797), 2nd son of Charles Sloane, 4th Baron (later 1st Earl) Cadogan, was an Anglican clergyman and vicar of Chelsea.

3. Colin Campbell of Carwhin (1763–1792) was the brother of John Campbell (1762–1834), 4th Earl of Breadalbane. Colin's connection with Robert Auriol Hay Drummond (1751–1804), 9th Earl of Kinnoul, and the subject of this reference are obscure and need not be political. See Adam, *Pol. State,* notes on Perthshire.

4. Taunton is described by the *H of P* as "an open borough" whose "contests were frequent and violent." Since the 1760's the principal interests in the borough had been split between a Government-supported corporation and an organization called the "Market House Society," apparently composed of Dissenters and manufacturers who were excluded from and hostile to the corporation. In 1784 the Market House Society had returned two members unopposed, Alexander Popham and Benjamin Hammet, both of whom had local connections and gave an independent general support to Government during the ensuing Parliament. At the general election of 1790 Popham and Hammet were again returned.

5. The right of election in Tregony lay in about 150 inhabitant householders. Lord Falmouth, who had been the principal patron

of the borough, had sold his Tregony estate to Sir Francis Basset in 1788 in return for Basset's support at Truro. But Basset then sold the Tregony property to Richard Barwell, the nabob and Government supporter; and the transaction seems to have been completed before the general election, perhaps even before the date of this letter. There was apparently some Oppositionist feeling that Barwell's interest might be tested and shaken before it had opportunity to become deeply felt.

Duke of Portland *to* William Adam
24 *October* 1789

Bulstrode Saturday 24 Octr: 1789

Dear Adam

I am to meet Baker tomorrow noon *exactly* at B. House [1] & have sent to Tom Grenville to come there at one—I have no particular desire to see H–[2] but I shall remain in town till between 2. & 3 when I must leave it as I have promised to return here to dinner. Your News if confirmed & not *reversible* will be very distressing, unless it gives an opening for Ld P [3] & Ld Holland [4] which I should hope under the present circumstances Wilkins [5] might not be averse to cooperate in.

Yours ever

P

I have full powers from Ld Fitzwilliam
to use what arguments I think fit, with Grenville

NOTES

1. Burlington House.
2. Possibly John Halliday (?1737–1805), a London banker with a family estate near Taunton. He had been member for the borough 1775–1784; after an early period in Opposition he had generally supported Government. In 1784 he had not stood, expecting Government preferment to office which would disqualify him

from membership in the House. The preferment was never forth-coming, and in 1790 he sought Opposition support and once again contested Taunton.

3. Possibly Lord Porchester, who had an estate at Christian Malford, Wilts. Alternatively, Henry Temple (1739–1802), 2nd Viscount Palmerston, a consistent Northite supporter of Opposition and intimate of Whig society; in 1790 he was in need of a seat.

4. Henry Richard Vassall Fox (1773–1840), 3rd Baron Holland, was at this time not yet sixteen years old. His grandfather, 1st Lord Holland, had exercised a considerable influence in the politics of Malmesbury; and his uncle, Charles James Fox, had been member for that borough 1774–1780. As a British peer Holland was a member of the House of Lords; reference here is to the cultivation of the family political interest.

5. Edmund Wilkins of Malmesbury.

Duke of Portland *to* William Adam
26 *October* 1789

Address: To / William Adam Esqre. / Lincolns Inn Fields / London
The bottom half of the portion of the sheet on which the letter was written has been torn away.

Dear Adam

Baker will not engage & all I can bring Grenville to without disclosing the whole *secret* to Him or insisting positively upon his trying B.[1] is a promise to undertake upon Moysey's[2] coming *to town* ⟨unless⟩ M–[3] should be of opinion that Ld R.[4] would be a preferable Candidate. You must think & find me a good man for E.[5] I think I shall be in town on Thursday Evening but certainly on Friday & by noon if I don't come on Thursday.

Your's ever
P

Bulstrode Monday night
26 Octr: 1789

108

NOTES

1. Bath.
2. Abel Moysey (1743–1831), M.P. Bath 1774–1790, was the eldest son of a distinguished Bath physician. He began his parliamentary life in Opposition, but in 1777 he was appointed a judge on a Welsh circuit and henceforward adhered to North's government. He opposed Shelburne, supported the Coalition and followed it into Opposition. A local opposition to his interest began to rise at Bath in 1784. William Pitt himself was asked to stand against him; and although he refused to stand, Pitt still received 12 votes to Moysey's 17. Apparently Moysey did not choose to stand in 1790.
3. Moysey.
4. Lord Robert Spencer.
5. Evesham.

Duke of Portland *to* William Adam
[31 *October* 1789?]

Endorsed by Adam's clerk: Duke of Portland / 1790. Octr
Although there is no salutation, spacing indicates that this is a complete letter. Portland's script is much larger than usual, probably the result of haste. The negotiations mentioned in the text clearly indicate a date in late October 1789, rather than 1790; the 31st fell on a Saturday.

I would not send after Tollemache [1] till I knew G–N–s [2] determination, I have now sent, but dare say he is out of town, & if matters press so much You had better write to Blair, [3] I am anxious for T–G'–s [4] determining to stand for Bath that I may have Ld Robts [5] for Evesham—It will be necessary for me to see Trevanion [6] again, & I need not say that I shall be happy to have his authority to make the proposal to Ld N— [7]

Sat: half past 12
I shall be in town again on Wednesday for one night—

NOTES

1. Wilbraham Tollemache.
2. George Augustus North.
3. Blair cannot be clearly identified, but the constituency suggested for Tollemache may be Dover.
4. Thomas Grenville.
5. Spencer.
6. John Trevanion (*c.* 1740–1810), a London merchant, M.P. Dover 1774 to 1784, and 14 January 1789 to 1806. Trevanion had steadily opposed North's administration and had supported Shelburne's peace preliminaries. In 1784 he stood at Dover with the support of North, who was still Lord Warden of the Cinque Ports, but was defeated by a Government candidate. He was again returned at the bye-election of 1789, however, with Opposition support and in opposition to another Government candidate.
7. Lord North.

Sir David Carnegie *to* William Ross
31 *October* 1789

Address: Montrose thirty first Octr 1789 / Mr William Ross sollic-
itor / Boswells Court near / Lincolns Inn / London
Postmarked: NO 5 89 *and* NO ⟨...⟩
Endorsed by Adam's clerk: D. Carnegie / 30th. Octr. 89

Sir David Carnegie (1753–1805), 4th Bt., of Southesk, had been member for the Aberdeen Burghs since 1784 and was the Opposition candidate again in 1790. A friend and relation by marriage of Sir Gilbert Elliot and revolving in Opposition circles, he had opposed Pitt in the Parliament of 1784.

Dear Sir

I wrote Mr William Adam two days ago to use his influence to obtain a *strong* letter from Mr Frances Aberdeen (a servant about the person of the Prince of Wales) [1] to his brother William Aberdeen a councillor of this borough, to give me his vote & interest. In case

Adam is not in town or has not got my letter, I request you will not lose a moment to get Anstruther[2] or some one of our friends to make the application as it is of great consequence to me, I am so hard pusht—& I wish it instantly. Yours in haste

DAVID CARNEGIE

Montrose 31st Octr 1789

NOTES

1. In 1801 "Frank" Aberdeen was identified by the Duchess of Devonshire as a "porter" of the Prince of Wales and formerly her own servant (Earl of Bessborough, ed., *Georgiana* [London, 1955], pp. 243–244).
   2. John Anstruther the younger (*d.* 1811).

Duke of Portland *to* William Adam
8 *November* 1789

Bulstrode Sunday 8 Novr: 1789

Dear Adam

I will Keep both the Letters I received from You this morning till we meet, which may be on Wensday Evening if You have no particular engagement as I shall be in town on that day & have sent to Ld Torrington to meet me at dinner to talk over his publick & private business.[1] But I dare say I shall be at liberty by nine, besides I shall not leave town, at *soonest* till Friday afternoon so as to get here by dinner, & possibly not till Saturday. We want a great *set off* for the long Letter & I am sure I know of *none*. Have You seen or heard any thing of Sir J. Morshead?[2] Besides Cornwall, is any appointment ordered for Skinner's friend, the Revd: John Wilgress D.D.?

Your's ever
P

I wish Simpson [3] had complied punctually with Our wishes, & sent *Us* the Letter We desired Him to write—I send You Bridgeman's [4] & only keep the *long* Letter.—

NOTES

1. George Byng (*d.* 1812), 4th Viscount Torrington. The "publick business" may have concerned the borough of Wigan, where Torrington's family had been involved politically in the past and where Portland still retained a considerable personal interest. By 1784 the return of both members for Wigan seems to have been principally in the hands of the Bridgeman family, whose interest Portland had supported in the past. All three Bridgemans had voted with Opposition during the Parliament of 1784.

2. Sir John Morshead (1747–1813), 1st Bt., M.P. Callington 1780–1784, Bodmin 1784–1802. During his first Parliament he had become attached to North's administration, particularly to Lord Sandwich, and in 1784 he followed his friends into Opposition. During the Parliament of 1784 he was drawn into Carlton House politics; by 1791 he was deeply involved in political and patronage management connected with the Duchy of Cornwall. See especially A. Aspinall, ed., *The Correspondence of George, Prince of Wales 1770–1812,* II, *passim.*

3. John Bridgeman Simpson (1763–1850), 4th (and 2nd surviving) son of Henry Bridgeman (M.P. Wenlock 1768–1794). M.P. Wenlock 1784–1785, 1794–1820.

4. Probably Orlando Bridgeman (1762–1825), 3rd (and 1st surviving) son of Henry Bridgeman and elder brother of John Bridgeman Simpson. M.P. Wigan 1784–1800. His return at Wigan in 1784 had been supported by Portland. It is of course possible that this reference is to Henry Bridgeman, the father. It is less likely that the entire subject concerns Wenlock rather than Wigan, since Portland had no interest in Shropshire and the old alliance between the Bridgeman and Forester families seems to have continued at Wenlock into the Parliament of 1790 with the return of two family members. At the general election the Bridgemans once again returned Orlando at Wigan. Portland returned John Cotes (?1750–1821), as he had done since 1782.

Henry Erskine *to* [William Adam?]
8 *November* 1789

Endorsed by Adam's clerk: H. Erskine / 8th. Novr. 89
H. Erskine was usually less formal with Adam both in salutation and closing.

Hill wrote concerning Perthshire in early 1789: "The present candidates for the County are General [James] Murray [of Strowan, M.P. Perthshire 1773–1794], the uncle of the Duke of Athole, who is supported by the Duke and Administration; and in opposition to him, Mr. [John]Drummond of Megginch [M. P. Shaftesbury 1786–1790], who is supported by many independent men in this County, not from an opposition to Mr. Pitt's Administration, but in order to break the influence of the family of Athole, of which they are extremely jealous. Mr. Drummond is also supported by the Earl of Breadalbane, and by the friends of the Opposition, and it is to be hoped that the support he receives from them will attach him to the same measures with them in Parliament in case he is returned" (Adam, *Pol. State,* p. 257). Drummond had voted with Pitt during the Parliament of 1784. Murray was returned at the general election 67 votes to 39 (Mackenzie, *Pol. State,* pp. 154–159).

Edinburgh
Novr. 8. 1789

My Dear Sir

Col. Hunter of Knap[1] is a Voter in Perthshire—He will be entirely swayed by the D. of Clarence—Lord Kinnoul is extremely anxious that the Duke should apply to him. I must therefore beg you will take the best means to secure this—You know how Valuable a Friend Ld. Kinnoul is and how important the County of Perth is to our Interest.

I am Dear Sir
with the most perfect regard
Your's ever
HENRY ERSKINE

The Sooner I can communicate to Lord Kinnoul the result so much the better—

NOTE

1. "Peter Hunter of Knap. A Colonel or Major in the Army. In easy circumstances. The estate sold to Lord Kinnaird, but the vote reserved during life. Messrs. Hunter, Hop Merchants, London, may have influence" (Adam, *Pol. State,* p. 263).

Francis Humberston Mackenzie *to* William Adam—10 *November* 1789

The enclosures do not appear to be among the Blair Adam MSS.

This letter has been included not only for the information it contains but also to provide an insight into the extraordinary complexity of Scottish politics—its busy, gossipy, highly personal and even petty quality—and into the personalities of the magnates who played this game of family aggrandizement and made it a way of life. In such a political environment "party" on a national level could only impose itself upon a situation whose dynamics were essentially independent of it. Nevertheless such conditions are scarcely uncommon even in more modern political situations; and it would be incorrect to conclude that, when successfully imposed, national party sentiment and attachment could not be real and effective even in late eighteenth-century Scotland. Certainly the hope of both Government and Opposition in this period was precisely to make it both real and effective.

The political geography of the Northern or Tain Burghs was exceedingly complex in the 1780's. The constituency was composed of five burghs in four counties. By 1784 Sir John Sinclair of Ulbster, at that time a Pittite, had formed an alliance with the Sutherland interest (Elizabeth, Countess of Sutherland, who in 1785 married Lord Gower), a staunch supporter of Government; this alliance controlled the burghs of Dornoch (Sutherland) and Wick (Caithness). Sir Thomas Dundas had meanwhile formed an alliance with Lord Ankerville, giving them control of Kirkwall (Orkney), Tain (Ross) and Dingwall (Ross). The oppositionist Dundas–Ankerville alliance had thus carried both the general elec-

tion of 1784 and the bye-election of March, 1786, by 3 votes to 2.
At the bye-election of June, 1786, the burgh of Tain changed sides,
however, and the Administration candidate, Sir Charles Lockhart
Ross of Balnagown, was returned by 3 votes to 2. According to the
H of P, "the shift in power was the result of a deterioration in
Lord Ankerville's affairs, which had forced him in 1786 to part
with much property, and cost the family its control over the burgh
of Tain." Tain, then, was at this time the key to control of the
Northern Burghs; and it was in Ross-shire, where Tain was located, that the power of F. H. Mackenzie and Donald Macleod of
Geanies was centered. Mackenzie, who had succeeded his brother
to the head of the clan Mackenzie, was in the process of rebuilding
the family estates and political influence in the North and particularly (though not exclusively) in this county. He was a most indus-
trious and ambitious politician and supporter of Opposition, principally because they were against the established Government
magnates in the county. He was an invaluable correspondent,
always, as he says, "with a view to the main chance." Although left
deaf and almost dumb by scarlet fever early in life, he was a man of
wide interests and vigorous personality. At the general election of
1790 William Adam was unanimously returned for Mackenzie's
seat in Ross-shire (Mackenzie, *Pol. State,* p. 170). In the burghs
the Opposition interests were able to retain control of Dingwall
and Kirkwall but not of Tain; they did not contest the election,
therefore, and Sir Charles Lockhart Ross was unanimously returned (Mackenzie, *Pol. State,* pp. 229–230).

My Dear Adam/   Seaforth Lodge 10th. Novr. 1789

I had long ago answered yours of the 19th. Sepr. had I
had any thing particular to say but there has ever since
the Election of Tain Magistrates been a business in agitation that I did not chuse to write about till I coud [sic]
say something decisive. I am sorry to say things have not
gone as I coud [sic] wish & as in Pols it is always best to
be clear I must say we cannot look on the Northern Burroughs as a sure seat but we still as you will see have a
good little to fight. I wish you to communicate this to the

Duke [1] as a too sure reliance on this seat might create a distress at the Election [2]—I send you two of Geanies letters for your information & shall only so far comment on them as to say it turned out afterwards the Sollicitors [3] letter was merely a thing of supposition wrote to Major Ross [4] to spur him to exertion & detailing every thing the Solicitor thought possible *as really to happen* some part of the Solicitors information will soon let *you* see that neither he or Geanies himself know what is actually intended in our arrangements—The Election mentioned in the letter of the 1st. of Octr. left us in a minority of 5 to 7 for 3 of the Council are disqualified from voting for a delegate of these 7 Sir John Ross,[5] Major Ross & Barclay [6] are three—Sir John is literally dying & certainly will never be able to go to Tain the Major is also in a very bad state of health as for Barclay *I think we have caught him again*—I acted as the Jack Robinson on this memorable occasion—I had occasion to know that B. was deeply hurt at his own conduct & *still more* at a disappointment of a little place he expected from the Admiral encouraged by this I sliped an old gentleman at him to encourage this disposition & with such good success that two days before I left the country B. went to Old Gillanders [7] my factor to desire him to apply to me to make his peace with Geanies this I readily undertook & have since concerted with Geanies a plan that must fix him ours—Geanies has three undersherriffs one for Tain one for Dingwall & one for the Lewis [8] he did the duty for Tain himself but has agreed to appoint Barclay his substitute which is a very generous attempt of Geanies as it takes £50 a year out of his pocket—Thus you see we need not despair we have 5 staunch & suppose the old gentleman not to attend or to dye we are sure of Barclay which instead of 5 to 7 will make us six to five you will see at first glance that though not so well as one coud [sic]

wish we are still much better than last year we have got
Geanies on the list & kept Sir Johns second son & Agent
off—At Dingwall all is quite well for not chusing to trust
to *may bes* I turned off the doubtfull sans ceremonie &
brought on my Brother Sandy & another in their place &
got myself elected Provost—The commotions of these
Burroughs have a good deal alarmed the Enemy as you
will see by the inclosed from my & Lord Gowers common
Agent it alludes to a hint I gave three years ago when I
first got Dingwall in answer to it I declined as civilly as I
coud [sic] on the ground of difference of Politics & my
looking on myself to act with Sir T. Dundas with whom I
had been friendly ever since I had the Burrough but it
was not only *our* business but Sir John Sinclairs that
alarmed them you no doubt know all about the battle at
Caithness between him & *the Duchesses son in Law* [9] during the conflict it was said Sir John intended to stand for
the Burroughs if he lost the County, whither this is true
or not it is worth your while to fish out, as also the truth
of what follows which I have from good Authority &
know Major Ross is much alarmed—It is said that although Sir John has declared he looks on himself as engaged to Lord Gower he has at the same time declared
that hitherto Lord Gower has made him no propositions
on the subject—On Sir John's return from Caithness he
had an interview with the Major—The Major said to a
friend of mine *the conversation was satisfactory to him
as far as Sir Johns engagement to Lord Gower went*—If
Lord Gower has not acquainted Sir John with his wishes
it is a riddle I cannot make out, yet what gives some
colour to the idea is that at Dornoch the Major is the declared candidate but at Wick all is still doubt & surmise &
I know that as yet no one has mentioned the Major *from
Authority*—Your part of the world is now the only place
to find out all this perhaps Lord Gower kept aloof of the

knight till he saw the event of the Caithness contest. If this is the case I shall soon know it—If you have not heard what passed in Caithness & have any inclination so to do write to me but as I foresee this letter will run into some length I do not see any good in increasing its bulk— Geanies as you will easily conceive looked very blank on his overthrow [10] in which he was really singularly unlucky he spoke to me not without tears about it. I encouraged him & he has that reliance on & attachment to me that he has engaged not to give up the contest but still act with vigour & attention but let me Adam put you in mind of the son he wants to get to Bengal as a writer you know the last time I suped with you I consulted you whither I shoud [sic] be justified in hindering Geanies from accepting a writership offered by Dundas & you told me by all means to do it for that you coud [sic] get the business done for god sake take care & do not let me injure the family of a friend who has for some time been implicitly trusting to me but hurry on this appointment which Geanies well deserves & it will much forward your own Election in the county with unanimity—The Lads name is Hugh McLeod his age 18—Woud [sic] it not be well in you to write to Geanies not as if hearing from me now but as if in consequence of what passed between you & I in winter & tell him when it can be done—I assure you last month Major Ross repeated Dundas offer & Geanies very handsomely told me of it & said he would act as I desired only if he took it he trusted you & I would not at the General Election ask him to oppose the interest of the man who provided for his Eldest son. I told him in answer it was for himself to judge which party he woud [sic] make friends with but that I was sure we coud [sic] manage this business for his son as I told him before— He was cut at the coldness I affected & swore I was not his friend if I did not know on which side his heart was &

that *he* had rather starve in the Duke of Portlands cause than live with Dundas but asked me what a man was to do with 14 children! He has declined the offer again on the ground of not having determined what to do with his boy yet think of all this & stir your stumps & I know you can do it at once—All is quite safe in the County of Ross. I have canvassed a few of the trusty & secured a considerable Majority but whither we shall bring it to unanimity or not I know not—In case of a sudden dissolution you must come down here to me immediately & if the parliament outlives the summer it would be a good plan if you coud [sic] come & spend a fortnight or so with me & I would carry you about among *your constituents*. Applecross [11] Kilcoy [12] Ord [13] &c:&c: are our own, & with my troops make a Majority of at least two to one—I go over to the Main [14] again at Xmas always with a view to the main chance—I must tell you that the Gordon family who have as you know treated Inverness both shire & town a little cavalierly are at the instigation of Dundas altering their conduct & sweetening upon the good folks very quickly—The Dutchess escorted by Lenox & Sir Robert Sinclair was to be last week at Inverness to attend the Northern meeting a Society she has hitherto treated with marked contempt as I know this motion to be merely political I have a trusty friend to watch all her motions & if I learn any thing will let you know [15]—What says *our* friend Harry Erskine to *his* friend Ross of Shandwicks [16] conduct? I told Harry two year ago what a rotten pear this Creole was, but he then thought I refined too much he now sees I judged right for this very shandwick has given Dundas some idea of his importance by boasting of a greater degree of friendship & intimacy with Erskine than he ever possessed—While I was last at Buchan Shandwick was sent for express to Dundas at Edr. & gave out he was called for to oppose Ferguson of

Raith who you know intends to bring in Crawfurd Geanies brother in Law [17] it is however thought it was not *for that* but it is known that Shandwick has offered Dundas to support him firmly & to spend £4000 if Dundas will get him a seat this I had from an intimate of Shandwicks—I am sadly mortified at my disappointment in Brookes [18] but it cannot be helped & we must hope better things. I know one of the black balls well & if you recollect the most blackguard of all our scotch members (which is a bold word) you have the man. I'll tell you why at meeting—This letter is unconscionably long yet I must beg your advice on a personal subject—You know many Estates in this part of the world hold fen of the Crown these fen dutys except in particular instances have never been called for & were looked on as merely nominal yet all of a sudden the treasury have ordered the exchequer here to inforce payment not only in time coming but of all arrears (in some instances 30 40 50 & even 60 years by gone [sic]) & not only of the fen dutys but of all Chapelry holdings &c: which were looked on as still more nominal. What galls us all here still farther is that it is not the public who are to benefit by this cruel oppression but the creatures of Mr. Pitt among others all the Chapelry holdings that is all arrears of them now due in this & some neighbouring countys are granted to one Rose a factor of Lord Fifes & to give you some idea how oppressive this is I am told there is a small holding of this sort where the arrears will amount to above ¼ of the fee simple—The arrears of fen duty here I mean on Lewis where it is about £120 pr. annm. are above £4000. of this about three are due by Lady Caroline & the rest by me sure it is a barbarous inhumanity in Government to let them run up in this manner & then on a sudden call them in to the ruin of many many families—I am told the fen dutys are not yet granted but the grant given to Rose is in

terrorem & the rest will be held over till the General
Election when *good boys* will get a grant of their own
arrears & perhaps of some of their refractory neighbours
into the bargain—Is not this a curious kind of bribery?
Do tell me if you think any thing can be done did not
your friend Lord North give up some plan of a similar
nature in wales? For god sake forgive this long long
scrawl but the first part of it I was keen to make you master of pray return my letters & any news you can tell me
will be acceptable—Does Dr. Willis work hold? & are the
great mans upper timbers still tight? [19] Are we to have a
war or interfere in france?—Pray make my respects acceptable at Burlington House & with best compliments &
wishes to you & yours I am

> Dear Adam
> yours Affectionately.
> F. H. MACKENZIE

My wife was delivered of a daughter five days ago all
well— Did you get the fish & potted Moor fowl I sent
you?—Pray look out the Roshire petition about the head
Burrough I sent you two years ago as I will present it next
Session— Keep it till we meet but I hope it will be at
hand—

NOTES

1. of Portland.
2. The previous May, before the election of the Tain magistrates, Mackenzie had looked upon the burghs as "already secure
. . . *if secrecy is observed"* (same to same, 3 May 1789, Blair
Adam MSS).
3. Robert Dundas of Arniston.
4. Charles Lockhart Ross of Balnagown.

5. Admiral Sir John Lockhart Ross (1721–90), 6th Bt., father of Charles Lockhart Ross.

6. On 8 October 1788 Mackenzie had written Adam of how he intended attacking the Lockhart Ross interest in Tain at the next election of the burgh's council: "Barclay the attorney at Tain is the man we must begin with. He is *getable*, & just now very discontented at not being appointed factor to the Admiral [John Lockhart Ross]. Barclay can bring us two or three more. . . ." (Blair Adam MSS).

7. George Gilanders of Highfield.

8. Donald Macleod of Geanies was sheriff of Ross-shire.

9. "Sir Robert Sinclair of Murkle, who was lately married to a daughter of the Duke of Gordon, has also a considerable estate and interest in this County, and is spoken of as the Ministerial candidate against Ulbster" (Adam, *Pol. State,* p. 77, section on Caithness).

10. At Tain.

11. Thomas Mackenzie of Applecross, listed with F. H. Mackenzie in Adam, *Pol. State,* p. 295.

12. Capt. Charles Mackenzie of Kilcoy, brother-in-law to F. H. Mackenzie (Adam, *Pol. State,* p. 297).

13. Thomas Mackenzie of Ord, whom Hill had aligned with F. H. Mackenzie (Adam, *Pol. State,* p. 298).

14. From Lewis, which is an island.

15. On 3 May 1789 Mackenzie had written Adam that the party had no "game to play in Invernesshire" (Blair Adam MSS). At the general election Norman Macleod of Macleod was unanimously returned (Mackenzie, *Pol. State,* p. 111) with the support of Henry Dundas and apparently against the Gordon interest (Furber, *Dundas,* pp. 214, 227). By the session of 1792–1793 Macleod had gone over to the new Foxite Opposition on the question of parliamentary reform.

16. William Ross of Shandwick.

17. John "Fish" Craufurd, who was to be brought in for the Dysart Burghs.

18. The Whig dining and gaming club.

19. Reference is to the King's illness.

Donald Macleod of Geanies *to* William Adam—9 *November* 1789

Address: Willm Adam Esqr.

Dear Sir

Our Mutual Friend Mr McKenzie of Seaforth Informed me by Correspondence last Spring, & Verbally since, of your Friendly Intentions towards me, & the Probability there was of your Procuring my Eldest Son being Sent out the Ensuing Spring as a Writer to India on the Bengal Establishment.—When he was with me here lately, he engaged to Write you again on this Subject, when he was to Explain to you the Particulars of a Contest in which I had been Engaged & in which you had an Eventual Interest.—His Distance in the Island of Lewis, & the Circuitous mode of Communication with you through that Channell being so Tedious, has Induced me to give you this Trouble, that I may particularly know how far the Business I have alluded to is Settled or in a Train of being so, as it may be necessary Soon to order the Young Gentleman over from Holland, where he has been for two years back, in order to his Equipment for the Voyage.—I am particularly Anxious to have his Destination fixed for Bengal, as his Cousin Mr Ross Lord Ankervilles Son means to take a Particular Charge of him.—His Name is Hugh, his Age is about 19, both which I have been told are necessary to be known.—I Propose being in London about the End of January, when I shall have an Opportunity of Thanking you in Person, for your Friendship in this Case—Till when & Always Believe me with the most Perfect Regard

Dear Sir
your much obliged & obedient humble Servant
Dond McLeod

123

Geanies 9th Novemr.
1789.
My Address is by Tain

EPILOGUE

On 27 March 1790 Adam wrote his father: "I am to represent the County of Ross in the next Parliament. McKenzie wishes to retire & I have every reason to believe that I have united all the interests—by means of Geanies—whose honour, public spirit & friendship I have the greatest reason to applaud & admire. It has been some comfort to me that I have been able to reward it. It was his object to get his son to India a Writer. Yet he declined the proffers of Dundas. And I have got him his object through the P[rince] of W[ales]. The means is flattering—& the result an Honourable & sure seat in Parl[iamen]t to me w[ithou]t expense or trouble" (Blair Adam MSS). For Geanies's decisive role in Cromartyshire, where he was also sheriff, see Furber, *Dundas,* pp. 229–230.

Memorandum *from* William Fergusson of Raith *to* Sir William A. Cunynghame [*ante* 10 *November* 1789]

Endorsed in hand of writer of memorandum: Memorandums from / Mr. Furgesson / [*added by Adam:*] of Raith
This memorandum is not in either Adam's or Cunynghame's hand; nor is it likely Fergusson would have misspelled his name. A note on the wrapper of the bundle in which this paper was found assigns it a date of 1789. F. H. Mackenzie to Adam, 10 November 1789, *supra,* indicates that Raith had by that date already decided to bring in Craufurd of Auchinames for the Dysart Burghs.

Mr: Furgesson of Raith Desires the following things may be attended to respecting his Election
Provost Hamilton of Kinghorn Deputy Comptroller of Excise in Scotland to be wrote to to support Mr Fur-

gesson with his interest in the Borough of Kinghorn—
—Scott a Tide Marker at Kirkaldy was removed to
Alloa by a Treasury Warrant—Mr Furghesson desires
to have him brought back to Kirkaldy as he has some in-
fluence in the Borough—
One Lock who had been fifty years in the Customs at
Kirkaldy, & bed ridden was reduced to the superannuated
list of £12.10 on account of his attachment to Mr
Furghesson who therefore wishes him replaced to the Sit-
uation he held which was £25 :— —

These Memorandums were given by Mr. Furgesson to
Sir Wm: Cunynghame, with an earnest request they
might be complied with by his friends when in power—

Henry Erskine *to* William Adam
12 *November* [1789]

Endorsed: Novr 12th 1790 / H. Erskine / Dumfermline Bghs
The date in the endorsement has been squeezed in at the top and was obviously added later. The date clearly has to be before the general election,
and the contents conform to a dating of 12 November 1789.

Sir James St. Clair Erskine had been proposed as Opposition candidate for the Stirling Burghs (of which Dunfermline was one). In
the event Lord Loughborough again secured Erskine's return for
Morpeth on the interest of Lord Carlisle, while William Fullarton
became the Opposition candidate for the Stirling Burghs.

Edinburgh Novr. 12
My dear Adam

In Consequence of your's I have sounded the Ground
of the Dunfermline district of Burghs and have written
the Result to Sir Thos. Dundas, to whom (for Reasons I

shall hereafter communicate) I have left to inform You
—The Bussiness may possibly be settled but unfortunately not for the Candidate proposed.—

Pray let us know what our friends think of the Convention—

Your's ever truly
HENRY ERSKINE

Sir David Carnegie *to* William Adam
14 *November* 1789

Endorsed by Adam's clerk: Davd. Carnege / 14th Novr. 89
Endorsed by Portland: 21 Novr / Adam

Dear Sir

I am much obliged to you for your dispatch in obtaining the Letter to Mr Aberdeen, & likewise for the anxiety
you express to know the state of my canvass. As to Mr
Aberdeen, I believe he had not declared against me before he ought to have received his brother's Letter; but I
cannot learn whether that has had a proper effect upon
him or no; & perhaps I shall only know at last by the answer he gives his brother, of which you will be good as
get notice & inform me. I am sorry to say that the state of
the matter is such, as not to warrant me to be sanguine,
though I do not look upon it as desperate. The history of
it is briefly this—after many private assurances & an apparently favorable michaelmas election, I took the field;
& in a couple of days after my circular Letter, Montrose,
Aberbrothock, & Brechin gave me answers, signed by almost every individual in each council, that they would
support me. I went to [the burgh of] Aberdeen to endeavour to make the matter sure by securing them, but I
found they had already associated against me at the insti-

gation of Mr Barclay of Ury.[1] In the mean time Mr
Scott,[2] the India Director, & our county member elect,
started Mr Callander [3] against me at Montrose; & the
arguments used by these nabobs there have had such an
effect that, of seventeen who signed my letter, nine have
avowed a determination to break their engagement, &
they are joined by two others who had not signed;
making the division at present eleven against me; & eight,
partly for me & partly undetermined: of the last number
is Aberdeen, though he signed the Letter to me. It is possible that I may reclaim some of the eleven; but besides
that many of them may be secured by *presents,* the share
that they all expect in the distribution of custom house &
other places fascinates them—& they cannot be disappointed, as my opponents openly avow that it is the duty
of every member for scotch boroughs to support the
Minister of the day; & that if a change were to happen,
they would wheel about of course. This system may not
appear a bad one alltogether to *you*—in the contemplation of future events; but I cannot combat such strong
arguments myself; & they treat me very disagreably in
Montrose, where contrary *to precedent* all custom house
places have been given to strangers ever since I was their
representative. I would however state one idea for your
consideration, & I shall not press it, if thought improper.
There is a belief at Montrose that the collector of the
customs has not long to live, & the hopes of succeeding
him has certainly drawn off one principal man, if not
more from me: Views of inferior posts have probably
debauched others. Now though it is common to consider
those offices when once obtained as being for Life, I think
myself, that in a case where they are obtained by such uncommon perfidy as the breach of a written engagement,
common rules should not be observed; & that I should
have authority from our friends to say, if I see it proper,
that should *they* ever have the power, they will at my re-

quest dismiss such rascals from whatever employments they may chance to have got possession of. This threat might be of use, & I would not employ it if I did not find a proper occasion. As I must have tired you with this long Letter I shall only add to it that if any change happen for the better I shall let you know—& I hope if you have any good news to communicate, you will not let me be the last to be informed of it. I am with great regard

Dear Sir
Yours faithfully
DAVID CARNEGIE

Kinnaird 14th Novr 1789

NOTES

1. Robert Barclay Allardice (1732–1797), of Urie (Kincardine). He had inherited and acquired through his second marriage large estates in Kincardineshire and the Aberdeen Burghs. He was attached to Government, it was thought because he was seeking to revive the Scottish Earldoms of Strathearn, Monteath, and Airth in his wife's line. In 1788 he had been returned for his county with the assistance of Henry Dundas; he voted with Government on the Regency. See Adam, *Pol. State,* pp. 12, 183–184, and *H of P.*

2. David Scott (*c.* 1746–1805), of Dunninald, M.P. Forfarshire 1790–1796, Perth Burghs 1796–1805. He was the Ministerial candidate for the county (Adam, *Pol. State,* p. 158).

3. Alexander Callander (1741–1792), of Crichton.

Duke of Portland *to* William Adam
[*post* 14 *November* 1789]

Endorsed by Adam's clerk: D. Portland
Endorsed by Adam: Respecting Sir D. Carnegie

The upper portion of this letter has been cut away, but portions of the writing of the line above are evident. It is clearly in reply to Carnegie's to Adam of 14 November 1789 (*supra*).

128

You have not said more to Sir David [1] than I would have said myself & the good opinion I have of his Understanding & Judgement inclines me to believe that he will be satisfied himself that as much has been said as could be with propriety. It would be a very doubtful question with me, did I possess the means of giving effect to his suggestion, whether it should be adopted, but a very little cool reflection will incline, sir D. himself, to be of opinion as I imagine, that prudence can not admit persons in our situation to authorize such a threat as he mentions to be held out. I can not fancy, unless the prospect of enforcing it was much nearer than it appears to me to be, that it could operate otherwise than to his & indeed to our general disadvantage, During the short Administration of −83 we had the opportunity of trying the effect of punishments, & experience may have convinced us of the little impression they make when unattended by their powerfull antidote the means of rewarding services—I wish to hear about Mr Hennah [2] that I may be able to write into Cornwall. Macbride writes me word that two of the persons nominated for Sheriff of that County are hostile—

Your's Ever

P

NOTES

1. Carnegie.

2. The *Universal British Directory* for 1797 (IV, 612) lists a "Thomas Hennah, Gent." as a member of the Tregony corporation. A memorandum of Adam, addressed to Sir John Morshead and dating probably from 1789, recommends that "Thomas Hennah, Butcher, Alderman of Tregony Supervisor of Tin to be succeeded by Mr. William Puckey of Fowey—" (Blair Adam MSS).

Duke of Portland *to* William Adam
17 *November* [1789]

Endorsed: Duke Portland / 17th. Novr. 89

Bulstrode Tuesday noon 17 Novr:

Dear Adam

Though I hope nothing will prevent our meeting to-morrow, I can not help expressing my wishes that You may be able to inform me of T. Grenvilles final determination respecting Bath, & whether Ld Robt: [1] will stand for Evesham. I have a very pressing Letter again today from Lavender, with an assurance of the cordial disposition of the Electors, & that the expense will not exceed 3000 & probably not 2500£. I have also a very satisfactory report from Bampfylde [2] of his Canvas at Exeter, where he tells me he has met *with the greatest success,* & that he had a person with him, who is extremely active & a *confidential* friend of his at Exeter, who assures him that *one* seat may be had at Honiton [3] for less than £3000. Have You ever spoke to Ld Loughborough upon the subject of Mr Gifford for that place?

Your's ever

P

I send You both Lavender's & Bampfylde's Letters which You may return me tomorrow—

NOTES

1. Spencer.
2. Charles Warwick Bampfylde (1753–1823), 5th Bt., M.P. Exeter 1774–1790, 1796–1812. Although irregular in attendance, Bampfylde had been connected with Opposition since his entry into Parliament.
3. This report seems most unlikely. Honiton had a wide franchise composed of men of low social and economic standing. It was a notoriously venal borough with frequent and expensive contests.

The principal local interest was that of Sir George Yonge, Pitt's secretary at war; Sir George and his father had held one seat in the borough since 1715, but they had been able to do so only with enormous expense. Lord Courtenay, who had a secondary interest in the borough, was in the habit of cooperating with Sir George. Honiton was not contested by an Opposition candidate in 1790.

Duke of Portland *to* William Adam
21 *November* 1789

Dear Adam

I send You the inclosed which I have just received by a special Messenger from Lavender, I have referred him to You, & have informed him that I had written to Lord Robert,[1] desiring him to address himself to Lavender, & that I had also written to Him (Lavender) acquainting Him with the steps I had taken.

Your's Ever
P

Bulstrode Sat: 5. P.M.
21 Novr: 1789

NOTE

1. Spencer.

Duke of Portland *to* William Adam
24 *November* 1789

Dear Adam

I am very sorry to send You the enclosed, because the more I consider it, the more I am convinced of the *unfit-*

ness of Ld R–[1] for E–[2] or any place where a *permanent* interest may be created. We must find another person. I will follow this Letter as soon as I can & hope to be in town before *one*. I mean & wish to return here this evening, & should therefore be glad to see You, & *possibly* Lavender as soon as I can, You know best whether it is *now* necessary for me to see H.R.H.[3]

Your's Ever
P

Bulstrode Tuesday morn : 24 Novr : 1789
9 o'clock

NOTES

   1. Lord Robert Spencer.
   2. Evesham.
   3. Prince of Wales. The subject undoubtedly concerns the Prince's debts.

Lord Robert Spencer *to* [Duke of Portland]—[22 *November* 1789]

The letter is datable from Spencer's letter to Adam of 23 November 1789 (*infra*). It is undoubtedly the letter Portland enclosed in his to Adam of 24 November (*supra*).

My Dear Lord,

I am much obliged to you for your letter, but I hope you will excuse me if I decline the proposal of standing for Evesham : My objection is not to the risk of the expence of the Canvass, but to the trouble, that I am sure must attend that sort of Borough, besides a probability of an opposition in case I vacate my seat. Upon the whole

I should very much prefer a more expensive seat without trouble.—However, if this refusal on my part to stand for Evesham is any distress to you or interferes with your plans—I beg you will not take my refusal, but let me meet Mr Lavender either at Coventry or Birmingham on next Saturday night; but I must in this case beg the favour of you to make the appointment with him as there would not be time for me to make it after getting your answer—Coventry would suit me best—& as I don't know the Inn—we had better appoint the Post Office. If our meeting can be put off till about Tuesday fortnight, I could meet him at Stratford upon Avon in my way to town, which is much nearer Evesham. I shall be at *Quorn near Loughborough* on Thursday night where I will beg the favour of an answer to this. I am ever Yours

Most Sincerely
R SPENCER

Langton Sunday

Lord Robert Spencer *to* William Adam
23 *November* [1789]

Endorsed: Ld. R. Spencer / 23d Novr. 89

Langton Monday
Novr 23.

Dear Adam

I have received your letter with the paper enclosed which states the thing with great clearness in every respect and undertakes very gallantly that the expence shall not exceed a certain sum: But to tell you the truth I had rather be damned than undertake a popular canvass of

133

this sort, especially at this distance from the election. I should not so much mind just at the moment of a general election trying any thing of this kind that might offer: The trouble would in that case soon be over, but in the present case I must beg the D. of P [1] to look out for another Candidate. If I did not decline the thing for these reasons, I should have trusted implicitly to the Duke's account & yours and nothing would have been necessary but to fix a day for the Canvass which I should have fixed for Wednesday fortnight. This You'll think looks like yielding, but that is not the case. I wrote yesterday to the D of P to desire to be off. I am now going for 2 days to Ld Fitzwilliam's & then to Quorn. If you have any thing to say to me—direct tomorrow and next day to Milton near Peterborough after that to Quorn near Loughborough.

Yours most sincerely
R SPENCER

NOTE

1. Duke of Portland.

Duke of Portland *to* William Adam
28 *November* 1789

Dear Adam

I think when You have fulfilled all Your intentions You will have nothing to reproach Yourself with on the score of Evesham, I am going to B–[1] & shall return [2] on Thursday for *one* night—I shall dine at home on Thursday & be very glad to see You if You have nothing better to do. I have received a Letter from Vanneck, in which he tells me that he has no thoughts of Ipswich, because he

finds the Politicks of that place would render him liable
to receive instructions; which he could not follow consistently with his principles & political attachments. He
does not say a word of Suffolk,—he means to be in town
in about ten days.[3]

Your's ever

P

Sat: ["noon" crossed out] 28 Novr: 1789
¼ past one P.M.

NOTES

1. Bulstrode.
2. To Burlington House in Piccadilly.
3. Sir Gerard Vanneck had been returned unopposed for the
family seat at Dunwich since 1768. In 1790 he stood for the county
in Suffolk and was defeated after an expensive contest. His younger
brother, Joshua Henry, was meanwhile returned for Dunwich and
voted with Opposition during the two sessions of 1791–1792. Sir
Gerard had voted with Pitt on parliamentary reform in 1783, but
he does not appear on the division list of those supporting Pitt's
motion in 1785.

Lord John Townshend *to* William Adam
2 *December* 1789

Endorsed by Adam's clerk: J.T. from / Bath / 3d. Decr. 89
The letter is in the hand of Lord John Townshend.

Bath Decr. 2d— 89—

Dear Adam

Is there any chance of our being able to get any money
towards discharging the Westminster debts or any part
of them—or have any steps been taken yet for this purpose? Cocker [1] has received a very peremptory letter

from Mr White the Committee Clerk at the House of Commons,[2] & various other applications on this subject which embarrass him not a little; & by all I hear, I am afraid if something is not done soon, we shall come to great disgrace, & Fox's interest will suffer very considerably—Pray have the goodness to talk over this, the first opportunity, with Ld Robert;[3] & try what can be done—Perhaps you may think it right to speak again to the D. of Portland about it.

Pray let me have a line from you here as soon as you can.

Yours Ever believe me most sincerely &c
J : T.

NOTES

1. John Robert Cocker, an attorney, of Gerard Street, Westminster, had been secretary of the general committee for Townshend's contest in 1788 (*The Times,* 15 July 1788). He had filled a similar role in Fox's Westminster contest of 1784 (Cocker to Gilchrist, copy, 18 October 1786, Blair Adam MSS). Part of his duties on both occasions had been to oversee the accounts. He was a member of the Whig Club, having joined 6 December 1784 (*Whig Club,* 1788 ed.).

2. Regarding expenses arising from Hood's petition.

3. Spencer.

Sir David Carnegie *to* William Adam
3 *December* 1789

Sir David Carnegie lost his election to Alexander Callander. Carnegie carried Brechin and Arbroath (or Aberbrothock, as it was then spelled). Callander carried Aberdeen, Inverbervie, and Montrose. Carnegie was unable to find another seat until 1796. Callander did not appear on Opposition minority lists and seems to have supported Government until his death in 1792.

Dear Sir

I have received both your Letters & as I conjectured it is only through your means that I have learnt the effect of the application upon Aberdeen, which is less than was expected, by those who pointed out the channel to me. His account however of the state of the council is not unfair, with this difference that it is not easy to say how those men can be determined to vote against me—since they can in as few days *change their determinations.* As far as yet appears I may depend upon my other two boroughs, & if I could muster a party in Montrose, much of the success of the election would depend upon circumstances of *various* kinds. The fact however at present is that of the nineteen there, I can only depend upon five; & that bad as my chance is ostensibly, it is still worse in reality. You will I dare say agree with me nevertheless that the best face must be put upon it, & that no exertion should be spared; & in that view I wish that Aberdeen should be further pressed either by his brother or yourself as you think best. He can be told that the favor is the same whether I succeed or not; & that if in his opinion there is so decided a majority against me that his vote can be of no use—It can be of as little to my oponent who of course will not thank him for it. But eleven out of nineteen cannot be considered as a great majority; & that in fact there is reason to hope & believe that his vote may be of the greatest service. That as a young member of council he may have an opportunity of bringing himself forward upon such an occasion, & by being of use to his friends to lay an obligation upon them to make him proper returns when it is in their power. But above all that he ought not to let himself be carried away by wicked example to lose sight of all that is honest among men, by being guilty of a breach of the most solemn engagement that can be made;

for that he may depend upon it, loss of character will follow such a step among all ranks & parties as soon as the foment of the moment is over.

I wrote you in such a hurry that I do not recollect if I mentioned that Aberdeen was one of the seventeen who engaged themselves to support me at the election—or if I sent you a copy of their Letter. In case I did not, you have it now & it will serve both to show you the situation in which Aberdeen stands, & the strong reasons I had for thinking the perfidy of those men almost unexampled, & worthy of the most severe punishment that is ever inflicted upon a change of ministry. I subscribe perfectly to the Duke's [1] sentiments, for they have long been my own upon general grounds—but still there are particular cases, where punishments may be salutary in every point of view. I disapprove of impeachments in general though I voted for that of Mr Hastings—But we shall let this matter rest & say no more about it. I am only sorry at one expression in his Grace's Letter, which as I return it you, I shall leave you to guess—but we have friends more *sanguine* than the Duke—& it is necessary they should be so.

If any thing new occur, I shall not fail to trouble you again, & in the mean time I remain

Dear Sir
Yours truely
DAVID CARNEGIE

Kinnaird 3d Decr 1789

NOTE

1. Portland.

Sir William Cunynghame *to* William Adam—20 *December* 1789

Livingstone Sunday
20th. Decr. 1789

My Dear Adam

For your kind Letter of the 26th. of last Month, accept my best thanks, had it not been for breaking in upon your more Essential Bussiness, I should have done this long ago, to have requested of you to assure my Friends, how much I feel myself obliged to them, for their kind Concern about my Election, The Fate of which is at yet uncertain, but if the Court of Session does me Justice, and puts on the Six Claims,[1] which were rejected at Michaelmas, I should then think my Chance as good as theirs, if the Election happens before the first of July; At all Events assure our Friends, that I shall neither Bitch for Money, nor Pains either of Body, or Mind, & the Treasurer[2] has done me the honor to say, that the Damned Fellow Cunynghame, has cost him more trouble than the half of Scotland. And if his Exertions are at last crowned with Success, I have the Satisfaction to think, that I have established such a Party in this County, as must secure the Election for any Friend of ours, when any Change of Government [sic], and although it has cost me a great deal of Money, this appears to me more for the advantage of our Party, than if I had bought an English Borough. As I said in the first part of my Letter, I should not have troubled you upon this Subject, had I not at all Events been to write you, to enquire after poor Keith Elphinstone, whom I really pity beyond Measure, & confess that in his present very Weak state, I dread the Worst of Consequences. Lady C. joins me in desiring to be remembered to him in the kindest Manner, should you

139

not be able to spare time to write me a few Lines, pray desire One of the Miss Elphinstones to do it, Say every thing that is kind from me to Mrs. Adam, Lady C. joins me in wishing that her & you were in this Country to pass your Xmas with us, where you would meet several of your Buff & Blue [3] Friends, Tomorrow I kill my best ⟨Stott⟩ & Sheep for them, and in the End of the Week the Fatted Calf, and a Hog. With these, a little Claret and ⟨Nil Gow⟩, we shall make the long Nights pass. I do not intend being up before the Middle of February, should you expect any Bussiness sooner, pray let me know, as you may depend upon me if required; Excuse this long Scrawl and believe me ever with much real regard and esteem

Yours Sincerely ⟨While⟩
W A Cunynghame

P.S. David desires his best Compliments to you adieu

NOTES
1. Reference is to litigation over the roll of freeholders for the county, which were made up annually at the Michaelmas head court. The Court of Session had appellate jurisdiction over the decisions of the head court.
2. Henry Dundas was Treasurer of the Navy.
3. The colors associated with Fox and the Whig Opposition.

Duke of Portland *to* William Adam
22 *December* 1789

Bulstrode Tuesday 22 Decr: 1789

Dear Adam

I have received just such an answer from Ld Plymouth [1] as I expected, that he is very sorry that it is no longer in his power to render any service to Mr Thompson,[2] having been engaged *ever since last spring* by his neighbour & old acquaintance Sir John Rushout[3] to support Him & Mr Sullivan[4] jointly—Fitzherberts[5] visit to me last Tuesday morning was to notify his intentions of retiring from Parliament till we were actually or at least within a certainty of being again in power, or in other words, in which I will do him the justice to say he was so explicit as not to be easily misunderstood, he was not disposed to be at the expense of purchasing a Seat till he could be sure of having his disbursement repaid with *liberal* interest. Trevanion whom I also saw the same morning seems to think it may be for his advantage to have a Collegue,[6] & appears very well inclined to join G. North,[7] he is of opinion that the Election if properly & discreetly managed need not cost above £2000 or at most £2500—but I perceive he would be very scrupulous in advising any one to stand, least he should involve him in an expense to double or treble that amount, which he says is not impossible & of which considering what he has already spent & the probable certainty of his own seat he would not undertake to pay the half or to exceed a sum which he would previously stipulate to pay provided the whole expense amounted to the double of what he would propose to give for his quota, & if less in proportion. But when he returns to Town he will be ready at any time to meet & give all the information & assistance in his power to enable any friend to judge of the expediency of being a Candidate at Dover. He complained to me again of the misapplication of the Lord Warden's[8] Patronage, & of a Plot having been lately made, as was pretended, by the interest of Lady Holdernesse[9] to whom Mr Lane said the promise had been made five or six years ago. The enclosed is from a Clergyman who has no other claim upon me than that of his late Father's having been benefited by my private Patronage but he is well connected in Cumberland, & supposing Ld Guilford & Ld North were totally unprovided with Claimants or expectants, I believe my Correspondent would do them no discredit, but You will understand that I don't mean to ask it for Him unless they are perfectly indifferent to every other Candidate— Have We any chance of Your looking in upon us during these Holidays? It would give me infinite satisfaction to be *assured by You* that *all* the Bonds to *Forth* had been cancelled in the D. of Clarence's apartment—as it was promised they should be, in the space of 24 or 48 hours at farthest.[10]

sincerely Your's &c
P

I have received a very temperate Letter from Sir F. Basset, & very friendly & cordial to me personally. But from the wishes & expectations he expresses respecting Hennah I can not answer for the effect of the wanton disposal of the Supervisorship that has been so long vacant—I hope no farther steps have been taken for the removal of Ld Eliot [11] or Sir E. Bayntun [12]—

NOTES

1. Other Hickman Windsor (1751–1799), 5th Earl of Plymouth. He had voted with the Opposition on the Regency (Stockdale, *Debates in the House of Lords on the Subject of a Regency,* p. 190).

2. Thomas Thompson (c. 1768–1818), of Piccadilly, Westminster. He had now been selected as the Opposition candidate for Evesham, where he was elected in 1790 and continued to sit until 1802. He joined the Whig Club 19 January 1790 (*Whig Club,* 1792 ed.) and voted with Opposition throughout the Parliament of 1790.

3. Sir John Rushout (1738–1800), 5th Bt., M.P. Evesham 1761–1796. He began the Parliament of 1784 in Opposition, but by the Regency he had gone over to Pitt and in April, 1789, applied to

him for a peerage. He continued to act with Pitt in the Parliament of 1790 and in 1797 was granted his peerage.

4. A Mr. Sullivan, the Government candidate, came in third on the poll at Evesham (Oldfield, *An Entire and Complete History . . . of the Boroughs,* 2nd ed., II, 263).

5. Thomas Fitzherbert (?1746–1822) was a man of obscure origins but who had long been involved in naval contracts in Portsmouth. In 1780 he approached the Government for a seat and at their suggestion was returned for the expensive borough of Arundel after a contest. He supported North's administration, opposed Shelburne, and was absent at the division on Fox's India Bill. He was returned again for Arundel in 1784, this time without opposition. Contrary to expectations, he opposed Pitt and divided with Opposition on every major party division during the Parliament of 1784. In 1793 the party still owed him £200 as reimbursement for election expenses at Arundel, but for which election is not certain (William Adam to Lord Fitzwilliam, 19 September 1793, Milton MSS, Northamptonshire Record Office).

6. At Dover.

7. George Augustus North.

8. Lord North.

9. Mary, widow of Robert, 4th and last Earl of Holdernesse (*d.* 1778).

10. Regarding these bonds and the debts of the princes, see Aspinall, ed., *The Correspondence of George, Prince of Wales 1770–1812,* II, 96–97, 148–149.

11. Edward, 1st Baron Eliot (1727–1804), one of the most formidable political magnates in the southwest of England and a supporter of Pitt, was receiver general of the Duchy of Cornwall. He had inherited the office from his father and was to retain it until his death.

12. Sir Edward Bayntun Rolt (1710–1800), 1st Bt., M.P. Chippenham 1737–1780. He is not known ever to have voted with a parliamentary opposition under George III. He had held the office of surveyor general for the Duchy of Cornwall since 1751 and was to continue to hold it until 1796.

Duke of Portland *to* William Adam
23 *December* 1789

Dear Adam

Bulstrode Wednesday 23 Decr: 1789

I am certainly not less surprized than Tollemache at the contents of Galloway's Letter which I dare say You will immediately communicate to Lowten [1] from whom I hope He will receive a serious lecture for his pertness. The paragraph in Tollemaches respecting Cheshire perhaps makes me feel more sore than I otherwise should as I am persuaded that had Galloway's answer been such as I think I had reason to expect all ideas of Cheshire would have been forgot & lost in this new pursuit— [2]

Your's ever

P

NOTES

1. Thomas Lowten, of King's Bench Walk, Temple, was an attorney frequently employed by Whig political society. He had joined the Whig Club at its foundation, 13 May 1784 (*Whig Club,* 1788 ed.).

2. Tollemache's principal seat was at Calveley Hall, Cheshire. He had been sheriff of Cheshire 1785–1786.

Duke of Portland *to* William Adam
27 *December* 1789

Addressed: To / William Adam Esqre: / Lincolns Inn Fields / if out of town not to be forwarded to Him / but by a safe hand

Dear Adam

Bulstrode Sunday 27 Decr: 1789

I am not at all surprised at the expectations You mention to be entertained &, I hope without committing any

144

one, I have not been wholly inattentive to the means of fulfilling them, but on the part of the expectants a preliminary step must be first taken which is to give precise & accurate information of the extent of their expectations. However I will defer any farther discussion of this subject to our meeting—Braddyll is ready to undertake what Clive declines, & I shall inform the D. of N. accordingly [1]—From the nature of the P-s property I should be inclined to suppose that his influence would be greater in the County than in any of the Boroughs, but where is the prudent & discreet person to be found who is to exert it?[2] What You tell me respecting Morland[3] is not a very auspicious omen with regard to every other concern of the kind, but We must go our own way & not mind these little rubs, You will though, I hope, see Sheridan[4] & prevail upon him to take no step without inquiry—I will apply again to Ld Beauchamp[5] distinctly for the persons You name. By a Letter I received from Him yesterday He desires me to acquaint Mr Thompson, as He is ignorant, (& indeed so am I) of his address that Mr T— may depend upon the Votes of all those who may be influenced by Him (Ld B) & he adds that it is generally said in his neighbourhood that T—s Canvas would have promised more success, had not many of the Voters been fearfull of being deserted by T— as they had already been by Ford, & consequently declined promising their votes till their doubts in that respect were removed. I will also write to Ld Spencer[6] & Sir Wm Codrington,[7] to Anson[8] I have already written & am in daily expectation of his answer. I sent him the names of Geo: Hand[9] & two others I don't recollect—Ld Tracy[10] & Edwards Freeman[11] I fear are desperate. But I have a channel of application to the first which will be tried tomorrow. As for Freeman, You seem to have forgot that his Son[12] who died last year was Member for Steyning upon Sir J. Honywood's[13] interest at the recommendation of The Ministry[14]—Grenville wishes to have an application made to Vaughan of Golden Grove[15] for the chance of his influence with a Mr Nichols a Surgeon in Queen Square Bath who comes from Vaughan's neighbourhood. If I am not mistaken, which I shall be glad to find myself, Vaughan did not act very handsomely in the beginning of −84. But whether I am right or not, I never had any acquaintance with Him myself & must therefore refer the inquiry & application intirely to You—I shall be very glad if Payne [16] has satisfied Tollemache, He will expect to hear from me, but I will defer it for a day or two till I hear again from you. sincerely Your's &c

P

I have a very comfortable Letter from little Philipps,[17] he thinks his Majority so decisive as to believe it will be unnecessary to trouble Ld Verneys friends,[18] whom I had engaged for Him, to go down—& the Canvas for Ld V− in this County [19] exceeds our most sanguine expectations—

NOTES

1. It is not clear whether reference is to an intended contest at Horsham or Carlisle; possibly it is to both. Charles Howard (1746–1815), 11th Duke of Norfolk, who was lord of the manor at Horsham, had begun buying up burgages in that borough since 1786 with a view to challenging the hitherto dominant Irwin interest. He did challenge that interest at the general election of 1790, and Wilson Braddyll was one of the members he returned. Braddyll (1756–1818) had been a supporter of the Rockingham Opposition while a member for Lancaster 1780–1784; he had declined a contest in 1784 and did not sit in the ensuing Parliament. In 1792 Braddyll was unseated at Horsham by a committee of the House of Commons. But he had also unsuccessfully contested Carlisle at the general election, and in 1791 he had been declared duly returned for that borough by another committee of the House. At Carlisle his patron had also been the Duke of Norfolk, who since 1784 had placed himself at the head of the anti-Lowther party in that city. It is striking that Norfolk was involving the party in his personal opposition to the Lowthers in Cumberland during a period when approaches were being made to Lonsdale to accept party candidates such as Anstruther and Cunynghame for family seats. The Lowthers had only recently come over to Opposition

during the Regency debates; they were to return to Pitt by the session of 1791. Edward, Lord Clive, was member for Ludlow from 1774 until he was raised to a British peerage in 1794. Ludlow was rather securely in the hands of his family, and it may be that the party hoped to secure Clive a seat elsewhere to create an opening in that borough.

2. Reference is to the Prince's influence in Cornwall. Sir John Morshead offered his services as such a manager in 1791 (Aspinall, ed., *The Correspondence of George, Prince of Wales 1770–1812,* II, 216–217), but his offer seems not to have been accepted.

3. William Morland (*c.* 1739–1815), M.P. Taunton 1796–1806. Morland was a partner in the banking firm of Ransome, Morland, and Hammersley, of Pall Mall; during this period his house was deeply involved in the financial affairs of the Prince of Wales. It was perhaps through this channel that he recommended himself to Adam, who was managing the financial affairs of the royal princes, and to Sheridan, who was an intimate companion and adviser to the Prince. See Aspinall, ed., *The Correspondence of George, Prince of Wales 1770–1812,* II, 96–97 n, 151–153. At the general election of 1790 Morland and John Halliday unsuccessfully contested Taunton. Morland was apparently building a private interest in the corporation (Oldfield, *History of Boroughs,* 2nd ed., II, 54–55).

4. Richard Brinsley Sheridan (1751–1816), the playwright, was also a leading member of the Whig Opposition.

5. Francis Seymour Conway (1743–1822), styled Viscount Beauchamp, eldest son of Francis, 1st Earl of Hertford. M.P. Lostwithiel 1766–1768, Orford 1768–1794.

6. George John, 2nd Earl Spencer (1758–1834), a Portland Whig. A lord of Treasury March to July, 1782, First Lord of the Admiralty 1794–1801, Home Secretary 1806–1807.

7. Sir William Codrington (1719–1792), 2nd Bt., of Dodington, Glos., M.P. Beverley 1747–1761, Tewkesbury 1761–1792. An old Rockingham Whig.

8. The reference is not clear, but this could be Thomas Anson (1767–1818), M.P. Lichfield 5 December 1789–1806. His father had been a supporter of Rockingham, and young Anson was to become a close friend of Fox. The Ansons had the return of one member for Lichfield, the Pittite Marquess of Stafford the other. At one time there had been an independent party in the borough, which in 1766 had asked Portland (without success) to join them in sponsoring a candidate; but since 1761 there had been no contests. In 1790 the two incumbents were again returned, apparently without a contest.

9. A George Hand is listed as a proctor of Lichfield in 1797 (*Universal British Directory,* III, 610).

10. Thomas Charles Tracy, 6th Viscount Tracy (1719–1792), whose principal seat was at Toddington, Gloucestershire, near Tewkesbury.

11. Thomas Edwards Freeman (?1726–1808), of Batsford, Glos., had been M.P. for Steyning 1768–1780 on the interest of his distant relation, Sir John Honywood (*c.* 1710–1781), 3rd Bt., who had supported the Opposition to North. Edwards Freeman "seems to have been completely independent, to the point of self-contradiction in his votes and speeches" (*H of P*).

12. Thomas Edwards Freeman (1754–1788), M.P. Steyning 1785–1788.

13. Sir John Honywood (*c.* 1757–1806), 4th Bt. M.P. Steyning 1784–1785, 1788–1790, etc. He had been a staunch supporter of Pitt during the Parliament of 1784.

14. The only recorded vote of young Edwards Freeman was on Richmond's fortifications plan in 1786, when he voted with Opposition; but there were a large number of normal Government supporters who voted with Opposition on that occasion, particularly among members who represented constituencies in the south of England. Codrington, Tracy, and Edwards Freeman were all propertied in Gloucestershire, and this portion of the letter seems to refer to a contest in that county. The constituency may well be the borough of Gloucester, where the resurgent interest of the Duke of Norfolk had fought an exceedingly expensive and close, but unsuccessful, contest at the bye-election the previous February (the Pittite candidate had been returned by a single vote on a poll of 1673). The two incumbents, one Oppositionist and one Pittite, were returned at the general election, apparently without a contest.

15. John Vaughan (*c.* 1752–1804), of Golden Grove, Carmarthenshire, M.P. Carmarthenshire 1779–1784. While in Parliament he had been a highly independent supporter of Government. His record during 1783–1784 does seem equivocal. "He voted for Shelburne's peace preliminaries, 18 Feb. 1783; was classed by Robinson in March as 'doubtful'; did not vote on Fox's East India bill; and in Stockdale's list of 19 Mar. 1784 appears as 'absent' " (*H of P*).

16. Sir Ralph Payne?

17. John George Philipps.

18. Lord Verney had been member for Carmarthen 1761–1768, when he had been supported by Philipps's father; but in 1768 Verney had unsuccessfully opposed the Philipps interest.

19. Buckinghamshire.

William Robertson *to* William Adam
15 *January* 1790

The *H of P* describes the Stirling Burghs as "one of the most venal" constituencies in Scotland. But although "no one family secured a lasting interest," the Campbells of Tuerechan and Inverneil had held the seat since 1774. The Opposition candidate seems to have withdrawn before the poll in 1790, for Sir Archibald Campbell was returned unanimously (Mackenzie, *Pol. State,* p. 234).

My Dear Sir

I communicated your letter to the Dean [1] & some of the persons from whom I have received information with regard to the state of the Burghs.[2] As there never was any declared Candidate Fullarton [3] may surely come in the place of Sir James St Clair [4] without difficulty, for as none of our friends were engaged to Sir James or to any other individual Candidate the same views which would have induced them to support one respectable man of our side, will lead them to espouse the interests of any other with equal zeal. A transference is sometimes difficult when a Candidate is declared, but in the present instance it will not be known that Fullarton was not the person originally in view. At the same time I look upon Sir James's interest as of great importance particularly in Dunfermling [sic] & Inverkeithing & Fullarton's cause will be powerfully aided by its being understood that he is supported by Sir James & *his friends*.

For the state of the Burghs I must refer you in a great measure to my letters to Sir James, which contained the substance of what could be committed to writing in a business of so much delicacy. In Dunfermling things remain in the same situation as when I wrote last & recent intelligence leads me to think that both Inverkeithing & Queensferry are still more favourably disposed than formerly. It is impossible to enter into any detail but the opinion which I have formed from an attentive examination of the ground is this. To attack a set of venal burghs in the possession apparently even of another person is always hazardous, & no man ought to embark in such an adventure unless he has made up his mind to being involved in considerable expense. At the same time Fullarton knows to his sad experience that a well established burgh interest may soon be overturned, & in the present case the opening is so good as to encourage any man who does not lay it down as a fixed principle that he will not in any situation engage where there will be a contest. Sir A:C:[5] will take the field with Stirling & Culross, Dunfermling is in that situation that an early exertion can scarcely fail to secure in our interest the other two[6] are disaffected to Sir A:C: & are entirely open to conviction, although Inverkeithing will depend much on the exertions of some of Sir James's friends with Mr Walker.[7] In short there is such an opening as I should be sorry to see neglected, there is ground & good ground to go upon, but let no man embark who is determined to avoid a contest.

Be so good as to shew this letter to Fullarton to whom I need not write as I can give him no farther information. I cannot conclude without urging the necessity of coming to some determination very speedily. Our friends in Dunfermling have fought a good battle without any foreign aid, but they find that they can do so no longer, we have amused them with the hopes of some respectable man coming forward, they will be discouraged & soon fall to pieces if that is not done, more particularly as the enemy have now taken the alarm & have been busy. It is not adviseable that any man should publickly appear as a Candidate, but we should be authorised to say that Fullarton or some other man is ready to come forward in proper time, & some supply must *immediately* be sent as an earnest of his being seriously embarked in the busi-

ness. If that is not done quickly the game is up. I am My
Dear Sir

Most faithfully Yours
WM ROBERTSON.

Edinr 15th. Jany.
1790:

NOTES

1. Henry Erskine.
2. Stirling Burghs.
3. William Fullarton (1754–1808), of Fullarton, Ayr. M.P.
Plympton Erle 1779–1780, Haddington Burghs 1787–1790,
Horsham 1793–1796, Ayrshire 1796–1803. A wealthy man with
extensive East Indian connections, Fullarton had been an effective
Opposition debater in the House, particularly on Indian affairs. He
had been raised with William Adam in Edinburgh, and had formed
close political ties with Lords North and Stormont, the former
having brought him in for Plympton. The Lauderdales had
brought him in for the Haddington Burghs; Thomas Maitland, the
younger brother of Lord Lauderdale, was returned for those
burghs in 1790.
4. Sir James St. Clair Erskine.
5. Sir Archibald Campbell (1739–1791), of Inverneil, Argyll.
M.P. Stirling Burghs 1774–1780, 21 August 1789–1791.
6. Queensferry and Inverkeithing.
7. Robert Walker, "late Bailie of Inverkeithing," is listed as a
Fife vote of Sir Robert Anstruther in Adam, *Pol. State,* p.
126. He was delegate for Inverkeithing at the general election
(Mackenzie, *Pol. State,* p. 234).

Duke of Portland *to* William Adam
[25 *January* 1790]

Endorsed: Duke of Portland / Jany 25th 1790— / Oakhampton

Dear Adam

I wish You would take the trouble of sending the D. of Bedford [1] (directed to Him at Brooks's) a list of such persons in the present Parliament as are not provided with seats in the next, & are willing to take trouble & spend some money for the sake of being returned to the next Parliament, & it would not be amiss to add the names of such other persons who are inclined to offer themselves, as may be supposed to be within the circle of the Dukes acquaintance—For Your better direction it may be right to tell You that he would not like such a man of the description of our gallant Evesham Candidate,[2] & that the place for which he wants one is Oakhampton, where he would give any such person the trial of a Canvas *gratis,* & where the Duke is also disposed to assist him further *pecuniarily,* if on his return from his Canvas he should be of opinion that it is worth his while to stand a poll—

Your's ever

P

No such person as Ld Lichfield [3] exists. The late Lds property is in possession of the present Ld Dillon [4]— Lady Hereford [5] (who is the Widow of the late Lord) was once a Maid of Honor & is decidedly hostile to Us. Walwyn [6] & Ld Beauchamp I will write to. & Fox is the person to consult about Ld Egremont [7] though perhaps Hare [8] or Ld Foley [9] may be the most proper to mention Morland's wishes to Him—

[added on verso by Portland:]

The D. of B. wishes to have
the list to night
he dines at the D. of York's—

NOTES

1. Francis Russell, 5th Duke of Bedford (1765–1802), and Lord Spencer were the two patrons of Okehampton at this time; but the actual management of the borough had long been in the hands of the Luxmoores, a local propertied family. Bedford and Spencer had joined their interests; but in 1784 the perfidy of one branch of the Luxmoore family had plunged the two patrons into an expensive and embarrassing contest (the borough had the reputation of being safe). The patrons' candidates were seated only on petition. After 1784 both Bedford and Spencer had thought of selling their property in the borough; and by December, 1789, Spencer had actually done so, though secretly, so as not to disturb the interest of the new owner. John St. Leger and Robert Ladbroke, both supporters of Opposition, were seated for Okehampton in 1791 after a double return.

2. Lord Robert Spencer.

3. Robert Lee, 4th Earl of Lichfield, died in 1776, at which date the title became extinct.

4. Charles Dillon Lee, 12th Viscount Dillon (1745–1813). His mother, Charlotte Lee, eldest daughter of George Henry Lee, 2nd Earl of Lichfield, had become sole heir to the estates of Lichfield upon the death of the 4th Earl.

5. Henrietta Charlotta Keck Tracy, daughter of Anthony Keck (1708–1767), M.P., of Great Tew, Oxon. In 1774 she had married Edward Devereux, 12th Viscount Hereford. Lord Hereford died in 1783.

6. James Walwyn (1744–1800), of Longworth House, Hereford. M.P. Hereford 1785–1800. Sheriff, Herefordshire 1784–1785. A Foxite and connection of the Duke of Norfolk.

7. George Wyndham O'Brien, 3rd Earl of Egremont (1751–1837). Toward the middle of the century the 2nd Earl had possessed the chief interest at Taunton, but that interest had since declined.

8. James Hare (1747–1804), M.P. Stockbridge 1772–1774, Knaresborough 1781–1804. An intimate companion of Fox and favorite of Whig society.

9. Thomas Foley, 2nd Baron Foley (1742–1793). M.P. Herefordshire 1767–1774, Droitwich 1774–1777. Another close friend of Fox and, like Hare and Egremont, a devotee of horseracing.

Lord Daer *to* William Adam
[*ante* 26 *February* 1790]

Address: Mr W Adam / Lincolns Inn fields
Endorsed: Lord Daer— / Election for Glasgow / question of
the / Eligibility of the / Eldest son of a / Scotch Peer—
The bye-election for the Glasgow Burghs occurred on 26 February 1790,
which dates the letter.

In October, 1789, the sitting member for the Glasgow Burghs, Ilay
Campbell, was appointed Lord President of the Court of Session
and retired from Parliament. For some reason neither of the candidates intending to contest the general election came forward during
the bye-election. Ministerialist Glasgow adopted a member of their
city council, John Dunlop, as an interim candidate; Opposition,
apparently after some misunderstanding with Lord Daer, put forward John Craufurd of Auchinames, who had been member for the
burghs during the Parliament of 1780. The Opposition seems to
have caught the Government interest by surprise; and Craufurd
was returned by capturing the delegates from Dumbarton and Renfrew, the returning burgh. Eldest sons of Scottish peers were
widely held incapable of representing Scottish constituencies, and
this explains Daer's apprehensions about eligibility and the party's
second thoughts about his standing for the Glasgow district;
though the law seems not to have been entirely settled as yet (John
Hatsell, *Precedents of Proceedings in the House of Commons*
[London, 3rd ed., 1796], II, 18–19 and especially 20n, which
indicates that prior to February, 1792, Daer himself was unsuccessfully testing this law in the Court of Session, where he defended his
right to be enrolled as a freeholder in Kirkcudbright. For his appeal
to the House of Lords, see Debrett, XXXVI, 143–145).

Jermyn Street Sunday forenoon

Dear Sir,

You have perhaps heard I am not off for Scotland. Mr.
Craufurd I found had still some idea that he might stand
at the general election; which would rather have been a

dissappointment to me, had I been found eligible, & born all the expenses of this surprize, which opened the way to his success for next Parliament. However I believe that would not have stopped my journey, as I should have trusted his laziness would recoil from so laborious an attack: When very luckily, & [I] shall owe Craufurd thanks for it, he read a part of a line he got from the Duke of Portland; in which (though I understood the Duke had written to Harry Erskine agreeing to make this election subservient to my views, if it could be done safely) I saw he was under such apprehensions of its marring their plans & prospects, which I confess I am not in the secret enough to comprehend, that I determined to be off; & wash my hands of the business. I have no notion of teasing a man against his opinion to give you the priviledge of paying 500£ for a six weeks seat, with the comfort into the bargain of bearing the blame, & perhaps the weight upon your conscience, of all future miscarriages; in a business, where perhaps your interference might have a bad effect, but where at any rate, the chance of miscarriage is at least ten to one; for such I look upon the chance of any known oppositionist carrying these Boroughs at next turn against the Minister.—I shall cut rather a droll figure after telling all my friends I was going off, to be found sitting here quietly. I thought it necessary even to write an apology to the Duke for not going, after he had written for me; so I am explaining a little what were my views.—I feel much indebted to him for his civility on this occasion; & to Craufurd too, for his obligingness & open manner. Adieu. I should have dined with you, but Mr Craufurd & I had not settled till six oclock.

Yours sincerely
DAER

Duke of Portland *to* William Adam
3 *April* 1790

Dear Adam

I wish with all my heart it was in my power to fulfill Mr Royds's wish as there is no man who can have a better claim to any service I can render him but my presentation has been long engaged, I may even say before I became a Governor of Christ Hospital & I had had at least a dozen applications before I received Mr Royds's which in justice to our excellent friend Baldwin [1] Mr R. should know had been made to me by Him the night before I left town. I beg You to say every thing for me to Mr Royds, but perhaps it will be best to shew him this Letter for I can not speak with more Truth or feel more concern than I do at not being able to gratify Him —There may be much talk but I can not believe it will be any thing more serious in Surry, it is adviseable however that Our friends should be alert & at their posts [2]—I dare say the *settlement* You have made is a safe one at least without risk [3]—I hope to see You in less than a week after You get this—In the mean time if there are any Letters which should be written by me send me the names—

Your's ever

P

Welbeck Sat: even 3 April 1790

NOTES

1. William Baldwin.
2. Surrey was contested in 1790. The two successful candidates were Lord William Russell and William Clement Finch (1753–1794). The latter was a Government candidate and in 1791 received £500 secret service money for election expenses (A. Aspinall, ed., *The Later Correspondence of George III* [Cambridge, 1962], I, 116 n). Sir Joseph Mawbey (1730–1798), who had been member for the county since 1775 and who had supported Pitt, failed to receive support from the Government interest during the election and was never again returned to the House (*H of P; cf.* Oldfield, *History of Boroughs,* 2nd ed., II, 128).
3. This seems to refer to the financial affairs of the royal princes.

Sir Godfrey Webster *to* William Adam [*ante* 14 *April* 1790]

For dating, see note 1, below.

Crewe's Act of 1782 disenfranchising revenue officers had raised particular havoc at Seaford. Since 1784 a fierce, expensive, and prolonged struggle had been waged by the Treasury interest, which was trying to maintain itself against a resurgent Pelham and insurgent independent interest. The years between 1784 and 1786 witnessed three elections, two of which were voided, and three petitions. Henry Flood on the independent interest (though he voted with Pitt on the Regency) and Webster on the Pelham interest were finally seated in April, 1786. In 1790 the Opposition offered a second candidate on the Pelham interest, John Tarleton (1755–1820). The poll in 1790 closed with John Sargent 92, R. P. Jodrell 91, Webster 48, Tarleton 48. The Pelham candidates petitioned once again against the Treasury nominees; the petition was not considered by the committee of the House until March, 1792, when Tarleton and John Sargent, one of the Treasury candidates, were declared duly returned. Oldfield, *History of Boroughs,* 2nd ed., 11, 348–393.

Seaford Wednesday

My Dear Adam,

Tarleton & I have been Here five Days – Going on very Well —All Hitherto has been Festivity, & *Tranquillity,* but as Our Opponents are Expected to Night, I Look for a Small Contest if Not a Battle in Ecclesiá, to Morrow, When We choose Churchwardens — My only fear is a petition, for if the least Colorable pretext Exists, the Bailiff, our Foe, will Return our Opponents; & after three petitions, I am not ambitious for a fourth— However I shall fight it out like a Man— Trusting that when I act With Men of Honor, I shall Experience the Same Conduct from them, that I have shewn to them—

I got this morn a Circular Letter for Wednesday 14th: on the Tobacco,[1] As My presence Here does Much Service, I most probably shall not leave Seaford for Some Days, You will thereore if You please get Me a pair, As I certainly shall not be in Town, on that Day—

> I remain with Great Regard
> My Dear Sir
> Your Most faithful
> & Obedient
> G WEBSTER

NOTE

1. On 8 March 1790 Sheridan moved that the House resolve itself into a committee to consider a number of petitions which had been received from throughout the kingdom praying for the repeal of the excise duty on tobacco. The House did not meet on Wednesday, 14 April; but on Friday, 16 April, Sheridan moved the order of the day and the House resolved itself into a committee on the petitions. Debrett, XXVII, 226, 403.

Duke of Portland *to* William Adam
30 *April* 1790

The two sitting members for Southampton, John Fleming (1743–1802) and James Amyatt (1734–1813), had both supported Pitt during the Parliament of 1784. Amyatt was once again returned in 1790 and continued to sit for the borough until 1806; Fleming did not stand and was not again returned to the House. The second member returned in 1790 was Henry Martin (1733–1794), later 1st Bt., who is listed in the *Official Returns* as residing in Stratford Place, London. Martin had been the commissioner resident at Portsmouth Dockyard 1780–1790; from 1790–1794 he was comptroller of the navy (Robert Beatson, *Political Index* [London, 3rd ed., 1806], II, 81, 89). He appears on no Opposition lists for the Parliament of 1790. The *H of P* classes Southampton as an "open borough." "Of the eight Members who represented Southampton 1754–90 every one was a Hampshire squire, and none a naval officer—Southampton never ranked as an Admiralty borough, although Government influence in it was of a certain importance. There was in the borough an independent local element, but . . . no genuine burgess represented the borough" from 1754 to 1790. Of the eight members returned during that period, five (including the elder Dawkins) were members of two West Indian interests and one was a nabob. Martin seems to have been the first candidate in decades who was neither a local squire nor an East or West Indian but a Government candidate connected with the Admiralty. By the general election of 1796 Oldfield lists George Rose as influencing the return of both members, and it may be that he was behind Martin's candidacy in 1790 (A. Aspinall and E. Anthony Smith, eds., *English Historical Documents 1783–1832* [London, 1959], p. 230).

Dear Adam

Inclosed You receive the Lists, of which I have no copy—There can be no occasion to send for Pembroke till I have seen Daukins [1] which I will endeavour to do in the course of tomorrow, & time enough for the Post—I dont expect Ld Fitz & beg You will not think of moving at this time of night. I did not propose to Him to come here upon account of his dinner—but we had much conversa-

tion & I found him perfectly disposed & ready to meet
whenever we pleased—Baldwin is the Key stone of all
our business ² & if he declines we shall all fall to pieces—
The Meeting was deferred till one tomorrow upon account of the Ds of Y– & C–s unavoidable absence.

Your's ever

Friday night 30 April 1790   P

NOTES

1. Henry Dawkins (1728–1814), a wealthy West Indian with
estates in Wiltshire and Oxfordshire. In 1757 he had inherited his
brother's estates in Hampshire. M.P. Southampton 1760–1768,
Chippenham 1769–1774 and 1780–1784, Hindon 1776–1780. In
1784 he had given up his seat at Chippenham (where he was
establishing a family interest) to his son, James; he and another
Foxite then offered themselves as candidates at Southampton in
opposition to three Pittites, but they were forced to withdraw
without a poll. Later correspondence indicates that Adam procured
the Southampton writ in 1790.

2. Relating to the princes' debts.

Duke of Portland *to* William Adam
1 *May* [1790]

Address: To / William Adam Esqre / Lincolns Inn Fields
Endorsed: D of P. / 1st May 90 / inclosing one / from Mr Dawkins

Dear Adam

I send You Dawkins's answer inclosed, can You save
this nights post—& bring P–¹ to town tomorrow & answer the other question?

Sat: 1 May   Your's ever
past 5 P.M.   P

NOTE

1. Pembroke.

James Dawkins *to* Duke of Portland
1 *May* 1790

This letter was found enclosed in Portland to Adam of 1 May 1790.

James Dawkins (?1760–1843), 1st son of Henry Dawkins, was M. P. Chippenham 1784–1806, 1807–1812, Hastings 1812–1826, Wilton 1831–1832. He had supported Opposition during the Parliament of 1784 and continued to do so through the session of 1791–1792.

My Lord Duke

I did myself the honor of calling upon your Grace about half an hour ago, after I had conversed with my father on the subject of your Grace's note of this morning. My father desires me to express in the strongest terms the sense he has of your Graces goodness to him on this occasion, & to say how very sorry he is, his health is in so indifferent a state as to prevent his having at present the honor of waiting upon your Grace to make his personal acknowlegements. He will be very glad to engage with Mr: Pembroke & wishes to set out with him for Southampton on Monday morning next, if it would be possible for Mr. Pembroke to be ready by that time. Will your Grace further have the goodness to allow me to ask you, in what manner Mr. Pembroke is to be satisfied on this occasion. I have the honor to be

My Lord Duke
your Graces
most obliged & faithful Servant
JAMES DAWKINS

Harley Street
May 1st: 90—

Henry Erskine *to* William Adam
9 *May* 1790

Endorsed: Edinr 9th May / 1790 / Hy Erskine

The Independent interest in Sutherlandshire seems to have split at the general election. Three candidates stood the poll. General James Grant, the incumbent and Sutherland–Gower candidate, was again returned with 9 votes. Robert Bruce Aeneas Macleod of Cadbole received 5 votes, including that of John Gordon of Carroll, a brother-in-law of Macleod of Geanies and a near connection of Lord Dumfries (Adam, *Pol. State,* p. 341). Robert Home Gordon of Embo received 3 votes. Only 17 out of 35 enrolled freeholders voted, then, and the absentees included such potential Opposition votes as George Dempster, Lord Ankerville, and Sir David Carnegie of Southesk (Mackenzie, *Pol. State,* pp. 186–189). The party seems to have decided not to intervene in Sutherlandshire. The Marquess of Stafford, Lord Gower's father, did not die until 1803; the Portland–Fox Opposition predeceased him by a decade.

Edinburgh May. 9th
1790

My dear Adam.

Some Months ago you will remember that I wrote you my opinion that a successful attack might be made on the County of Sutherland in Case the *nominal* Votes should be set aside. But you Wrote me in return that our friends did not chuse to oppose Lord Gower who they thought but for his Father would be friendly. From that time I thought no more of the Matter—Now however a Candidate has started—Mr Gordon of Embo [1]—one of our principles & who if elected will vote with us—His Friends have applied to me for our Support—I have given no definitive Answer but I beg you'l immediately consult our Friends on the Subject and if they think now that an opposition does exist they can Support it I have little doubt it will be successful & that we shall gain a County by the Shift—If our Friends can take a part Measures must be taken to Secure Geo. Dempster. Ross of Cromarty [2] can make Houston of Creech [3] and keep right the Gordons of Pulrossie [4] one of them Lieut. Gordon is now in London—The sooner I can know Your resolves on this Bussiness the better.

I much fear you have trusted too much to G. Graham's [5] Generosity. I can't draw an answer from him though Sir M. Malcolm [6] & S. H. Moncrief [7] have made his going with me [8] a Condition of their giving him their Votes [9] and I hope Bruce [10] will do the same—I wish K. Elphinstone would write Mercer [11] to follow the same line. Graham might then be driven to the point to which I am affraid he is very averse and I fear much that by supporting him unconditionally you'l find him on the wrong side of the Post.

Your's in great haste

H. E.

NOTES

1. Robert Home Gordon of Embo was added to the roll of freeholders for Sutherlandshire at the head court meeting of July, 1790. Hill had anticipated this in his "state," and noted: "Has an immense estate in the West Indies. Mr. Cooper Lee, Attorney-at-Law, has influence" (Adam, *Pol. State,* p. 343).

2. Alexander Gray Ross of Cromarty.

3. Hugh Houstoun of Creech, a wine merchant at Brora. Hill thought he would "lean to the Gower interest" (Adam, *Pol. State,* p. 342). At the election he voted for Macleod of Cadbole (Mackenzie, *Pol. State,* p. 188).

4. Hill noted that Capt. Charles Gordon of Pulrossie was "Independent. Not in good health. About to sell to Mr. Dempster." Gordon's three sons were "inrolled on votes from him." Adam, *Pol. State,* p. 341. The Gordons of Pulrossie did not vote at the general election, and only two of the sons (both lieutenants in the army) were still on the roll of freeholders (Mackenzie, *Pol. State,* pp. 186–189).

5. George Graham (1730–1801), of Kinross. M. P. Kinross-

shire 1780–1784, 1790–1796. Kinross was Adam's home county. Adam had persistently refused to oppose Graham's interest at the general election or to believe that Graham would not support Erskine in Fife. In the event Graham was not opposed in Kinross; and although he first said he was committed to the other side, on 23 June he wrote Adam that he would gladly support Erskine (Blair Adam MSS). The contest in Fife was not taken to the poll, however; William Wemyss of Wemyss, the Pittite incumbent, was unanimously returned (Mackenzie, *Pol. State,* p. 97). Graham appears on no Opposition division lists during the Parliament of 1790.

    6. Sir Michael Malcolm of Lochore.

    7. Rev. Sir Henry Moncrieff Wellwood (1750–1827), of Tulliebole. Appointed chaplain to the Prince of Wales in 1785 and to George III in 1793.

    8. In Fife.

    9. In Kinross-shire.

    10. Thomas Bruce of Arnot.

    11. G. K. Elphinstone was married to the eldest daughter and heiress of William Mercer of Aldie (Adam, *Pol. State,* p. 192).

Duke of Portland *to* William Adam
22 *May* 1790

Address: To / William Adam Esqre.: / at the Honble: Captn: Elphinstone's / Grafton Street

Dear Adam

I am very sorry I missed You, not that I had much to say to You, but to tell You that I had represented to Sheridan the impossibility of my being concerned in the negotiation with de Beaume or any other upon terms less advantageous than those agreed to with Hankey or suffering any negotiation of that sort to proceed without communicating it to Hankey or being a party to or concerned in any negotiation the terms of which could not be publickly avowed [1]—Sturt [2] misunderstood You with regard to the Letters, but said he would send them this evening. But as my company did not break up till past 11, I doubt my receiving them in time for Lowten to have them before he sets out. Ld Sheffield will be in town tomorrow. I have left a note for him saying that it seemed to be the opinion of his friends that he should set out for B.[3] & canvass R–[4] in his way, & that I should be in town on Tuesday Evening before ten, at which hour should he be then in town I should be very happy to see Him. Do get me an answer from Ld North respecting Swann or send it to Ld Ludlow [5] & let me know if any thing has been settled with Stephens [6] respecting the press musters at Sandwich.

Your's ever
P

Sat: night 22 May 1790

NOTES

1. This passage concerns the financial affairs of the royal princes.

2. Perhaps Charles Sturt (1763–1812), M.P. Bridport 1784–1802 on his family interest, and a Foxite. If so, the "letters" could be intended for the contest at Bridport, or even for the county of Dorset, for which Sturt's father, Humphrey Sturt, had been member 1754–1784. Sturt's interest in the county had been increased in 1788 by his marriage to the daughter of the 4th Earl of Shaftesbury. The two sitting members were returned for Dorset, both of whom had voted with Pitt during the Parliament of 1784. The second member returned for Bridport in 1790 was James Watson, also a Pittite. Alternatively, reference may be to Charles Stuart, the journalist.

3. Bristol. On 13 May 1790 Adam received the following note from Samuel Heywood, a leading metropolitan Dissenter who had long and with some success been seeking the party's support for the repeal of the Test and Corporation Acts: "Thus saith a Letter I got to day from Bristol: 'Mr. Cunningham has taken ground I did not suspect, he is among the Dissenters promising every thing—He

will do mischief—Ld. S—must be at B—soon or all chance of his doing any thing—or of the Tories not starting *two* will be over—I am in silence doing all I can & I think not with out some good prospects—If the Dissenters as Dissenters bring a man forward, we are undone—The Church will be a prevailing enemy—I wish Ld. S—had been within call a week ago—' " (Blair Adam MSS). These remarks may help explain why reform issues—even when deeply felt—did not appear on the surface of electoral politics in this period.

4. Reading was a frequently contested and "remarkably expensive" borough; but during the mid-eighteenth century "the Members were almost invariably neighbouring landowners: outsiders . . . fared badly" (*H of P*).

5. Peter, 1st Earl Ludlow (1730–1803), M. P. Huntingdonshire 1768–1796 on the interest of the Duke of Manchester. A staunch old Rockinghamite.

6. Philip Stephens (1723–1809), M. P. Liskeard 1759–1768, Sandwich 1768–1806. Stephens had been Secretary to the Admiralty since 1763 and had long carefully nursed the Government interest in that borough. Oldfield (*History of Boroughs,* 2nd ed., II, 314) wrote: ". . . at the last election [1790], Sir Horace Mann [*d.* 1814, nephew and heir of the diplomat and friend of Horace Walpole], who resides in the neighbourhood, having the largest Kentish estate of any man in the county, and is so much respected for his hospitality and convivial talents, that no other person would have stood the smallest chance of success in opposition to government, became a candidate on his own interest, in opposition to lord Parker, comptroller of the household, (who was supported by government, in conjunction with Mr. Stephens . . .) was successful. . . . Thus the independent interest succeeded, for the first time, in the election of one of their members." Mann voted with Opposition over Oczakow in 1791, but he appears on no other Opposition division list during the Parliament of 1790.

J. Jackman *to* Charles Whiting
[1 *June* 1790]

Address: Mr. Whiting— / Salopian Coffee house. / Charing Cross.
/ London.
Postmarked: 74 FOLKSTONE *and* JU 3 90
Endorsed by Adam: J. Jackman
The first of June fell on a Tuesday in 1790.

Hastings, Winchelsea, and Rye are grouped closely together on the coast of Sussex. New Romney is nearby on the Kentish coast. All four boroughs were Cinque Ports, the number of qualified voters in each had been greatly reduced by Crewe's Act of 1782, and each had an old and well-established patron who—with the exceptions of Nesbitt, who was in process of selling his interest, and the momentary revolt of Lamb in 1784—invariably returned Government nominees or supporters. None of these constituencies either returned or were contested by Opposition candidates in 1790. It is difficult to see what provoked Jackson's extraordinary investigation —unless it grew out of the Winchelsea negotiations of September, 1789—indeed it is not altogether clear who initially conceived and authorized it. But it is precisely its extraordinary and speculative nature and its having been sponsored and financed by Adam and at least countenanced by Portland which makes this investigation so highly significant. Jackman had been editor of the *Morning Post* for several years before his dismissal *c.* 1783. Under his editorship the paper had supported Government and seems to have received a subsidy from the end of 1780, but it is not certain what Jackman's personal politics were at this time. Nothing certain is known of his activities after 1783 (Lucyle Werkmeister, *The London Daily Press 1772–1792* [Lincoln, Neb., 1963], pp. 44–47), although the *Universal British Directory* for 1797 (I, 190) lists a J. Jackman of 1, Gough Square, as a "French and Irish Agent." Nothing is known of Charles Whiting.

Folkstone Tuesday:

Dear Sir.

I was favored with your letter of Saturday — This morning I saw Mr. Mathew Robinson of Houghton, formerly Member for Canterbury,[1] and a very remarkable Gentleman in this County. He, and a variety of other people have assured me, that Parliament will be dissolved shortly after the birth day— Whether this be an affectation of superior intelligence, or a well grounded assertion, I am unable to determine—At all events, I shall proceed in my business with every possible dispatch.

Under their respective heads you will find in this letter, a laconick statement of facts and a few observations on the several places in Sussex, which have been objects of my particular attention—My being on the Spot, hath furnished me with *secret information,* which may be of infinite service, as well on the present occasion, as hereafter— Some Gentlemen consider themselves perfectly secure in what they call *their boroughs*— I know the contrary, and that a spirited manoeuvre, would shove them "from their stools"— Read the following observations with attention, and I think you will be of my opinion.

Hastings—

I have in a former letter, mentioned what hath passed between Milward,[2] and myself. You must understand that nothing can be done at this place, but through the medium of this extraordinary Man— Without a ray from erudition, he professes an astonishing fund of natural sagacity. He constantly talks of his honor, his integrity, and his consistency, and yet, he will at some moments betray himself, if you flatter him with caution, and which will convince you that his morality is constantly in Masquerade— Appear to do homage at the shrine of his authority, and you have him—This I found to be his weak side, and I made my own use of it.

On the receipt of this letter you must get Mr. Adams to furnish me with the names of two Gentlemen as candidates for Hastings— My Folkstone friend, who stands so well in Milwards confidence informs me, he will go no

further in the treaty without knowing who the Gentlemen
are, that look to his friendship, on the next general election— In my opinion you have not a moment to lose in
this business.

Winchelsea

W. Nesbitt [3] is generally supposed to possess the power
of returning the members for this borough. He has done
it hitherto, and lately bargained with Barwell, who I understand is a man of considerable property— Lord Somebody — they say is to be the other Member— Now I
must inform you, (*but I conjure you be secret as to
names*) that a Mr. Martin [4] at this place who is steward
to Nesbitt, could as easily return the members for
Winchelsea independent of his employer, as I could direct
this letter to you— Nesbitts estates here are all in Mort-
gage, and of course that lessens his influence— But in a
secret conversation which I had with Martin, (for I have
attended to him very particularly) he told me *in confidence,* that notwithstanding there were but six voters,[5]
(the rest being placemen and rendered incapable by Grenvilles act) [6] all of whom he had at his command, Mr.
Nesbitt could not procure him, or did not think proper to
obtain a place for him at Winchelsea of about 120 gs per
annum, which had been in his family for Sixty years, and
was given to a stranger who possessed ministerial influence—He added *very gravely*—"I am bound however
to Mr. Nesbitt by *gratitude*"—
    I shall make no comment on this matter, as I believe it
to be unnecessary— Mr. Adams no doubt will make
proper use of this information—
P. S. Martin is one of the qualified voters—

Rye—

I have seen the Mr. Lambs,[7] whose influence at this place
no human power can shake— I was (as Mr. Adams di-

rected) particularly tenacious respecting Rye. But hearing from undoubted authority in the neighbourhood that
neither Mr. Long or Mr. Dickenson would be returned
again, I waited on the old Gentleman, who gave me a
very gracious reception—After a conversation, which
gave me to understand that one seat was vacant, he told
me, that he had delegated all his influence in the corporation to his Son,[8] who is the present Mayor, and lived but
a few ⟨roods⟩ out of the Town— I requested to know
if I had his permission to wait on the Mayor— He said
"by all means"— Very fortunately Young Lamb was an
old school fellow of my friend the Aldermans—I accordingly paid my compliments to the Mayor, and in company
with the old Gentlemans nephew— The reception I met
with was exceedingly flattering, and very candid— He
said, that until he knew the name of the candidate it was
impossible for him to say any thing conclusive on the subject— He said likewise, that he was just returned from
London, and that he had *partly* engaged his interest at
Rye—

The fact is one seat may be had here, but I understand
for not less than 4000 pounds or Guineas— Pray see Mr.
Adams immediately and say, what I am to do respecting
this place—

New Romney–

In a few words I can assure you that Sir Edwd. Deer-
ing,[9] stands exactly in a similar situation respecting New
Romney, as Mr. Nesbitt does at Winchelsea. The acting
Man at present in Sir Edwards affairs is a Mr. Woodgate, who I understand is at present in London with Sir
Edward— Major Murry is no longer an acting Trustee,
and Woodgate has no influence here— A Mr. Walter [10]
(here I must again request an absolute silence as to
names) informed me that Sir Edward Deerings influence
at Romney was *on the go*— I give you his own words,
and he is a leading man in the corporation—These sev-

eral informations could not be had without being on the spot, and they may be of the highest consequence, if properly attended to—

You now have a history of these places—also what can, and what cannot be done— I must request therefore you will immediately furnish me with instructions, and the names of those Gentlemen, who are to be candidates for each place—Mr. Adams will select those places he is most desirous of attaining, and no pains shall be wanting on my part to accomplish the business with every possible dispatch—

I am Dear Sir very truly
Yours J. JACKMAN

I must get you to send me an immediate remittance as My money is nearly all gone—

NOTES

1. Matthew Robinson Morris (1713–1800), of Horton, near Canterbury, Kent. M. P. Canterbury 1747–1761. He retained a lively and active interest in national politics after his retirement from Parliament, wrote pamphlets criticising the American policies of North's government and advocating parliamentary reform, and —like Fox and his friends—"rejoiced at the outbreak of the French Revolution, but disapproved of its subsequent course" (*H of P*). He was a notorious eccentric in his personal habits and appearance, which made it difficult for many to take him seriously.

2. Edward Milward had been the Government manager for Hastings since the days of Newcastle and had inherited that position from his uncle. After Newcastle's fall he continued to serve the interests of successive Governments, never failing to return two Treasury nominees. Although there seems to have been a latent opposition to Milward within the borough, there was no contest at Hastings during the period of his management until 1784, when Stephen Lushington and Sir Godfrey Webster made a poor showing. It may well be that after so long a period Milward's interest in the borough had become personal, but he still had a place in the customs to protect. In 1790 John Stanley, an incumbent Government nominee, and Richard Pepper Arden, Pitt's Master of the Rolls, were returned.

3. Jackman has mistaken the initial. This should be John Nes-

171

bitt (?1745–1817), of Keston Park, Kent. M. P. Winchelsea 1780–1790, Gatton 1790–1796, Bodmin 1796–1802. Nesbitt had inherited the principal interest at Winchelsea from his uncle, Arnold Nesbitt (?1721–1779), who had finally succeeded to a dominant position in the borough at the end of the 1760's. John Nesbitt was connected with the Prince of Wales and had followed the politics of Fox since 1782. The estates which he had inherited from his uncle were heavily encumbered. By 1789 he was teetering on the brink of bankruptcy, and shortly before the general election he sold his Winchelsea estates to Richard Barwell and Lord Darlington for £15,000. At the general election Barwell himself and Lord Barnard, uncle of Lord Darlington, were returned. Both were supporters of Pitt. *H of P;* Oldfield, *History of Boroughs,* 2nd ed., II, 342–343.

4. Thomas Marton. According to Oldfield (*History of Boroughs,* 2nd ed., II, 347), Marton became the agent for Barwell and Darlington, by whom he was "allowed two hundred pounds a year for the management of the borough."

5. Oldfield (*History of Boroughs,* 2nd ed., II, 344–345, 347) believed they numbered only three.

6. Crewe's Act of 1782.

7. Thomas Lamb, "a tally-cutter in the exchequer, a place of 400l. a year, and cursitor of Hampshire," who had succeeded his father some forty years earlier as Government manager of the borough (Oldfield, *History of Boroughs,* 2nd ed., II, 330, 336). Crewe's Act of 1782 had reduced the legal voters in Rye to some half dozen persons who did not hold disqualifying places of the Treasury. In these circumstances Lamb attempted to assert his personal influence in returning one member for the borough, and in 1784 he returned William Dickinson, a Northite and opponent of Pitt. But apparently he found such independence of Government risky, and in 1790 he returned Charles Long, who had come in for the Treasury seat at the bye-election of 1789 and was to become joint Secretary to the Treasury in 1791, and Robert Banks Jenkinson, later prime minister as 2nd Earl of Liverpool and son of the "King's Friend."

8. Thomas Phillipps Lamb, "cursitor of Kent, and late a king's waiter of the customs at this place, which he has given to his son, Thomas Davis Lamb, a minor" (Oldfield, *History of Boroughs,* 2nd ed., II, 336). The mayor was the returning officer of the borough.

9. Sir Edward Dering (1732–1798), 6th Bt., of Surrenden Dering, near Ashford, Kent. M.P. New Romney 1761–1770, 1774–1787. Five generations of Dering's immediate ancestors had

sat for the county of Kent. Sir Edward had inherited estates near New Romney through his first wife and had established his interest there by 1760, from which date he had wholly controlled the return for both seats. He had invariably returned members nominated by or friendly to Government. In 1794, when applying to Pitt for a peerage, he claimed credit for having refused "some very advantageous offers" made him by Opposition during the Regency Crisis (quoted in *H of P*), which perhaps explains Portland's reaction to Jackson's report on New Romney (*infra*). In 1790 Dering returned the incumbent Richard Joseph Sullivan, who had been nominated to his seat by Pitt at the bye-election of 1787 and who had supported Pitt in the House, and Sir Elijah Impey, who with Warren Hastings was the object of the famous Whig-managed impeachment.

10. Probably Jacob Walter (*H of P*, article on New Romney; Oldfield, *History of Boroughs*, 2nd ed., II, 325, 326).

Duke of Portland *to* William Adam
4 *June* [1790]

Endorsed: D of P. / 4th June 90

Dear Adam

I want or rather am wanted to set out for Bulstrode. I therefore shall leave this at the Gate—I take Romney & Rye to be quite out of the question, & I should doubt the other two [1]—But yet I should not despair of either but there can be no use or occasion to give any names till I see You which I hope for on Sunday Evening when I shall return at 9 or between 9 & 10 at latest.

Your's ever

P

Friday noon
4 June

[added by Portland on verso:]
Ld Suffolk is beat at Malmesbury.[2]

173

NOTES

1. Hastings and Winchelsea.

2. Henry Howard, 12th Earl of Suffolk, had originally established Edmund Wilkins as the family's political manager in Malmesbury; but Wilkins had later deserted John, the 15th Earl (1739–1820), in 1768 and established his separate interest. It appears that Opposition supported an attempt by Suffolk to revive his interest in Malmesbury—perhaps persuaded him to do so—but since the election at Malmesbury was held 21 June, it is clear that Suffolk had withdrawn his candidates before the poll.

Sir Grey Cooper *to* William Adam
4 *June* 1790

Rickmansworth June 4. 1790

My dear Sir.

By yesterday's post I had the honour of a letter from the Duke of Portland, & I have answered by that of this day.— Whatever may be the event of this business, I acknowledge my obligations to you for the readiness with which you undertook to remind his Grace of my application—I omitted when I saw you last to tell you what Lord Cassillis, (just before he left London last week in a better state of health than he has been the whole winter) intreated me to mention to the Duke, namely to shew all the attention & give all the assistance in his power to Sir Andrew Cathcart in his contest for Ayrshire: Lord Cassillis said he doubted whether Mr Broughton [1] had been applied [to] by the Duke.—

Yours ever very Sincerely
GREY COOPER

NOTE

1. James Murray (1729–1799), of Broughton, Wigtown, and Cally, Stewartry of Kirkcudbright. M.P. Wigtownshire 1762–1768, Kirkcudbright Stewartry 1768–1774. Hill credited him with the largest single interest in Kirkcudbright Stewartry and noted: "A great estate. Married a sister of Lord Galloway's, but separated from her. No children. Leaning to Opposition, though of late he has meddled little in politicks" (Adam, *Pol. State,* pp. 195, 211). Murray was not himself a freeholder in Ayrshire, but he seems to have had influence with two who were (Adam, *Pol. State,* pp. 34 [Alexander Stewart], 40 [John Bushby]).

Roger Wilbraham *to* William Adam
4 *June* 1790

Address: William Adam Esqe M:P: / Lincolns Inn Fields / London
      Postmarked: JU 7 90

Lanhydrock near Bodmin
June 4th 1790

Dear Adam

I have this day seen Mr Tocker [1] and left him perfectly satisfied as to the £150. I see that he and his Friends are very anxious to have what they call a private Canvass, which I discouraged as much as possible, and you will probably hear from Some of them Soon; they want to know where they may draw for any part of the first Sum of £500 and when. In short they wish to have a little money, the danger and impropriety of which I represented Strongly. There appears to me to be some little apprehension from the Jealousy between Mayne [2] and Perryman [3] on the one part, the Persons patronized by Sir J. Morshead, and our Friends [4] on the other. I can not suppose this Jealousy will reach Sir John, but I think it would be as well if the D of P. would conciliate him as much as possible. I find he wanted a ——— [5] for Sir J. Frederick,[6] which I should have been as glad of as he could possibly be, but he wished it on easier terms than those at ———.[7] You will naturally take no notice of this letter unless to the D of P.[8]

All goes on at Bodmin for Sir J. Morshead and myself as well as we could wish it, in short we have no doubt of Success.[9]

I am Dear Adam Yours most Sincerely
R WILBRAHAM

If you have anything new pray give me a line.

NOTES

1. Thomas Wheare Tocker, an attorney at Tregony and in 1797 a member of the corporation (*Universal British Directory*, IV, 612).

2. Probably Dr. Thomas Mein, a naval surgeon and Portreeve (returning officer) of Fowey, who was connected with Morshead and seems to have taken a lead in the Opposition interest for the borough (Aspinall, ed., *Correspondence of George, Prince of Wales 1770–1812*, II, 213–214, 216–217, 223–224; *Universal British Directory*, III, 128).

3. "Richard Perryman, Gent.," was listed as a member of the Tregony corporation in 1797 (*Universal British Directory*, IV, 612). He was apparently to have managed the election.

4. Sir Francis Basset's?

5. Seat?

6. Sir John Frederick (1750–1825), 5th Bt. M.P. Newport 1774–1780, Christchurch 1781–1790, Surrey 1794–1807. He had supported North's administration, opposed Shelburne and Pitt. Frederick had exceedingly bad luck with patrons: his patron for Newport sold his interest before the general election of 1780, and Hooper had lost his interest in Christchurch by 1789. Frederick was now in search of a seat, and Morshead thought of him for Tregony.

7. Christchurch?

8. Duke of Portland.

9. The principal interests in Bodmin were the Treise–Mors-

head and Hunt of Lanhydrock. The Pitt of Boconnoc interest had not contested the borough since 1762. Sir John Morshead had been member on the family interest since 1784 and was to be returned again at the general election. Thomas Hunt, a brother of George Hunt of Lanhydrock, had been returned for the other seat in 1784; but Hunt had died in 1789 and had been succeeded by George Wilbraham (1741–1813), his son-in-law and elder brother of Roger Wilbraham. This was George's only excursion into parliamentary politics, and Roger was returned for the seat in 1790.

⟨Charles⟩ Whiting *to* William Adam [7 *June* 1790?]

Address: Wm. Adam Esqe—
Endorsed: Whiting—June 90
This letter seems to have been written on Monday, 7 June 1790, the day before Adam's to Hodgson of 8 June (*infra*).

> Salopian Coffee house
> One oClock
> Monday

Sir

I am truly sorry to hear of your indisposition—I received your's by Mr. Walsh [1] who I understand has made you auquainted [sic] with the Situation he found me at Rye, and have the further mortification to add that I stayed at Rye till 7 oClock on Sunday Night but could not find *Jackman,* I was told he was gone to Maidstone thats all I could learn—I determined therefore to come immediately to Town—to get Letters of introduction to *Milward* and to auquaint you of my unpleasant situation —This morning at four oClock I meet [sic] Mr Walsh about 40 Miles from London on his Way to Hastings. I cannot convey to you an Idea how distrest I feel myself by *Jackman's* Conduct, who I am apprehensive has be-

trayed his trust—Would you wish me to return to Sussex
—Or can I be useful any were [sic] else—

> I am with the greatest Respect
> Sir Your Most obedient
> Humble Servant
> ⟨CHAS⟩ WHITING

NOTE

1. Walsh had been employed as a clerk in the office of the
Secretary of State for the American Colonies under the administration of Lord North. He had continued in that position when the
Rockinghams took office in 1782. When the third Secretaryship was
abolished, he apparently continued in government service as a clerk,
for Adam found him employed writing letters for the Coalition
Government in 1783. But when the Coalition Government fell,
Walsh gave up his government position, apparently voluntarily,
and continued to work for the Coalition while in opposition. He
was given an office in an upper floor of Carlton House, and his task
was to write letters on behalf of the party requesting attendance in
the House or at meetings whenever an occasion particularly de-
manded it. He seems also to have acted as a special messenger. He
continued to perform these tasks for the party until at least as late
as 1793, and was given a remuneration by the party according to
the extent of his services. William Adam to Lord Fitzwilliam, 19
September 1793, Milton MSS; Blair Adam MSS, *passim*.

William Adam *to* George Hodgson
8 *June* 1790

Address: George Hodgson Esqr / Charles Street / St James's
Square
Endorsed: To Geo Hodgson / from / Mr. Adam / June 8th. 90
A copy. The text and address are in Adam's hand, the endorsement in
that of his clerk.

George Hodgson, an attorney of Charles Street, St. James's
Square, had joined the Whig Club at its founding on 13 May 1784
(*Whig Club,* 1788 ed.).

Lincoln's Inn fields June 8th
1790

Dear Sir

In a Matter of great Trust & confidence I take the
Liberty to apply to you: & to request of you to repair to
Folkstone & deliver this Letter to Mr Jackman who
has as I confidentially informed You been very usefully
employed at Hastings & Elsewhere—As you are particularly instructed, I need not say more in this Letter, but
that I trust implicitly to your Judgment & his to bring the
Business in hand to a good conclusion: & I am sure this
Letter will give you full & implicite confidence with a Person of the Liberality & Good Sense of Mr Jackman; It
being quite unfit to Trust to a common messenger a Matter of such Delicacy & Importance.

I am Dear Sir
Yours most faithfully
WILLIAM ADAM

P.S.
Enquire for Mr Jackman by the Name of Fleming at
Folkstone.

William Robertson *to* William Adam
8 *June* 1790

The subsequent history of this pamphlet is unknown. The party
had expended funds in the writing, printing, and distribution of
pamphlets during the Regency Crisis, but their publishing activities
for the general election are obscure.

My Dear Sir

About fourteen months ago when there was a rumour
that Parliament was to be dissolved, I sent to you a small

Tract to be published in case that event should take place; & you signified your opinion to me that it might do some good. As a speedy dissolution seems now certain you may perhaps think it adviseable to send it to the press, but I leave you entirely at liberty to do so or not as you shall think proper, only if it is printed I hope it may be so managed as to cost me nothing. If it is published send a few copies to me. I ever am My Dear Sir

Yours most faithfully
WM ROBERTSON.

Edinr 8th. June
1790:
W : Adam Esqr

William Windham *to* William Adam
[9 *June* 1790]

Address: William Adam Esqr / Lincolns Inn
Endorsed: Wm. Windham / 9th. June 90

William Windham (1750–1810), M.P. Norwich 1784–1802, St. Mawes 1802–1806, New Romney 1806–1807, Higham Ferrers 1807–1810. Chief Secretary to the Lord Lieutenant of Ireland April–August 1783, Secretary at War 1794–1801, Secretary for War and Colonies 1806–1807. Windham was one of the principal leaders of Opposition in the lower house. Henry Hobart (1738–1799), M.P. Norwich 1786–1787, 1787–1799, was a Pittite, though the younger brother of John Hobart, 2nd Earl of Buckinghamshire, a Foxite. Adam was also asked and arranged to have writs sent to Opposition candidates at Lincoln and Sandwich.

Dear Adam

Hobart assures me, that He will do all that is necessary about the writ, for the dispatch of which He has an equal interest with myself, and that He can ensure its being at Norwich on Sunday, that is, the day after its being issued: that Norwich being a county by itself the writ goes directly to the Sheriffs of the place, & not to the Sheriff of Norfolk.

Notwithstanding all this I will be obliged to You, if you should have an opportunity, to talk to Hobart, and, if any doubt remains, to have recourse to the method, which you mentioned.—

Yours truly
W WINDHAM

Wednesday night.—

F. H. Mackenzie *to* William Adam
10 *June* 1790

Endorsed by Portland: 10 June 1790 / Mr Humberston MacKenzie / to / Mr. Adam / Rx 17

C. B. 10th. June 1790

My Dear Adam/

I received yours containing the Ultimatum of Lord Loughborough &c: & things shall be done accordingly though I confess it is an awkward thing to me & may eventually be of serious consequences by the light it will strike other liferenters in & may give a blow to my interest—As to the expressions in my letter which you quote I will explain them at meeting the point they allude to is past—You are doing every thing very right but if not too late pray do not send the Turtle till the dissolution is fixed or till Sepr. I mean my turtle for I jestingly told Geanies [1] to advise you to get one for your Election dinner but that was mere joke—I mean to give a Turtle feast here to the freeholders either after the Dissolution or about Autumn—Be very very secret as to what I now

am going [to] say & let no one except the Duke [2] & Sir
Thos. Dundas know of it—I have great hopes of getting
Tain even though the Dissolution should take place before the Michalmas [sic] Election of Magistrates. I had
a long & confidential (on his part) conversation with one
of the heads of the Enemys troops who I am pretty sure
we shall draw to us as soon as Geanies comes down—
This man wanted much to throw himself *on me* & gave
me more than oblique hints that if I thought his attachment worth acquiring I should have it—Geanies knows
nothing of this yet as his motions were so uncertain I did
not choose to write to him—Added to this Admiral
Ross [3] died yesterday—You are not enough acquainted
with the partys to make it necessary for me to enter into
detail nor coud you understand me if I did but you well
know I have never deceived the Duke in any thing I have
stated to him & I therefore expect you to rely on me when
I tell you I have *very* good hopes but by no means a certainty of success there—& now my dear Adam let me
throw myself on the Candour of the Duke & Sir Thos. &
ask if we succeed here whether I ought not to be allowed
the nomination of the Borrough member this turn. I have
never interfered before in the nomination but as you will
know have chearfully & unremittingly laboured for the
common cause & in this point particularly have stood in
the front of the battle at some risque. I appeal to you for
the great trouble I have taken to secure this seat & you
know *I* have brought it twice to the brink of success when
once all my plans were ruined by the sottish bad conduct
of General Ross [4] & the second time by the too sanguine
confidence of Geanies this time if no unexpected bad
management takes place I strongly hope to carry my blow
home. I will write to you more at large when I have consulted Geanies—I need not say the Duke may be sure I
should name no one but one firmly in his interest. I rely
on his friendship to put this in a fair light to Sir Thos. as

I really think it is but justice to me—Assure the Duke I am & shall be indefatigably attentive to his interest in this neighbourhood & believe my Dear Adam that I am

ever yours
F. H. MacKenzie

NOTES
1. Donald Macleod of Geanies.
2. Portland.
3. Admiral Sir John Lockhart Ross.
4. Major General Charles Ross of Morangie (?1729–1797), M. P. Tain Burghs 1780–1784. Reference is undoubtedly to the bye-election of 1786, when the general stood unsuccessfully for the burghs.

Roger Wilbraham *to* William Adam
10 *June* 1790

Lanhydrock near Bodmin
June 10th 1790—

Dear Adam

I have been labouring since I have been down in Cornwall both by letters and interviews to conciliate and unite the discordant and Jealous interests at T–[1] and hope by the assistance of Sir J. Morshead, who has given over all Ideas of it for Sir J. Frederick, that I shall succeed. They are now very impatient to know their Candidates, and indeed to see them down, and if there is any foundation in the Reports, which come very well authenticated to me, of an immediate Dissolution, it is high time they should canvass the Town. Pray, if possible, by the Return of the Post let me know who they are, and when they will be down. Mr Hunt [2] who has considerable property in

183

and about the Town, and can influence several Votes, will send his agent to canvass with them. I trust that I need not give you any farther assurances of my wish to give them every other assistance in the power of—

Yours most Sincerely

R: WILBRAHAM

I am Sorry to find that all chance at St Mawes is at an end—[3]

NOTES

1. Tregony.
2. George Hunt (?1720–1798), of Lanhydrock, near Bodmin, Cornwall. M.P. Bodmin 1753–1784.
3. St. Mawes had long been in the hands of Robert, 1st Earl Nugent, and Hugh, 2nd Viscount Falmouth, each cooperating with the other and returning one member respectively. Falmouth had died in 1782 and left his interest in the borough to his illegitimate son, Hugh Boscawen, who again returned himself for the Parliament of 1784 and supported Pitt. Nugent died in 1788, and his property passed to his daughter, Mary Elizabeth, wife of George Grenville, 1st Marquess of Buckingham, the elder brother of Pitt's Home Secretary. Boscawen seems already to have sold his interest to Buckingham, who now had the borough entirely in his hands. He returned two Pittites at the general election. Apparently the ambitious Morshead–Basset gangs attempted to test Buckingham's interest before it had become firmly established.

Duke of Portland *to* William Adam
[11 *June* 1790]

Address: William Adam Esqre / Lincolns Inn Fields
Endorsed: D of P. / June 90
The letter is datable from Portland's incomplete draft to Morshead of 11 June 1790 (*infra*), which was apparently enclosed in this.

Dear Adam

Pray send me the paper of arrangements for I am not sure enough of the manner in which Our friends are

184

posted to insert their names properly—I have no answer
yet from Tollemache.

Your's ever
P

is it not Sir J. Frederick ⎱
            Purling [1] ⎰ Tregony. 3250. each
Ord [2] ⎱ Grampound—2500
        ⎱   4000.
        ⎰   or 3500

I send You also the beginning & nearly the whole of the
Letter I intend to write to Morshead—Carpenter should
be instructed not to consult Sir F Basset respecting
Tregony.

NOTES

1. John Purling (?1722–1800), M.P. New Shoreham 1770,
East Looe 1772–1774, Weymouth and Melcombe Regis 1774–
1790. A leading figure in East India Company direction in the
1770's and 1780's, he had supported North's government, opposed
Shelburne, and followed the Coalition into opposition. Purling and
Welbore Ellis were destined to lose their seats at Weymouth when
Pulteney bought Steward's interest.

2. Almost certainly John Ord, who had been returned for
Wendover in 1784 on an independent interest. John Baker Church
(c. 1746–1818) had purchased Wendover in 1788, and at the
general election returned himself and Hugh Seymour Conway
(1759–1801), both Foxites. Lord Eliot had the principal interest
at Grampound and had normally placed both seats at the disposal
of Government (for a price). In 1790 he once again returned two
Government supporters.

Duke of Portland *to* [Sir John Morshead]
11 *June* 1790

Endorsed: D. of P. / 11 June 1790.

This letter ends thus in the middle of a sheet, and is clearly an incompleted draft.

London Friday Even: 11 June 1790

My Dear Sir

I beg leave to recommend Mr Carpenter [1] the Bearer of this to Your Protection & to assure You that You may give him full credit & place intire confidence in his discretion & abilities. It has been thought adviseable to send him down to assist in the Elections at Tregony & Grampound where in consequence of the intimations which have been received from You & other Friends Sir John Frederick & Mr Purling, & [crossed out: "Ld Daer"] & Mr Ord

NOTE

1. In December, 1788, during the Regency Crisis, Lord Robert Spencer sent Adam a letter addressed from a Capt. Frederick to Edward Kent, who had been a principal agent for Lord John Townshend in the Westminster contest of that year. The letter, dated 5 December, contained the following paragraph: "As Emissaries have been sent all over the Country to solicit addresses of thanks to Mr. Pitt, I wish you would move whether it would not be adviseable to undermine such maneouvre, and endeavour to procure counter-addresses, which, in my humble opinion, is not very difficult. Should this idea meet with approbation, I shall beg leave to recommend the following Gentlemen as proper persons to be employed. Mr. Carpenter for the west. This Gentleman is an eminent Attorney, and of large fortune. He has great interest in that part of England, is attached to our party, and is very ambitious to be presented to the leaders, and render them some essential service" (Blair Adam MSS). He is listed as having joined the Whig Club 6 December 1791 with the address "Blackman-street, Borough, or Twickenham" (*Whig Club,* 1792 ed.). In 1797 the *Universal British Directory* (I, 373) listed him as an attorney at 4, King's Arms Yard, Coleman St., practicing in both King's Bench and Common Pleas.

William Frogatt *to* William Adam
[11 *June* 1790]

Address: Wm Adam Esq
Endorsed: Mr. Frogat / 12 June—90
The eleventh of June, 1790, fell on a Friday.

Frogatt delivered writs to Wendover and Seaford, and perhaps elsewhere, at the party's expense.

Dear Sir.

I am this moment returned from Wendover & have not been in Bed these two nights shall therefore be much obliged to You if You will deliver the ⟨Precept⟩ to the bearer my Clerk with which after two Hours rest I will set out for Seaford.

> I have the honor to be
> Sir Yours most obediently
> WM FROGATT

Fryday
12. at Night

Charles Carpenter *to* William Adam
15 *June* 1790

Address: Wm. Adam Esqr. / Burlington Ho. / London
Postmarked: TRURO / JU 19 90
Endorsed by Portland: Tregony 15 June 1790 / Mr Chas. Carpenter
to Mr Adam / Rx 19

My dear Sir!

Unpleasant as it is to me in any case to be the messenger of bad news, it is more particularly so, indeed mortifying beyond the bounds of description, to be so in a cause in which from my very Soul I have embarked yet I should be very ill deserving of the confidence you have placed in me were I not to lay before you a true state of things in the way I have proved them—Your Friends must not expect success at Tregoney or G— [1] We are too late for either—To morrow or the following day I will give you the particulars of what has been done—Since yesterday I have not looked forward to ultimate success & I have avoided expence as much as possible—Indeed I please myself with the thought that I have trod in the exact path you would have wished me—In all things however I have consulted Sir John Morshead & Mr Wilbraham & they have sanctioned my proceedings—Richards [2] Oates [3] Parker & some others & myself have just left these Gentlemen & tomorrow if there is not a better prospect than on the 1st. canvass (which I do not expect) I shall think myself justified in ceasing all expence. Post waits & therefore I am necessarily obliged to conclude—I am always

Dear Sir Your most faithful humble Servant
C : CARPENTER

Tregoney 15 June 90

With my duty to the Noble Duke [4] pray say I delivered his Grace's Letters to Sir Francis Basset & Sir John Morshead—The latter Gentleman & Mr W.[5] have no doubt of success at Bodmin.

NOTES

1. Grampound.

2. William Richards, Jr., an attorney at Truro (see *infra,* and *Universal British Directory,* V, 218).

3. Adam's correspondence indicates that M. Oates of Plymouth expended his personal funds on behalf of the party's candidates at Tregony; in 1792 he was still seeking partial repayment from Adam.
4. Portland.
5. Wilbraham.

Charles Carpenter *to* William Adam
17 *June* 1790

Address: Wm. Adam Esqr / Burlington House / London
Postmarked: TRURO / JU 21 90
Endorsed by Portland: Tregony 17 June 1790 / Mr Chas: Carpenter to Mr Adam / Rx 21

My dear Sir

You will not draw any conclusion from my last Letter —We have this day recommenced a very vigorous canvass & we stand much more favorable than when I wrote you last—Except Agency & about £50 more expences no further will be added which I think will all come within the £500—I have made a private contract with the principals among our Friends & it will be *worth their while* to use every effort to insure success—With the entire approbation of Sir John Morshead & Mr Wilbraham I shall, if we succeed, recommend a further sum of £700 making in all £7000 being paid—This recommendation is a part of the contract—I have been obliged from among my own friends to raise £1000 in hard Cash which together with my note for the residue I have deposited in the hands of one of the principals having taken proper security for its return in case—The *sight* of this has had good effect. I have drawn as directed for £500 on Herry & Co.[1] & I should think this sufficient—If absolute necessity compels me to advance another hundred I will draw for it but not otherwise—This I believe was a part of the instructions I received from you—

I have a correct list of the poll at the last Election together with the various determinations which took place at that time—I have engaged three very proper Agents for the Election which commences on *Saturday* next— Perhaps you may hear from Mr. Richards—Should he insinuate that he has not been properly attended to you will be good enough to withhold your judgment untill you hear from Mr Wilbraham—I am very sincerely

> Dear Sir
> Your most faithful & obliged Servant
> C: CARPENTER

Tregoney 17th June 90

NOTE

1. Sir Robert Herries & Company, bankers, St. James's St.

Charles Carpenter *to* William Adam
19 *June* 1790

Endorsed by Portland: Truro 19 June 1790 / Mr Carpenter to Mr Adam / Rx 22

My dear Sir!

It is with infinite regret I am under the painful necessity of informing you that after due deliberation with all our friends privately and together, I have thought proper to decline a Poll at Tregoney—Nothing less than a possitive assurance from us to about 120 Persons of their having at all events £20 Ppiece would, at the present moment, under many disadvantages & particularly that of a long previous canvass, have carried the

Election—9/10ths at least of the Electors are among the most wretched of mankind and I really feel with respect to about 16 or 18 of the poor men (who have been extremely active on our part) that I should not discharge my duty were I to omit recommending that some small gratuity might be made them—It seems 12 of the no. are Tenants to the Nabob [1] & they have not only received notices to quit their Tenements but are hourly in expectation of having their Furniture distressed for the Rent in arrear.—It may not perhaps apply to the present Candidates but I am confident that if these Men at the distance of about a fortnight from hence were to have a few Guineas given them it would have a greater effect on the minds of all the Electors at any future Election than £100 a Man some few days previous thereto, but this rests entirely with you & I have in mentioning the circumstance complied with the wishes of our Friends.

You will be pleased to take credit for the inclosed 18 (Falmouth bank) bills value £94.10 & I will send you my account of disbursements the moment I can collect them—

The Members returned for Tregoney are Messrs Montague [2] & Stevenson.[3] I am very sincerely

> Dear Sir
>> Your most faithful humble Servant
>> C: CARPENTER

Truro 19th. June 90

NOTES

1. Richard Barwell.
2. Matthew Montagu (1762–1831). M.P. Bossiney 1786–1790, Tregony 1790–1796, St. Germans 1806–1812. A Pittite.
3. John Stephenson (?1709–1794), another Pittite. The official return for Tregony was made on 19 June 1790.

Duke of Portland *to* William Adam
[*ante* 19 *June* 1790]

Address: To / William Adam Esqre
Endorsed: Duke of Portland / June 1790.
The Sudbury return was made on 19 June 1790.

The Suffolk Writ was to be sent either to Hippisleys [1] House in town or to Him at Sudbury but when Walsh comes here I will send Him to Hippisleys to learn whether any person waits there for it, & if not to prepare a Messenger to carry it.

Yours ever

P

NOTE

1. John Coxe Hippisley (1748–1825). M.P. Sudbury 1790–1796, 1802–1818, an Oppositionist and intimate in the circle of William Windham. Possibly this writ was for Hippisley at Sudbury and not for the county, which Vanneck was contesting.

Joseph Richardson *and* R. B. Sheridan
to William Adam—[*June* 1790]

Address: W Adam Esqr. / Lincoln's Inn Fields
Endorsed: Richardson & Sheridan / June 90. Reccomending / Reid—

Joseph Richardson (1755–1803), M. P. Newport 1796–1803, was a close friend of Sheridan and Fox. A playwright and a political writer of some talent, and possessed of a legal training, he had become involved in the proprietorship and editing of several newspapers during the later years of the American War. Probably some-

time in 1783 he had approached Sheridan with the offer of converting the *English Chronicle,* of which he was then editor, into a
Coalition paper. He asked in return that the Coalition enable him
to "buy up the types, etc etc" in case his fellow proprietors objected
to his converting the paper "into a strong *party one.*" In the event
the *Chronicle*—which had hitherto had "good intelligence," been
impartial, and enjoyed "a considerable sale"—lost its circulation.
Richardson's fellow proprietors had from the outset objected most
decidedly and he was given assistance with which to buy them out,
but he was left with a failing business venture. From that date,
probably from 1784, Richardson was in receipt of £200 per year
from the party's general subscription fund. He continued to receive
this sum until the party's financial dissolution in 1793. Lord Fitzwilliam always insisted that the payments were for "present"
rather than "past" services. The stipend was neither an annuity nor
a sinecure; whether it was a retainer or a salary is not altogether
clear, though the latter seems entirely likely. His services seem to
have been irregular and proportionate to the political pressures
upon the party and its activities. He contributed to party pamphlets
and newspaper publications and was particularly active as an agent
and manager during general elections. George Reid is far more
obscure a figure. For one thing, there were two George Reids,
father and son; and it is impossible in this instance, for example, to
determine which is involved. Their milieu, as well as their activities
for the party, seem to have been similar to Richardson's. See especially Werkmeister, *London Daily Press,* pp. 69–70; A. Aspinall,
Politics and the Press c. 1780–1850 [London, 1949], pp. 451–
452.

Dear Adam,

   Will you forgive me for the great Liberty of making
an Appeal to your Kindness, on a Subject perhaps not
strictly professional—It is simply this.—You are a Man
of Authority—Reid is a Man who would be glad of professional Employment—In these bustling Times, if you
will do so desperate a thing as to follow the rash Example of Milbank [1] & Sheridan [2] who have engaged me for
Durham & Stafford & employ Reid on a similar Business,
You will serve him, & I am convinced, injure no one, to

whom you may reccommend him—At all Events forgive me—

ever Yours

JRICHARDSON

[added at bottom in hand of R. B. Sheridan:]
please Adam do all possible for foresaid Vagabond

RBS.

NOTES

1. Ralph Noel Milbanke (*c.* 1748–1825), later 6th Bt. M.P. Durham County 1790–1812.
2. Sheridan was member for Stafford 1780–1806.

George Craufurd *to* William Adam
[*June* 1790]

Endorsed: George Crawfurd / Woodstock Street / June 1790

This could be George Craufurd, the 3rd son of James Craufurd, merchant, and cousin of John Craufurd of Auchinames (John Burke, *A Genealogical and Heraldic History of the Commoners of Great Britain and Ireland* [London, 1st ed., 1833], II, 386).

Sunday four o'clock

Dear Sir

Upon due consideration of what you was kind enough to mention to me this morning I have resolved not to give any thing like the sum required for a Seat in Parliament, though I have every wish of rendering myself usefull to your friends in that way, & shall hope for some favorable opportunity occurring in future. I consider myself how-

ever equally obliged to you, & wishing you better health &
a good journey to Scotland remain sincerely

Dear Sir
Your most obedient Servant
GEORGE CRAUFURD.

No 4 Woodstock street
   Oxford Street
William Adam Esqr. Lincolns Inn fields

Duke of Portland *to* William Adam
30 *June* 1790

Endorsed: D. of P. 30th June 90 / Rd. 16th July— / in Ross shire

Wednesday 30 June 1790

My Dear Adam

Having never heard of You since You left Grantham [1]
I trust Your journey has been as beneficial to You as I
wished it, & that Your health is perfectly reestablished—
Now therefore to business—I have received no other
Letters for You but those which I send inclosed by which
You will see that all Our Western Speculations have
failed completely, as I expected, & I am sorry to add that
those in the South have been equally unsuccessfull, at
which perhaps You will not be much disappointed. I dont
perfectly understand the amount of Carpenters expenses,
nor do I see any particular advantage to arise from the
generosity he recommends to be extended to the 16 or 18
poor men at Tregony but if the Opinion of our friends
inclines to the favorable side as an act of Charity I certainly shall not resist it. The draft mentioned in Yours
from Wall I have not heard of, but my silence I hope con-

195

vinced You of my readiness to attend to it as You desired. If Seaforth [2] succeeds I certainly shall be the last man in the world to object to his availing himself of his success in the way he wishes, & I should hope that Sir Thomas [3] will not refuse his assent. If it is to be put upon those terms which I think very fair & reasonable how would it suit Fullarton? I only throw this out without meaning to give *even a decisive hint.* Or what think You of Craufurd? [4] Or is there any other friend north of Tweed to whom it would be more desireable & adviseable to offer it? I suppose Seaforth is under no engagement, but I beg to be clearly understood, that notwithstanding, I don't wish to propose, if he has any thing like a preference in his own mind, or that our friends should be of opinion that the Cause can be better served by any other means. I heartily congratulate with You on Bakers success in Herts,[5] it is the most brilliant Event & as much so & as honorable in every respect as could be wished—The fate of Hants I dare [say] does not surprize You [6]—Surry is very satisfactory, Ld Wm: Russell had upwards of 1200 single Votes [7]—I tremble for Kent—Last nights poll brought Marsham within 55 of Honywood & all Knatchbulls split votes are thrown upon Marsham. For Knatchbull is 1342 above Honywood [8]—I am not dissatisfied with returns in general but I shall lose this nights conveyance as I have everyone for this week past if I add more. Pray tell H.E.[9] that I will endeavour to write by the same conveyance to Him, Lds Stormont & Lauderdale tomorrow or eightday at farthest.

Your's ever
P

NOTES

1. Adam was enroute to Scotland. His own election for Ross-shire was to be on 16 July.
2. F. H. Mackenzie.

3. Sir Thomas Dundas.

4. Undoubtedly John Craufurd of Auchenames, who had lost the Dysart Burghs.

5. The poll in Hertfordshire tallied William Plumer 1831, William Baker 1302, William Hale 1031. Baker also contested the borough of Hertford, but unsuccessfully, the poll being John Calvert 319, Nathaniel Dimsdale 290, Baker 223. Oldfield, *History of Boroughs,* 2nd ed., I, 312, 314. Plumer had been member for the county since 1768 and a loyal supporter of Rockingham and the Coalition.

6. The poll in Hampshire tallied Sir Wm. Heathcote 2013, William Chute 1805, Lord John Russell 1290, J. C. Jervoise 1232 (Oldfield, *History of Boroughs,* 2nd ed., I, 260). Heathcote and Chute were both Government supporters in the Parliament of 1790; neither had sat in the House before. Jervoise Clarke Jervoise (?1733–1808) was M.P. Yarmouth I.o.W. 1768–1769 and 1774–1779, Hampshire 1779–1790, Yarmouth I.o.W. 1791–1808. He had opposed North and supported the Coalition both in and out of power. Lord John Russell (1766–1839), later 6th Duke of Bedford, was the younger brother of Francis, 5th Duke of Bedford, and elder brother of Lord William Russell. Upon coming of age Russell had unsuccessfully attempted to come in for Windsor at a bye-election. A year later in 1788 he was returned for the family seat at Tavistock. On 27 December 1790 he was again returned for Tavistock in the place of Percy Charles Wyndham, who had elected to sit for Midhurst. Lord John strongly supported the Foxite Opposition, as did the other members of his family.

7. According to Oldfield (*History of Boroughs,* 2nd ed., II, 128) Finch and Russell were returned "by a considerable majority."

8. Charles Marsham (1744–1811) was M.P. Maidstone 1768–1774 and Kent 1774–1790. Marsham was a highly independent member of the House. He had been a co-chairman of the St. Alban's Tavern group which had attempted to reconcile Pitt and Fox in early 1784; Pitt's refusal seems to have offended Marsham, and he normally supported Opposition during the Parliament of 1784. Filmer Honywood (*c.* 1745–1809), M.P. Steyning 1774–1780, Kent 1780–1796 and 1802–1806, had generally supported Opposition since his entry into Parliament. There had not been a contest in Kent since 1754. According to Oldfield (*History of Boroughs,* 2nd ed., I, 321), the success of Sir Edward Knatchbull, the Government candidate in 1790, "was owing more to the want of a junction of interests between Mr.

Honeywood and the Hon. Mr. Marsham . . . than to the weight of all this [Government admiralty, ecclesiastical and personal] influence united." The final state of the poll was Knatchbull 4285, Honywood 3101, Marsham 2724 (*ibid.,* I, 324).

9. Henry Erskine.

Duke of Portland *to* William Adam
5 *July* 1790

Endorsed: London 5th July 1790 / Duke of Portland— / Rd. 18th July—

London Monday 5 July 1790

Dear Adam

As You say nothing of Your health, I am willing to conclude it is perfectly reestablished—I have seen Craufurd [1] again this morning & he will certainly go down to Renfrewshire if necessary, but I must say that our friend Shaw Stewarts accounts are so incorrect, or at least so lamely justify the conclusions he draws from them, that I do not much wonder at the Fish's reluctance, & wish Shaw had never sent *Him* any statement of the relative interests of Himself & Cunninghame [2]—Your information respecting Dundas [3] whether in Sterlingshire or the Orkneys is very satisfactory indeed, You may possibly have seen Your Brother K.E. [4] I hope the P–s [5] message to Him will intirely obviate any ill consequences which might have been apprehended from His Father in Law [6] —I think You had better take a friend who is willing to advance what is necessary than one who stands in need of assistance from the Fund, for I don't find it has flourished much since You left Us, nor have I much hope of its thriving—& I think either of the names I suggested in my last [7] would answer the purpose & be thankfull for the offer. The fish had been tampering with Geanies [8] to try if Ross [9] would not give up to Him, but unsuccessfully. Pray what is this story of Geanies's having broke his word with H. Dundas about the appointment of the Cromartie Election? If it is true, the first & great error consists in his having given D. any hopes.[10] I am not at all disappointed with respect to Roxburgheshire & I hope our friend [11] will have no reason to be so with his return for Helstone—I heartily wish You joy of little Thompsons success at Evesham, he was within 11 of Rushout & polled 257 single Votes.[12] I very much fear for Sir J Eden—He was 119 below Burdon on Friday the 5th: days Poll [13]—You must not be alarmed about Cornwall for Basset writes me word that we must expect, from various circumstances, too many to repeat, that Gregor will have the lead of St Aubyn for the two first days— Gregor polled the first day 189—& St Aubyn only 166 [14] —I see You leave the Peers to take care of themselves by not saying one word upon that subject—[15]

> sincerely Yours ever
>
> P.

Halliday has applied for assistance in case of a Petition, which I have not given Him the least hope of, & he calls a much *for immediate help.* The last account which was the tenth days Poll was as under—Hammet 166— Halliday 160—Popham 153—Morland 149. They never have polled above 40 *Voters* in a day.[16]

NOTES

1. John "Fish" Craufurd of Auchinames, who was credited by Hill with influence over three votes in Renfrewshire (Adam, *Pol. State,* p. 285).

2. Alexander Cuninghame of Craigends, Shaw Stewart's opponent.

3. Sir Thomas Dundas, whose principal interests were in Stirlingshire, the Orkneys, and the borough of Richmond (Yorks).

4. G. K. Elphinstone.

5. Prince of Wales.

6. William Mercer of Aldie, Kinross-shire, whose eldest daughter and co-heiress had married Elphinstone in 1787 and had died December, 1789.

7. Fullarton and Craufurd.

8. Donald Macleod.

9. Sir Charles Lockhart Ross of Balnagown, who was to be returned for the Tain Burghs on 12 July.

10. For this story see Furber, *Dundas,* pp. 229–231.

11. Sir Gilbert Elliot.

12. Oldfield (*History of Boroughs,* 2nd ed., II, 263) gives these figures: Rushout 418, Thompson 407, Sullivan 374.

13. Sir John Eden (1740–1812), 4th Bt., M.P. Durham County 1774–1790, elder brother of William Eden, 1st Baron Auckland, a leading Coalition man of business who had notoriously defected to Pitt in late 1785. Sir John had continued to support Opposition even after his brother's defection, but his attendance in the House was poor. It was said that his brother opposed his re-election for the county in 1790. Rowland Burdon (*c.* 1757–1838), an independent supporter of Government, and the Oppositionist Ralph Noel Milbanke were returned.

14. The highly independent Sir William Lemon, who normally supported Government but had voted with Opposition on Richmond's fortifications plan and had split his vote during the Regency, was again returned for the county. Gregor beat St. Aubyn for the second seat. The poll closed with Lemon 2250, Gregor 1270, and St. Aubyn 1136 (Henry Stooks Smith, *The Parliaments of England* [London, 1844], I, 36).

15. For the election of the Scottish representative peers which occurred on 23 July 1790, see Furber, *Dundas,* pp. 231–236; Mackenzie, *Pol. State,* pp. 1–40.

16. The final state of the poll at Taunton on 6 July gave Hammet 291, Popham 257, Halliday 239, Morland 183 (Oldfield, *History of Boroughs,* 2nd ed., II, 57). Halliday and Morland petitioned the House in December, 1790, but for some reason dropped the proceedings a few days later (*Journals of the House of Commons,* XLVI, 16 and 91).

George Reid *to* William Adam
[30 *June* 1790?]

Address: William Adam Esqr. / Lincoln's Inn Fields
This letter was found enclosed in Portland's to Adam of Monday, 5 July
1790. Portland's previous letter to Adam was dated Wednesday, 30 June.
It seems likely that this letter was written on Wednesday, 30 June, but
reached Portland too late for enclosure in that day's packet; note that the
letter first went to Adam's chambers, then was forwarded to Burlington
House, from whence Portland forwarded it to Adam in Scotland.

Basil William Douglas (1763–1794), styled Lord Daer, was the
1st surviving son of Dunbar Hamilton, 4th Earl of Selkirk. Since
1774 Lord Selkirk had led the independent party at the elections of
the representative peers. Lord Daer was also highly independent,
but he was a radical as well and became deeply involved in Scottish
reform politics in the 1790's. In 1790 he engaged with Lord Haddo
and the popular interest in a radical contest at Poole, where he may
have damaged the interest of another Foxite, M. A. Taylor (Oldfield, *History of Boroughs,* 2nd ed., I, 233–235) ; meanwhile he
was also the Opposition candidate at Canterbury, where George
Reid (Jr. or Sr.) and Edward Kent were his agents. Sir John
Honywood and George Gipps, an incumbent and another Pittite,
were returned at the election on 19 June. Lord Daer was unable to
find a seat.

Wednesday Morng
1/2 past 3

Dear Sir

I am this moment setting out to meet Lord Daer at
Canterbury from whence I shall return on friday or
Saturday—If therefore you are enabled to do any thing
in the matter mentioned by Mr. Sheridan it must be so
contrived as not to interfere with this engagement on

which account I trouble you with this letter—With many wishes for the restoration of your health I remain

> Yours very faithfully
> GEO REID

[by Portland on verso:]

> Wm: Adam Esqre
> I don't know to what the contents allude but something perhaps that may be embarassing unless Your absence is supplied *effectually*

Duke of Portland *to* William Adam
11 *August* 1790

London Wednesday 11 August 1790

My Dear Adam

Possibly on Your landing but certainly when You got to Edinburgh You learnt how unnecessary it was for You to proceed farther Southward till Your health was perfectly reestablished, & my first & principal wish & prayer is that all Your attention may be bestowed on punctually observing those directions which may be given You by the Faculty for the purpose of Your complete recovery. When that is effected & ascertained I shall be very happy in seeing You & all that belong to You at Welbeck[1] as soon as You please. I mean to be there myself some time next week, but the Antwerp business[2] (of the success of which I am *now* more doubtfull than ever from the Agents employed in it besides those who alone ought to be concerned in it) will probably detain me here till the end of it, & it is possible that I may not get there till Monday or Tuesday. But this is only troubling You

unnecessarily as I have not the smallest expectation of
meeting You there nor indeed do I wish it till You can
send me a clear Bill of health—Sir W. Cunynghame
dined here yesterday he gives me a good account of
Stirlingshire & does not despond in respect to Orkney or
the Aberdeen District.[3] I forgot to ask Him if there was
any chance of the Dysart Boroughs for which I heard
from Ld Loughborough that the Fish[4] was a Peti-
tioner.[5] Upon the whole Sir Wm reckons that we have
ten certain in Scotland,[6] which is exactly ⟨5⟩ more than
I took credit for after reading Mr Robertsons Letter
to You, & therefore You may judge of the extent of
my disappointment with regard to that part of the
Kingdom—Carpenter called here since his return from
the West, but I happened to be out, & have not seen Him
—Nor indeed does there seem any occasion for it—as I
concur in opinion with You, & can see no reason for
throwing away any part of our means. Considering the
event You must excuse my applying to Sir J. Frederick or
Purling, it is a subject I hate speaking to any one upon &
though I think they ought not to refuse I can not bring
myself to run the risk of it. By the death of Ld Guilford[7] what we shall have I think will be fully sufficient
for all the purposes required, & if Fredk: & Purling decline still I think we shall be able to replace the deficien-
cies of the Westmr: fund. I suppose You have heard
from Walsh. He said a word or two to me upon his
charges which he says he depended upon being defrayed
before this time. He talked of a Bill of 160 which would
become due in a few days & by what fell from Him *that*
did not seem to be the whole of His demand—I know
very little of Geanies's[8] Letter but by Report, & having
treated it as I do all Reports injurious to friends which is
by a declaration that I do not give the least degree of
credit to them I suppose I heard no more of it. Candour
is a very pernicious ingredient in the composition of any

party man, & ought to be used with the greatest circumspection—I have heard nothing of G Craufurd & wish I may not see Him till I can hear from You whether it would be adviseable for me to write to G [9] on the success of Your Election. The only thing leading to *Reform* which I have at all liked is H. Erskines tack to the Resolution of Perseverance [10] which I read in this mornings paper—& be assured that had it taken place, which God forbid, instead of our present numbers we should not have had half of them, & possibly should have lived to have been witnesses to the annihilation of Parliaments all together. I say nothing of the Norths, as I dare say You have the most authentick accounts from G [11] or some of the family—& of War & Peace I say nothing because I don't know what to say but still incline to the Latter, & believe there was no occasion for the Armament.[12] I think I have detained You quite long enough so I shall conclude.

Your's ever

P

NOTES
1. Portland's country house in Nottinghamshire.
2. The loan for the royal princes.
3. This is curious, as the election for Orkney was held on 28 July and for the Aberdeen Burghs on 12 July 1790; the Opposition candidates had lost in both instances, but only the Orkney candidate petitioned against his return.
4. John Craufurd of Auchinames.
5. MS. Petr: Craufurd did not petition.
6. Ten is certainly an overestimate. Only five Scottish members were returned whom the Opposition could with some reason count as reliable: John Shaw Stewart (Renfrewshire), William Adam (Ross-shire), Sir Thomas Dundas (Stirlingshire), Sir John Sinclair (Caithness), and Thomas Maitland (Haddington Burghs). These five had recently voted with Opposition and were to continue to do so during the period before the party split in late 1792. It is uncertain how the party should or would have classed William Grieve (Linlithgow Burghs), who had not sat before, voted with

Opposition in 1791 over Oczakow, but never again. They were perhaps disappointed in four additional members. Sir Robert Laurie, the Duke of Queensberry's member for Dumfriesshire, had normally been a Pittite during the Parliament of 1784 but had followed his patron in voting with Opposition over the Regency. He never voted with Opposition during the Parliament of 1790, however. Alexander Stewart (Kirkcudbright), who had deserted Pitt over the Regency and had been rebuffed by Dundas, apparently continued to seek military promotion and never again voted with Opposition; he became major-general in 1790 and colonel of the 2nd Foot in 1793. Adam seems also to have been somewhat sanguine about his neighbor, George Graham (Kinross), but Graham never voted with Opposition during the Parliament of 1790. More surprising, perhaps, and instructive of the persistently local dimension of Scottish electoral politics despite the interference of national party managers, there is not a single recorded instance of Duncan Davidson's (Cromartyshire) having voted with Opposition during the Parliament of 1790 despite Henry Dundas's having vigorously supported his opponent during the general election (see Furber, *Dundas,* pp. 229–231).

7. Guilford died 4 August 1790 and was succeeded by his son, Lord North.

8. Donald Macleod of Geanies.

9. Geanies?

10. On 4 August 1790 the "Convention of Delegates from the Burgesses of Scotland, associated for the Purpose of obtaining a Reform in the Internal Government of the Royal Boroughs," had met in annual session at Edinburgh. A motion introduced and passed the previous year, calling for burgh reform, was reintroduced and the delegates exhorted to persevere in their efforts to secure passage of a measure in the House of Commons. Henry Erskine supported the motion, but added a tack expressing the delegates' reverence for the British constitution and assuring the public that, far from wishing to alter it, they wished to preserve the constitution by an early reform of its abuses (Archibald Fletcher, *A Memoir Concerning the Origin and Progress of the Reform Proposed in the Internal Government of the Royal Burghs of Scotland* [Edinburgh, 1819], pp. 108–109).

11. George Augustus North, who was a very close friend of Adam.

12. The Nootka Sound crisis.

Duke of Portland *to* William Adam
1 *September* 1790

Endorsed: Welbeck Sepr 1st 90 / D of P— / Rd. at Edr Sepr 3d.

Welbeck Wēnsday morn: 1 Septr: 1790

My Dear Adam

The Principal object of this Letter is to let You know that I go to town tomorrow to meet one of the Antwerp People, & that by what I learn from Joweld I have great hopes of getting wherewithall to extricate, *the persons,* from their present difficulties & to put them, as far as possible, in a way of avoiding them in future [1]—I don't beleive Lymington or Melbourn [2] Port at all likely to answer the purpose You suggest. I wish they were. But think a little to whom they belong, & then hope if You can—Aldeburgh [3] is represented by Ld Grey (my nephew) [4] & Tom Grenville—so upon that score You may be easy I think. I don't know what else can puzzle You but shall be glad to solve any difficulties I can—G. North [5] goes of course to Banbury [6] & Titch: [7] must succeed Him at P—[8]—After what You know of the Election of the 16 [9] You can not be very much surprized at any incorrectness or rather inattention in the manner of their placing their Confidence. I am sure You do every thing that can be done for them, but if they do not assist You or rather relieve You You must I fear act, in such a case as this, contrary to Your feelings—I hope to be here again by tomorrow sevennight at latest—Your Politicians may be very right—but Peace is a good thing, & I believe there was not any occasion for risking an infraction of it—& that it was an engine for domestick political purposes—

Your's ever

P

NOTES

1. This passage concerns the loan to the royal princes.
2. Milborne.
3. Aldeburgh (Suffolk) was a pocket borough in the hands of Philip Champion Crespigny (*d.* 1803), M.P. Sudbury 1774–1775, Aldeburgh 1780–1790. Crespigny had supported North's administration, opposed Shelburne, and supported the Coalition both in and out of office.
4. George Harry Grey (1765–1845), styled Lord Grey, eldest son of George Harry, 5th Earl of Stamford. M.P. Aldeburgh 1790–1796, St. Germans 1796–1802. Stamford had married Portland's sister.
5. George Augustus North.
6. The old seat of Lord North and in the hands of the Earls of Guilford. It was now vacated by North's having been elevated to the House of Lords.
7. William Henry Cavendish Scott Bentinck (1768–1854), styled Marquess of Titchfield, eldest son of the 3rd Duke of Portland. Lord Titchfield had unsuccessfully contested Rochester at the general election (Oldfield, *History of Boroughs,* 2nd ed., I, 326). On 29 December 1790 he was returned for Petersfield in the place of G. A. North. Petersfield was a burgage borough in the hands of William Jolliffe, the other member for the borough since 1768 and a Northite.
8. Petersfield.
9. The representative peers of Scotland.

William Richards, Jr. *to* William Adam
1 *September* 1790

Address: William Adam Esqr: M:P: / Lincoln's Inn fields / London—
Endorsed: Truro 1st Sepr 90 / Richards / Rd Edin 9th / Sepr / 1790

Truo 1st: September 1790.

Sir

Some short time before the last general Election, Mr. Tocker of Tregony, whom you saw in London with me in March last, informed me that Mr. Rashleigh of St.

Austell,[1] who is Receiver of the land tax for this county, had made a demand on him for forty pounds due for Arrears of land tax from the borough of Tregony which Mr. Tocker, the collector, had not been able to receive from the inhabitants—& Mr. Tocker desired me to assist him in getting this Money, as he thought it would be exceedingly impolitic at that time to take any steps by law to compel the payment of it; My Advice to him was immediately to wait on Mr: Wilbraham who was then at Lanhydrock in this county the Seat of his uncle, Mr: Hunt, & acquaint him of the business, & to act in it as he Should think proper. Mr: Oates a person who lives at Tregony & myself accompanied Mr. Tocker to Lanhydrock, & on our representing the Matter to Mr: Wilbraham, & asking him if he thought it advisable to draw on you for the forty pounds—he said he certainly approved of our doing it, & that he would write you by the first post to let you know that such Draft was drawn, in consequence of what Mr. Wilbraham then said Mr: Tocker drew on you for the forty pounds in my favor, & obtained the Money from a bank here, which he paid the same day to Mr: Rashleigh. This Draft is returned, & I am called on to take it up, & pay the Money, this would be extremely hard, as I never saw one farthing of it, & only suffered Mr: Tocker to make use of my name, from Mr. Wilbraham having assured us that the Draft should be paid. Mr. Tocker tells me, that he has written you on the subject, & explained to you the reasons of our not having succeeded in the Tregony business, we from the first disapproved of Mr: Carpenter's conduct, & plainly saw that the plan he pursued would not be attended with success, had the management of the business been left to us as Mr. Tocker & myself understood from you was to be the case, we have no doubt but every thing would have answered our most sanguine expectations—The Money which Mr: Tocker & myself expended on our Journey to

London, *solely* for the purpose of fixing a plan of opposition, is upwards of fifty pounds, I therefore hope that
as the Draft was drawn with the intire approbation of
Mr: Wilbraham, who undertook that it should be paid,
you will not suffer me to be compelled to pay the forty
pounds, which ⟨ . . . ⟩ be case, should you refuse to
pay it yours ⟨ . . . ⟩

                    I am Sir,
                        your most obedient humble Servant
                            WM: RICHARDS JUNR:

                        NOTE

1. Charles Rashleigh (1747–1823), of St. Austell, Cornwall,
7th son of Jonathan Rashleigh, M.P. Fowey 1727–1764; and
younger brother of Philip Rashleigh (1729–1811), M.P. Fowey
1765–1802, an independent supporter of Pitt. Charles was also a
Steward of the Stannary Courts in the Duchy of Cornwall. In
1790 he acted as Barwell's agent. See Aspinall, ed., *The Correspondence of George, Prince of Wales 1770–1812*, II, 143,
171–172, 344.

Lord Robert Spencer *to* William Adam
5 *September* [1790]

Address: Willm Adam Esqr. / George Street / New Town / Edinburgh
            Postmarked: SE ⟨ . . . ⟩ 90
Endorsed: Lord Robt Spencer / Petworth Sepr 5th 90 / Rd Edr 9th
            / Sep / Wesmr Money— / Answered

                                        Petworth
                                        Sep. 5—
Dear Adam,

Finding that there is a prospect of raising very shortly
a sum of money equal to the discharge of the debts, I
called the other day to look at Sir T. Dundas's account at

Hercy's where I saw that you had drawn for 800£. Now I wish you would let me know whether that was applied to the payment of any debts standing on account in the list which Sir Thos Dundas possesses. If it was applied to any other purpose it really should at any rate be immediately repaid, for it would be excessively hard & provoking to those; who have now agreed to Subscribe a large sum, to find it unequal to the discharge of the whole debt, which was stated to them, and indeed it is on that condition, that the money is subscribed. Pray write me a line in answer to Berkeley Square as soon as you can. Adieu

Yours most sincerely
R Spencer

[the following is added in the hand of Adam:]
Wrote by return of Post. That £200 of the sum was on account of The Duke of Portlands advance for Country News Papers. That His Grace had authorised the application of it to General Election Purposes. That the remaining sum was for the same purposes. The subscription for that purpose not having been got in in time to answer the Purpose of the Dissolution—That by a late Letter from The Duke of Portland there was no doubt of its being repaid very shortly—

Sir William Augustus Cunynghame *to* William Adam—7 *September* 1790

N23 Berners Street
Tuesday 7th. Septr. 1790

Dear Adam

Accept our best thanks for your kind attention in lending us your Lodge, but of which from a Variety of Acci-

dents we have never been able to avail ourselves, nevertheless we are equally obliged both to you, & Mrs. Adam,
to whom & yourself Lady C. joins me in desiring to be
remembered in the kindest Manner. We have as you will
see, by the Date of this Letter, taken possession of
⟨ . . . ⟩ House, who proposes going abroad next Week,
and as we shall be here when you arrive, Lady C. and
I expect that you, Mrs. Adam and the Bairns, will
live with us, untill your own House is arranged. As you
advised I spoke last Week to Sheridan, who promised me
he would mention it to the Prince; Lord Lonsdale it is
said has come over to Opposition, if that is true, and the
Prince asks him, I may have some chance, as he has two
Seats [1] to give, one of which is held by Jenkinson [2] who is
to sit for Rye, and the other by Colonel Lowther; [3]
Lord Lonsdale I am well assured, is to be in Town by the
29th. Currant to arrange all his Seats, so that a very little
time must decide who [he] is to bring in. Dick Pen [4] who
was beat at Lancaster, will probably have one of the
Seats, but Ld. Lonsdale has not yet said so. I long much
for your coming to Town, as I have more dependence
upon your Friendship than any thing whatever. No News
except of a War, which is generally believed, and I imagine, that they do not intend, that Parliament shall meet
before November, Adieu and believe me ever with much
real regard and esteem Yours Sincerely ⟨ . . . ⟩

WA CUNYNGHAME

Wm. Adam Esqr.

1. Haslemere and Appleby.
2. Robert Bankes Jenkinson had been returned for both Appleby
and Rye at the general election. He elected to serve for Rye and
was replaced at Appleby the following January by William Grimston (1750–1814), brother of Lord Grimston and an independent
supporter of Pitt.
3. James Lowther (1753–1837) had been member for West-

morland since 1775. At the general election he apparently stood
also for Haslemere as a stop gap. The seat was taken by Penn in
December, when Lowther resumed his county seat.

4. Richard Penn (?1734–1811), M.P. Appleby 1784–1790,
Haslemere 20 December 1790–June, 1791, Lancaster 1796–1802,
Haslemere 1802–1806. He was a consistent supporter of Pitt, and
did not desert with the other Lonsdale members during the
Regency.

Duke of Portland *to* William Adam
25 *September* 1790

Address: William Adam Esqre / Lincolns Inn Fields

Welbeck Saturday night 25 Septr: 1790

Dear Adam

I am excessively sorry indeed to hear of G North's
loss, & most sincerely pity Him Her & the whole family,
for whom something like experience has taught me to
sympathize. I hope & am willing, from the stile of Your
Letter, to believe You found Your Son's health &
strength reestablished. I trust his Recovery is perfect &
that You will have no cause of future alarm. I have written to *Baldwin* from whom as well as from Yourself I
have received an unwelcome Letter this evening. I will
come up as soon as You or the P–[1] please after next
Thursday, notwithstanding I differ with You in opinion.
& think that no arrangement can be attempted till the
event of the Antwerp Negotiation is Known—I have sent
B.[2] my Letter to the P.[1] & have told Him that I was sure
You would let Yourself be employed by Him either as a
Scribe or a Messenger to H.R.H. Pray let me know if it
should be necessary for me to come up next Friday for I

shall not stir till I hear again from You or B.² or from the Prince—

Your's ever
P.

Basset writes me word that St Aubyn & Rogers have determined, (without prejudice to the present return & Petition) to give up Helleston upon account of the expense it puts them to. That they have signified their intention to the rest of the Corporation who immediately dispatched 3 of their Body to negotiate as B— *supposes* with the D of Leeds. He asks me if We have any friend who would engage in it—but how can he without the Corporation? In short what to make of this I don't even guess— ³

NOTES

1. Prince of Wales.
2. Baldwin.
3. For the ludicrous and complex legal situation in Helston, see *H of P* and Oldfield, *History of Boroughs,* 2nd ed., I, 83–85. John Rogers (1750–1832) was a former mayor, member (1784–1786), and presently recorder for Helston. The Duke of Leeds seems to have regained the dominant interest in the borough shortly after the general election. At the general election a double return was made; Sir Gilbert Elliot and Stephen Lushington were returned by order of the House of Commons on 23 December 1790. The displaced Government candidates were the incumbent James Bland Burges, who was Leeds's Undersecretary of State, and Charles Abbot, the future Speaker of the House.

William Adam *to* Lord Loughborough
[*ante* 28 *September* 1790?]

Source: Lord Campbell, *Lives of the Lord Chancellors* (Philadelphia, 2nd American from 3rd London edition, 1851), VI, 184–185. This letter was presumably written before the postscript in Portland's letter to Adam of 28 September 1790 (*infra*).

MY DEAR LORD,

The following lines are written in consequence of a conversation I had yesterday with the Prince of Wales, when I had the honor to be with his Royal Highness, and in which he expressed himself with the utmost anxiety, and at the same time under difficulty about the mode of obtaining what H.R.H. has so much at heart. At the same time that I am executing the commands of H.R.H., I need not inform your Lordship how much those commands coincide with the wishes of the Duke of Portland and all our friends.

It is understood that Lord Lonsdale has two seats yet to fill up—one for Haslemere and one for Appleby, and that he has not fixed upon the persons who are to fill those places. H.R.H. is extremely anxious that Sir William Cunnyngham should be recommended to Lord Lonsdale. But under the circumstances in which H.R.H. says he stands with Lord Lonsdale, he thinks it can not flow directly from him. What he has desired me to do, therefore, is to request of your Lordship to open this matter to Lord Lonsdale, to assure him of Sir William Cunnyngham's attachment to H.R.H., and *of his being ready at any time to vacate his seat, if Lord Lonsdale should signify to him his disapprobation of his politics;* and that if the Prince is referred to by Lord Lonsdale, his Lordship will find his Royal Highness most anxiously zealous for Sir William's success.

> Ever, my dear Lord,
> Yours most faithfully,
> **WILLIAM ADAM.**

Duke of Portland *to* William Adam
28 *September* 1790

Welbeck Tuesday Even: 28 Septr: 1790
My Dear Adam

The inclosed was put into my hands this morning by Sir Thos: Dundas who called here in his way back to Scotland, & we agreed that You were the best person to whom Sedley could be addressed. Sir Thos: answers for his attachment to the Party, & for his integrity in all respects, he is a sort of Banker or rather as Sir Thos: explained it a Remitter from Ireland. The Depositors are Ld Conyngham [1] & Sir John Leicester,[2] but S. intimated some doubt of the first upon account of his pretentions to a claim of Paramountship over the whole isle of Thanet in establishing which he fancies Government may do him much service. Sir Thos: had one or two conversations with Sedley, while he was last in town, upon this subject, & recommended it to him to try Fownes Luttrell [3] or Medlicott,[4] but I suppose he did not meet with them before Sir Thos: set out, & he accordingly wishes for the result of S— investigation to be communicated directly to You. If any conduct on the part of Mortimer could surprize me, it would be *that* which is taken notice of in the inclosed. I can not help doubting it, & yet even Bryant himself is not a very good surety for the good behaviour of Mortimer. I hope Your Son is quite & completely recovered—

sincerely
Yours ever
P

You must send for Sedley—for Sir Thos: does not mean to write to Him—Do You know any thing of the effect of the application in behalf of Sir Wm Cuninghame?—

NOTES

1. Henry Conyngham (1766–1832), 3rd Baron and 1st Viscount Conyngham, in 1816 created Marquess Conyngham in the peerage of Ireland and in 1821 Baron Minster in the peerage of the United Kingdom. He was a consistent supporter of Administration in Irish politics.

2. Sir John Fleming Leicester (1762–1827), 5th Bt., of Tabley, Cheshire, later created Baron de Tabley, son of Sir Peter Leicester, 4th Bt., M.P. Preston 1767–1768. M. P. Yarmouth (Hants) 1791–1796, Heytesbury 1796–1802, Stockbridge 1807.

3. John Fownes Luttrell (1752–1816), M. P. Minehead 1774–1806, 1807–1816. There is no record of his having voted during the Parliaments of 1784 and 1790; but he regularly returned himself and a Government nominee for Minehead, of which he was the patron.

4. Thomas Hutchings Medlycott of Milborne Port, who also normally returned a Government nominee. It is puzzling why Sir Thomas should have suggested these two men.

D. Sedley *to* Sir Thomas Dundas
24 *September* 1790

Address: Sir Thomas Dundas Bart / M.P— / Inkley / Leicester
Shire / If Sir Thomas has left Inkley / forward this ⟨ ... ⟩
ost to up Seatham.⟨ ... ⟩ York Shire
Enclosed in Portland to Adam of 28 September 1790 (*supra*).

The right of election in Shaftesbury lay in inhabitants paying scot and lot. Oldfield wrote of the borough in 1794 (*History of Boroughs,* 2nd ed., I, 196) : "This borough consists of about four hundred houses, two hundred of which are the property of Hans Winthrop Mortimer, esq. sixty belong to Mr. Bryant, Clerk of the papers at the King's Bench Prison; thirty to Paul Benfield, esq.

and about one hundred are divided amongst individuals in the town." Hans Winthrop Mortimer (1734–1807), M.P. Shaftesbury 1775–1780 and 1781–1790, a supporter of Pitt in the Parliament of 1784, had only gained complete ascendancy over the borough in 1784, and in 1786 he had been able to return a member without a contest. But shortly before the general election in 1790 his principal opponent in the borough had sold his property to Paul Benfield (1741–1810), a notorious nabob who had purchased an interest in Cricklade in 1780 and was known to fight elections by wholesale bribery. At the general election on 18 June 1790 two Government candidates had been returned on Benfield's interest, the state of the poll being Charles Duncombe 224, William Grant 224, Mortimer 67, William Bryant 67 (*ibid.*, I, 197).

Lisson Green London 24 Sepr. 1790

Sir

When I had the pleasure of seeing you on Tuesday last, a Circumstance escaped me which I intended to have Communicated to you, and that is, Mr. Mortimer gave me to understand that he should Sell Shaftsbury, therefore if you know of any of your ffriends that you should wish to have it, I shall with pleasure make all necessary enquiries for them, and I believe that the Estate, and Borough may be had a great Bargain, owing to his present situation.

You will observe that he intends to Petition against the present representatives, and I have great reason to believe that He will succeed, particularly as Certain People have held out a Compromise.

I suppose you have heard of the Death of the Duke of Montrose,[1] by his Demise, the Marquis of Graham[2] Ascends the upper House, and the Borough of Great Bedwin in Wilts lays open a new return, pray shall that strengthen your Interest.

I shall be glad to hear from you about the Certainty of what we talked of, for Young Men cant be well trusted with large Sums of Money, therefore when you are sure

217

of Success, I shall directly have the Money paid into a Bank where they shall have no power over it, and I think it is better it should be there in time, than to be looking for it in a Hurry when wanted, also it will be such a Tye on them as will keep their minds even, and prevent their Ideas from Wandering, for what Young Lads may be Mad for to Day, the Day following may be Obnoxious to them, therefore be so kind as to Advise me what you think of it.

You gave me to understand that you do expect another from a Quarter who you cant perfectly Ryly on, if so, on two more I believe I can do the same by them as by the others, at five thousand Guineas. I am Sir with great Regard,

> Your
>> most Obedient
>> and very Humble Servant
>> D SEDLEY

NOTES

1. William Graham, 2nd Duke of Montrose, died 23 September 1790.

2. James Graham (1755–1836), styled Marquess of Graham, eldest son of William, 2nd Duke of Montrose. M.P. Richmond 1780–1784, Great Bedwyn 1784–23 September 1790. Great Bedwyn was in the control of the Earls of Aylesbury, who supported Pitt and returned Government members during this period.

Donald Macleod of Geanies *to* John Craufurd of Auchinames—3 *October* 1790

Address: John Craufurd Esqr

My Dear Sir

I have very great Pleasure in assuring you that I never attributed your Silence to any neglect, Indeed far the Reverse. My letter to you was Explanatory of Circumstances, which I wished you to know, that you might make your Arrangements Accordingly, & did not in fact Require an Answer.—That I Possess your Friendship is a Circumstance highly flattering to me, & that I may Merit to Continue in the Possession of it shall be my Study.

With Respect to the Burgh's,[1] Seaforth & Sir Thomas keep their hold Firmly, & though Sir Chas. Ross has at the Michaelmass Election which has just taken Place, by the most Secret & underhand dealing & in Palpable Contradiction to his Avowed Declarations, outwitted me a little, & debauched two of those I considered my Friends on the Council, by which he has got an *Apparent* Victory, I consider myself to Stand on fully as good Ground as I ever did, if not better, as his Conduct gives me an opportunity of Acting Openly & Avowedly in opposition to him, which I had some Delicacy about before. To Secure the Point, The Sinews of War will be wanted, but not to any very Considerable Extent. £1000 at the utmost.—Is it prudent for me to lay out so much? My Idea is, that you call for Adam & Settle with him, that if *you* are at the outlay necessary to Secure Tain, you shall have Another two. If not, we must either Shop, or *they* must find me the means, & let whoever gets the Seat, Indemnify the outlay—I shall pledge my Honor that there shall not be a Shilling unnecessarily laid out, & that I shall render a faithfull Account as far as it is Practicable in such Circumstances.—I shall Still go further, that If I do not Succeed, the money I draw, I shall Consider as a loan & Indemnify Every Shilling—I hope this Proposal will meet with your Approbation for if I get the Town, I mean it Positively to your Disposal in the first Place, & failing of your Acceptance to the Prince's or Duke of Portland's—In case Adam may not be returned to Town You are best Judge whether a Communication with the Duke & Sir Th. Dundas would not Answer the Pur-

pose—I would have the money to be lodged with Sir
Robt. Herries or any other Banker you may chuse rather
than with Mr Coutts—on Account of Sir Hr. Munro's
Connection with that House—I shall Expect the Pleasure
of a few lines from you Soon & in the mean time I remain
with the most Sincere Regard My Dear Sir

yours most faithfully & Affectionately
DOND M'LEOD

Geanies 3d Octr 1790—

P.S. Though at so great a Distance from a General Elec-
ion it is necessary to make the Exertion now, as they have
commenced their Plans for Securing the Town in their
Interest, & if I once get hold, my Popularity in the Place
& neighbourhood, will Prevent their ever being able to
make any future Impression.

NOTE

1. The Northern (Tain) Burghs.

Lord Loughborough *to* William Adam
3 *October* 1790

Rudding Hall 3d Octr : 1790

My Dear Adam

You cannot doubt of the Satisfaction I should receive
from any share I could take to myself in serving Sir Wm.
Cunynghame, nor of my readiness to obey H : R : H:'s
commands; But my Situation with respect to Ld: Lonsdale precludes me even from bearing a message to Him
on the Subject of filling up any of his Seats, for He had
told me distinctly that in giving a Seat to Anstruther He
had postponed a friend of his own. It would be still more

impossible for me having recently received one obligation from Him, to appear to sollicit a second & I confess to You I feel that I should lose all credit with Him by the Attempt. The obvious Answer to me would be, You know that by serving a friend of yours I have still a friend of my own unprovided—I am aware that the Proposal ought not to come directly from H: R: H: though It would certainly be most likely in that shape to ensure Success. But the Reason applys with much greater force against the communication of the plea by me, and in my opinion the only way in which the chance can be tried is by finding some Person who at a proper time could Suggest to Ld: Lonsdale the Idea of making an offer to the Prince, & it would be best that this should be done by some of the Ladys of his own family.—

I had flatterred myself that there was a possibility of your calling here upon your return from Scotland as this place is but five miles from Wetherby, but the reason for your passing me was too good.

Adieu My Dear Adam & believe me ever most

Sincerely Yours,
LOUGHBOROUGH

Lord Daer *to* William Adam
3 *October* 1790

Endorsed: St Mary Isle Octr 3. 1790 / Lord Daer / Canterbury Accounts.

St. Marys Isle near Dumfries } Octr 3 1790

Dear Sir,

The Accounts about my unlucky Canterbury business are never yet all settled. Mr Kents [1] were delayed till you

221

should be in the way; as it was agreed you should settle them. I really cannot tell exactly what he has to account for, as several of my friends paid him & others money. But I believe it is 1,000. vizt 200 paid to himself, by my cousin; 300 paid through his hands to one of the name of Reid, whom he recommended; & 500 paid to his own account in some Bankers house, by Mr Chalmer. Of this, Mr Reid paid 200 to one Fox[2] & others in Canterbury which Fox has accounted for. Kent paid nothing of Canterbury expenses, only London & the carriages taking voters down & up. So that I always expected back a considerable ballance: but the sooner it is settled the better.—

May I also beg you to speak to Mr Baldwin about the information he got from one Wm Epps at Canterbury (Mr Beckfords agent)[3] of their being able to prove bribery against my opponents: & concert if tis worth enquiring into. Mr Reid wrote to me that Mr Baldwin had spoke to him about it.

I trust you will excuse the trouble I am thus putting you to.

Yours very Sincerely
DAER

I wrote to Mr Kent that I had got a letter from one in London by which it appeared that some of our people there were not yet satisfied. That should be done properly. But warn him to take care that whilst we are seeking for proofs of bribery against my opponents; nothing is done which can be interpreted as bribery against me.

Mr W Adam

NOTES

1. Edward Kent, of Gerard Street (in 1788) and Henrietta Street (by 1792), Westminster. In September, 1790, it was reported by Charles Hyndes, whose already pregnant wife Kent had

allegedly seduced and run off with, that Kent "was formerly in the Coal Trade, but broke." He had joined the Whig Club at its founding on 13 May 1784 and was probably active in supporting Fox during the Westminster election of that year. During the bye-election of 1788, in which he was an agent of Lord John Town-shend, he seems to have been in charge of the accounts and expendi-tures of the Select Committee of which Morrell was secretary and which met at Ireland's in Bow Street. This committee was respon-sible for detecting and exposing in the public prints any irregulari-ties, illegalities, or particularly any violent practises among the supporters of Hood. It may also have had charge of the Whig gangs. During the general election of 1790 he was Daer's agent at Canterbury and seems to have run assorted errands for the party in the south of England. In 1793, when Adam was winding up the finances of the party, he paid Kent £200 "for services at various times he never having received any thing." *Whig Club,* 1788 and 1792 eds. Charles Hyndes to William Adam, 27 September 1790, Blair Adam MSS. *The Times,* July–August, 1788, *passim.* Wil-liam Adam to Lord Fitzwilliam, 19 September, 31 October 1793, Milton MSS.

2. Samuel Fox, a freeman of Canterbury, was a woollen draper and mercer (*Universal British Directory,* II, 505).

3. A William Epps of Canterbury had joined the Whig Club on 10 November 1789 (*Whig Club,* 1792 ed.). He was a grocer by profession (*Universal British Directory* II, 505). Which Beck-ford is not clear; but Richard Beckford stood a poll at Leominster in 1790 on the Duke of Norfolk's interest. He ran third on the poll but was seated by petition to the House of Commons on 28 March 1791 (Oldfield, *History of Boroughs,* 2nd ed., I, 305–307; *Offi-cial Returns*).

Lord Robert Spencer *to* William Adam
4 *October* [1790]

Address: Willm Adam Esqr / Richmond Park / Surrey
Postmarked: THETFORD *and* OC 5 90
Endorsed: Lord Robert Spencer / Thetford 4 Octr 1790. / Westmr Subscr / refunding it—

Thetford
Octr fourth

Dear Adam,

If you can be absolutely certain of paying the whole in Novr; I see no great objection to your deferring it till that time. You are only to consider that Hercy & Birch [1] are considerably overdrawn, but I dont believe they mind that much if you make them some excuse for not paying the money immediately. I shall probably see you in the course of a fortnight & we will then talk over the other arrangements you mention. I do not quite despair yet of getting the debts paid, but the prospect is not so good as when I wrote to you last. I am yours

Most sincerely
R SPENCER

NOTE
1. Hercy, Birch, Chambers, and Hobbs was a banking house in New Bond Street.

EPILOGUE

On 25 October 1790 Portland wrote Adam from Welbeck (Blair Adam MSS): "To say the truth I do not perfectly understand the state of the account You sent me in Yours of the 17th: but this I am clear of, that if the balance is to be employed it had best be applied to the demands of H. & B. but if nothing presses I should rather wish it to remain in Your hands till we meet." Lord Robert Spencer wrote again from Milton on 18 November 1790 (Blair Adam MSS): "Although I see no way at present of our paying our debts I think it would be a good thing, if you would just look over your papers & memorandums before the meeting of Parliament for the purpose of ascertaining the exact sum that is wanted."

Duke of Portland *to* William Adam
5 *October* 1790

Endorsed: D of P. Welbeck / 5th Octr 1790 / Rd 9th Octr

Welbeck Tuesday Even : 5 Octr : 1790—
My Dear Adam

I should not have beleived it possible that Captn : B—
could have met with such a disappointment had I not
learnt it from You, or some equally good authority—I
have already written to Lushington [1] in the strongest
terms in which I was able to express myself, & dare say if
the case is remediable, that immediate redress will be obtained—I agree intirely in opinion with You, because I
never saw any thing in that quarter that was not straight
forward & direct, & I am persuaded that the reason
assigned for withholding the signature was the real one &
had made that impression upon his mind which he represented, though I do not see the force or the prudence of it
myself. I will write to Him whenever You think it necessary, but perhaps till it shall be so it may be as well to
defer it.[2] We must not expect to get rid of the people one
of whom You met & the other You heard of till we can
shew them to be unnecessary as well as prejudicial & there
is but one effectual means of bringing that to bear. I now
very much regret Coutts's [3] absence. It is a great loss, I
am sure, at this moment, & will, I fear, be felt in the remainder of this transaction.[4] I wish with all my heart
that the application for our friend Sir W.C.[5] had been
made *directly* & immediately, & yet I could not have advised that or any other to be made from the quarter from
whence my wishes would in this instance lead me to be-

lieve it most effectual. But I am generally an enemy to all applications from that quarter to any person of any description save one, & there I should not have the least objection to his applying daily—I shall be very happy to hear that all Your anxiety for Your Son is at an end by his being sent back to the Charter House.

sincerely

Your's ever

P

Pray *forget* to send the P.[6] the proposal. I am sure he will not remember it.

[the following is added verso by Portland:]

I don't know what to think of Sedley he has been asking Michl Angelo [7] if he would give FIVE. & I don't understand that he has any consideration even to *offer* for it. I have just got a Letter from Macbride, he is ordered for foreign service, though His Ship is very foul & has not been in dock for these 3 years—He has sent for his Law Agent to Portsmouth.

NOTES

1. Undoubtedly Stephen Lushington, who was currently a director of the East India Company.

2. The subject to this point seems to concern East India Company patronage.

3. Thomas Coutts (1735–1822), the banker, who with Adam was a trustee of the Duke of York.

4. This portion of the letter relates to the loan for the royal princes.

5. Sir William Cunynghame.

6. Prince of Wales.

7. Michael Angelo Taylor.

D. Sedley *to* William Adam
[11 *October* 1790]

Address: Wm. Adam Esqr.
Endorsed: Sedley. Lisson Green / 11th Octr 1790

Sir

On Saturday last I was favoured with a Letter from Sir Thomas Dundas, who desired me to wait on you, and to shew You his Letter, but as I have not been fortunate enough to find you at Home, if you will favour me with a Line by the Penny Post, and say when I shall wait on you, I shall avail myself the pleasure of doing so. I am Sir

Your
most Obedient
and most Humble Servant
D SEDLEY

Lisson Green
Monday morning

Should you happen to come to Town to Day, and write to me there, I shall not receive your favour untill to morrow Night, but if you will send a porter to our Counting House any time before 4 OClock to Day, to N 27—Nicholas Lane Lombard Street, directed to me only, I shall receive it, and wait on you when you please.

Sir Charles Bampfylde *to* Duke of Portland—30 *October* 1790

Endorsed by Portland: 30 Octr: 1790 / Sir Chas: Bampfylde Bt: / Rx 2 Novr:

227

The following was forwarded to Adam enclosed in a note from Portland dated Welbeck, 2 November 1790, which concluded with the postscript: "I have just received the inclosed, what hope is it possible to hold out to him?"

London 30th. October 1790

My Lord,

My embarrassments of which I apprehend Your Grace may be in part apprized, have imposed upon me a most mortifying and painful seclusion from all society; and being thoroughly conscious that in Your Grace's feelings I shall find a ready apology for the liberty I am about to take, I have the less repugnance in troubling you, with an unreserved statement of my very humiliating situation; a situation replete with every possible present inconvenience, and painful privation, and what is perhaps more formidable, with the greatest prospective danger of my personal liberty; even to the extent of my life—

It most unfortunately occurs that the nature of the greater part of the pecuniary demands upon me would render a retreat to the Continent as insecure as my remaining in this Country, where it is impossible to hope the most cautious privacy can avail me to a much longer period—

Had I the alternative of living abroad however contrary to my wishes, I should prefer all the inconveniences of Exile, to the subjecting Your Grace, to the smallest trouble on my account, and if I have presumed too far I trust it will be remembered, as some excuse for my having intruded myself upon your Notice, that this address is dictated, by the terrors of perpetual imprisonment, which, perhaps it may be in Your Grace's power to avert—

As I have no doubt Your Grace is informed, a Petition is ready to be profered by the Electors of Exeter, and if I can rely on the assurances of my Council, and those acquainted with the Demerits of Mr. Barings [1] return, the Event must necessarily make His Election void—

I have every reason to assure myself that Ministry will not venture a second Contest, and if they should, as I shall be able to meet it with much greater Energy, & a very large super addition of support, that I could not command at the last hard fought one, I am little less than certain that it would not be unsuccessfull—

I am aware, that there are not very many double returns, in the returned list, but aided as I am by the protection, & good wishes of the Prince of Wales, to which I am sure I may add those of Your Grace, and Mr. Fox, I have ventured to entertain a hope, that, some Gentleman devoted to you individualy, or to the party in general, might be induced by Your obliging intercession, to make a sacrifice of His seat, till the depending petition, in which I am so deeply interested, shall be decided—

Whether any person attached to the party & Your Grace, whose being in Parliament a year sooner or later was no very material objection to it, or Himself would not render it more essential service by such relinquishment, than in the holding of His Seat, is not a question for me to determine, but I cannot help suggesting, that the chance of the Petitions succeeding will be essentially diminished, by my not being able to attend its operation—

I will not now take up more of Your Grace's time, than to entreat, that when you reflect upon my situation, you will bear in mind, that mine is not a case of common convenience, but that the Alternative to my obtaining what I have now presumed to sollicit, is total and immediate ruin with respect to my self, & the consequent loss to the party, of the feeble support, yet strenuous and consistent attachment it has derived from me, through the whole course of my Parliamentary life— [2]

I have the honor to be, with the greatest Respect &
Regard,

My Lord, Your Grace's
most devoted & most
Obedient humble Servant
CHAS. BAMPFYLDE

PS:
Might I trouble Your Grace to address any answer you
might do me the honor to send to this Letter, under cover
to Messrs. Grahams, Lincolns Inn.

NOTES

1. John Baring (1730–1816), M.P. Exeter 1776–1802, a
Pittite in the Parliament of 1784. The poll at Exeter concluded
with James Buller 1106, Baring 588, Bampfylde 550 (Oldfield,
History of Boroughs, 2nd ed., I, 136). Bampfylde lost his petition.

2. In the Parliament of 1784 Bampfylde had voted with the
party against Pitt's Irish propositions, Richmond's fortifications
plan, and on the Regency questions—a good record.

Donald Macleod of Geanies *to* William Adam—10 *December* 1790

My Dear Sir

I did myself the favour of Writing you on the 14th.
Octr. last now near two Months Ago, & have not Since
had the Pleasure of hearing from you—I hope there was
nothing in my Letter Improper or any Circumstance Suggested that could Incur your Displeasure, or even Disapprobation; Even if there had your Representing the
Impropriety would have more readily brought about a
Correction, than Silence.—But I am perfectly Incon-
scious of any Intention either to Act Wrong or give
offence—I know well your Engagements & Avocations

are great, & I have some fears that bad health may have
had some Share of your time—But I do not Expect or
look for a frequent Correspondence, nor will I give you
the trouble of it on my Part, there were however two or
three Circumstances in my last Letter that I had reason
to Expect an Answer to; The Enquiry respecting A
Proper Academy for my two Boys which you was so
obliging as [to] Undertake when here—The Reminding
Mr Elphinston to obtain the ⟨Surgeons⟩ Appointment to India for Mr Gordon, And your opinion on the
Occurrences in the Tain Politicks. With respect to the
latter I am going on with my Complaint before the Court
of Session, & have assurance from my Counsel of Success
—It will however be a hard Case indeed, if by my Exertions in that Cause I forfeit the friendship & good Will
of some of my Country Neighbours, make myself Obnoxious to Sir Chas. Ross & his Supporters; & Receive
neither Countenance Advice or Support from those for
whom I am fighting this Battle—I shall however persevere untill I have the Decision of that Court; further I
shall not Say—As I wish to send the Commodore to Sea
this Spring, & as there is to be no War I wish to put him
in to The India Service, I have used the freedom to
Write a few Lines to Mr. Elphinston on the Subject, Requesting his Advice how he ought to be Placed & his
Assistance to get him out with Some Acquaintance, which
I here inclose, & you may deliver or not as you think my
Request Proper or otherwise—With Best Respects to
Mrs Adam & your Young Family I remain with great Regard   My Dear Sir

                         Yours faithfully
                         DOND M'LEOD

Geanies 10th. Decr.
          1790
    Mr Adam

William Adam *to* Donald Macleod of Geanies—[*post* 10 *December* 1790]

Endorsed: Copy to / Geanies— / Decr 1790
This is a copy in Adam's hand. It is clearly in reply to the previous letter.

Our idea is that at so long a period before any use could be made of the interest with the various chances of change of circumstances by deaths and otherwise it would be idle to make the advance—and I cannot disagree from any part of the Determination. And What has occured as the best determination to take is for you to have the complaint made in the Court of Session and According to the turn which it takes there we can decide what more can be done. To the extent of the expence of the Suit in the Court of Session there is no difficulty in finding the Mean's as it cannot be very considerable and According to what appear's there it can, or not, be decided to go farther. Because if the Law should prove to be Against us there would be no use in persisting upon any other ground than that of regaining the Council by Canvass—

This plan if you approve may be immediatly executed, and I will write to H Erskine and Wight who as a Party concerned will do the Law business Without Fees—

Duke of Portland *to* William Adam [20 *December* 1790]

Address: To / William Adam Esqre / House of Commons
Endorsed: D of P. / & Troward / Decr 20th / 1790

Dear Adam

I think You had better not move the writ for Petersfield without speaking again to Joliffe & if moved on

Wednesday it will answer all the purposes of its being moved today—Troward or Tierney is unintelligible for if Tierney has paid between 7 & 8000£ as he told me he had for Colchester Troward must surely be paid in full— ¹ I hope You are now quite well.

Your's ever
P

[added verso by Portland:]
You may keep Sir Wm ⟨Neclaer⟩ till after Wednesday by Fox's saying one word to Him.

NOTE

1. On 3 October 1806 (Grey MSS, University of Durham) Richard Troward, who had been Tierney's solicitor for the Colchester committee in 1788–1789, wrote Charles Grey, then Lord Howick, that his "exertions before a six weeks com[mitt]ee with 20 witnesses in town procured Mr. Tierney the seat, & that the whole expense was paid by me as solicitor to the great leaders then forming the heads of the party." Troward, without strict justice, appealed to Howick as "head of the party on whose account the debt was incurred" (Fox then being dead). He placed the total expense at £3400, of which he claimed he had received only £1000 "through Mr. Tierney." Grey's reply is not extant, and there is no evidence that Troward was ever further reimbursed. At the general election George Jackson, the Government candidate whom Tierney had unseated in 1789, was again returned for Colchester. Tierney did not return to the House until 1796.

Duke of Portland *to* William Adam
10 *September* 1791

Welbeck Saturday Even: 10 Septr: 1791

My Dear Adam

When I come to town which will probably be some time in the course of November I will take care to satisfy

233

Halliday, though I must confess he has not satisfied me, &
by this information I hope You will be able to quiet Morland & to procure at least a suspense from his vexation—
With respect to Ld Robt:[1] I can not but think there
must be some misunderstanding, & yet considering his
accuracy & great correctness I can not but suspect my own
memory, & even my account Book. I find there that on the
19th October 1789 I gave *You* an order on Child & Co:
for £200 on the account on which he says he is in advance
for me, & on the 15th February 90 I also find that I gave
him an order on Child & Co to Bearer for the like sum on
the like account. As for my other £50 due on this years
account You shall have it whenever You please & I would
advise You to apply to Ld Frederick[2] who is returned to
Twickenham Park for the subscriptions of the two
Georges[3] to whom I understood him to have spoken but
Ld John[4] is so unsatisfied with the conduct of the News
Writers that Ld F.[5] tells me he will not continue his subscription any longer & will not give his money to propa-
gate opinions which are not only not consonant to those
he professes but highly injurious to that Party of which
He is a Member & very pernicious to the Community at
large— What the D of C.[6] has told You & particularly
the latter part of it surprizes me very much, though indeed I ought to be ashamed of being surprized at any
thing of that sort that originates or happens at C.H.[7]
but I think it very necessary that Ld M.[8] should be informed of it & I shall write to him by this nights post for
reasons which I will communicate to You when We
meet— I can not fancy Parliament will meet till after
Christmas notwithstanding R–s intelligence. What is the
reason of the Weymouth expedition?[9] The Dss: is much
obliged by the good accounts of Her Godson & begs Mrs.
Adam's acceptance of Her best wishes for them both.

Your's ever

P

I should very much like to see the D of Y–s [10] Letter to You & Coutts.

I return You Morlands & send You one of Geo: Reids for your *amusement* & observation—

NOTES

1. Lord Robert Spencer.
2. Lord Frederick Cavendish.
3. Lord George Augustus Cavendish (?1727–1794), 2nd son of William, 3rd Duke of Devonshire and brother of Lords Frederick and John Cavendish; M.P. Weymouth and Melcombe Regis 1751–1754, Derbyshire 1754–1780 and 1781–1794. Lord George Augustus Henry Cavendish (1754–1834), 3rd son of William, 4th Duke of Devonshire, and brother of the 5th Duke; M.P. Knaresborough 1775–1780, Derby 1780–1796, Derbyshire 1797–1831. Lords Frederick, G.A., G. A. H., and John Cavendish each subscribed £50 annually to the party's general fund. The Dukes of Portland and Devonshire, Lord Fitzwilliam, and Lord Robert Spencer each contributed £200, while Lord Derby's subscription was £100 (William Adam to Lord Fitzwilliam, 4 July 1793, Milton MSS).
4. Lord John Cavendish (1732–1796), 4th son of William, 3rd Duke of Devonshire. M.P. Weymouth and Melcombe Regis 1754–1761, Knaresborough 1761–1768, York 1768–1784, Derbyshire 1794–1796. Lord John, and not the 5th Duke, was the political leader of the Cavendish family. He had been a lord of the Treasury under the first Rockingham ministry and Chancellor of the Exchequer under the second Rockingham and Coalition governments.
5. Lord Fitzwilliam.
6. Duke of Clarence.
7. Carlton House, residence of the Prince of Wales.
8. Probably Lord Malmesbury, who was enroute to Berlin to attend the marriage of the Duke of York and the daughter of the King of Prussia. He had been secretly commissioned by the Prince of Wales to negotiate a loan with the King of Prussia. See Aspinall, ed., *Correspondence of George, Prince of Wales 1770–1812*, II, *passim*.
9. The king had gone to Weymouth at the beginning of September. Following the Regency Crisis the Opposition was continually watching for signs of a break in the king's health.
10. Duke of York.

Richard Perryman *to* William Adam
2 *November* 1791

Address: William Adam Esqr. M.P.— / Lincolns Inn Fields– / London—

Tregony Novr. 2nd 1791

Dear Sir

I have made Free to trouble you with this Letter concerning the Borough of Tregony in the late Election as I am the only Person and manager of the whole Business in your behalf. I find there have been many persons applying to you and Mr. Carpenter for Cash. I much wonder at such large expences as I have taken all the Trouble and all my expences I never received one Farthing for it the Cash Mr. Carpenter put in my hands for this Business I returned to him again to Farthing which I hope you already know to be true. If some Persons had not interfered I would warrant the plan to succeed as I had carryed on the same plan for a great while with Doctor Mein of Fowey and attempt several Boroughs besides this all to my own expences. I wrote many Letters to Mr. Carpenter touching the poor Men and Myself to have something for them as he promised there should be a sum of money Distributed amongst them they have not received a Farthing to this Day nor myself. I spoke with Mr. Carpenter in Cornwall about Myself and they poor Men he told me the Gentlemen had not settled their Business as yet but will be soon done, I desired Carpenter to lay my Letter before you which I sent him as he promised me it should be done. I held a small sinecure under the Prince of Wales of Twenty pounds a Year and it is kept back from being paid me by whom I know not. No Man can't be served so ill as I am for doing all this for the party, only ⟨refer⟩ the whole Business to Sir John

Morshead and then you will be to a certainty of the whole affair. Please to shew this Letter to Mr. Carpenter and see if he have any thing to say against it or to Sir John Morshead. Your Answer Dear Sir will oblige Your

sincere Friend & humble Servant
RICHARD PERRYMAN

John Robert Cocker *to* Thomas Lowten
14 *November* 1791

Address: Thos. Lowten Esqr. / Temple

Nassau Street
14 November 1791

Dear Sir

I have used my utmost endeavors to make out another Account respecting my Concerns in the Election of Lord John Towshend, but finding it utterly impossible to do so with any tolerable degree of accuracy I waited in expectation of the arrival in Town of Sir Thomas Dundas when I hoped that the Accounts so long since delivered by me to Lord Robert Spencer (and which I understood after being laid by His Lordship before the Gentlemen who met at Sir Thomas Dundas's in the beginning of last Year had been allowed by them and a provision agreed to be made for the ballance) might probably be found amongst the other papers then submitted to the Consideration of those Gentlemen.

As His Lordship lately objected to the payments of fifty pounds and twenty five pounds which were made to Mr. Reid Junr. by desire of Mr. Sheridan and charged to the Club at Beckets [1] —I concluded that the same objection would be made to the three hundred pounds paid to Mr. Reid Senr. and charged in the Election Account—I have therefore claimed (but not received) that 300£ and the 50£ and 25£ from Mr. Sheridan and the amount must therefore be deducted from my Account.

I think it necessary to observe that when I sold out the two thousand pounds Stock to enable me to defray the Expence of defending Lord John Townshends Petition I acquainted Lord Robert Spencer with the Circumstance who then informed me that the Interest should be Repaid me—On this Account I have paid for two Years Dividends the Sum of one hundred and twenty pounds besides the difference of one hundred fifty eight pounds two Shillings and six pence which I also paid on replacing the Stock—After I have been encouraged to expect that I shall not be a loser by this transaction I am convinced (if His Lordships Memory still serves him) he will not now make an objection to these Charges—If however His Lordship insists on a deduction of the £120. Dividends and the £158.2.6 Loss on replacing the Stock besides the £82.10.9 paid to Messrs. Hercy for Interest the 300£ to Mr. Reid Senr. and the £75 to Mr. Reid Junr. my situation compels me to submit to His Lordships decision although each of those Sums were actually paid by me, and in that Case which I cannot consider otherwise than as extremely hard the ballance due to me will be reduced from twelve hundred eighty eight pounds and three pence to five hundred fifty two Pounds and Seven Shillings.

The Loss I shall sustain on this Account if My Claim is so settled will be nearly double the Sum which I received for the labour of eleven Months during the Westminster Election and Scrutiny in the Year 1784 independent of the delay which may happen in obtaining the 375£ from Mr. Sheridan.

> I am
> > Dear Sir
> > > Your most obedient Servant
> > > Jno Robt. Cocker

Thos. Lowten Esqr

NOTE

1. For a number of years the party had been in possession of apartments above the shop of Thomas Becket, a bookseller in Pall Mall patronized by the Prince of Wales. The rental of the apartments and the expense of furnishing them with such items as stationery and newspapers were defrayed from the party's annual subscription. The apartments were employed as a club or headquarters where the party's men of business might meet and work, over a glass of claret. It was in these apartments that the famous *Rolliad* seems to have been written in 1785; and, in addition to being a center for political writing of all kinds, they appear in this letter to have been an organizational center during Westminster elections. A Samuel Massingham was continuously attached to the club as a messenger. The party paid him one guinea a week (a total of £138.12.0) for his "attendance" at Becket's from 9 November 1788 (the outset of the Regency Crisis) to 22 May 1791, and by June, 1791, he also billed the party £36.1.2 for "Moneys Disbursted at Different times at Mr. Becketts." T. Becket to William Adam, 29 August 1789; S. Massingham to William Adam, 11 June 1791, Blair Adam MSS. See W. Sichel, *Sheridan* (London, 1909), I, 454-455; II, 87-93.

William Frogatt *to* William Adam
19 *April* 1792

Dear Sir:

If You will Indulge me with an Account of what You paid for the *Seaford Writ*—I will Introduce it into my Bill—

I have the honor to be
Dear Sir
Yours most obediently
WM FROGATT

Castle Street
19th April 92

Duke of Portland *to* William Adam
[*early* 1790?]

Address: To / William Adam Esqre
Endorsed: D of Pd— / Taunton
This letter was found among a bundle of Portland's letters to Adam of
1790.

As far as *one* I will take upon *myself* to answer unconditionally except with regard to H–s [1] engaging positively
to Us.

Your's ever

P

Friday one o'clock   if more is required I must
write to Ld F. & I like the *two*
in my way for M.[2] & L.[3] better
than *one* unconditionally—
[a line is drawn through the first
ten letters of the last word]

NOTES

1. John Halliday of Taunton.
2. Milborne Port?
3. Lymington?

Unknown *to* [William Adam?]
[1789 *or* 1790]

Endorsed by Adam: Bootle & Crewe
The final portion and cover of this letter has been lost. It was found
among a bundle of Adam's correspondence and papers concerning the
general election of 1790.

"The Grosvenor family, seated at Eaton Hall, four miles from Chester, had considerable influence in the corporation; and their record of parliamentary service to the borough was almost unique: between 1715 and 1874 they held one seat without a break, and for 42 out of these 159 years both seats" (*H of P*). Thomas Grosvenor (1734–1795), brother of Richard, 1st Earl Grosvenor (1731–1802), had represented the borough since 1755, as had Richard Wilbraham Bootle (1725–1796), of Rode Hall, Cheshire, since 1761. Both were independent supporters of Pitt in the Parliament of 1784. There had long been an independent party in Chester, but it had rarely contested the Grosvenor interest. It did so in 1784, however, when it unsuccessfully put forward as its candidate John Crewe, probably the only son of John Crewe (1742–1829), of Crewe Hall, Cheshire, member for the county 1768–1802 and close friend of Fox. In 1790 the elder Thomas Grosvenor was again returned. Wilbraham Bootle retired from Parliament, and Robert Grosvenor (1767–1845), styled Viscount Belgrave, eldest surviving son of Lord Grosvenor, was returned for his seat. The younger Thomas Grosvenor (1764–1851), third son of the elder Thomas, did not sit for Chester until the death of his father in 1795.

Dear Sir

I now sit down to answer, in as particular a manner as I am able your enquiry concerning the state of politics in this City & with what probability a stand might be made on behalf of the Whig-interest at the approaching Election—I shall first state what I apprehend to be the difficulties in the way of an opposition, and then the circumstances which may seem to encourage such an attempt.

In regard to your general question whether Lord G. intends to exert his interest for returning both members, there is not the smallest particle of doubt on that head—Indeed the papers I have just sent you will afford abundant proof that the Corporation, at his Lordship's instance no doubt, mean to maintain their ground to the last.

At the general Election in 1784 there were about 1200

freemen of whom 626 voted for Mr Bootle & 420 for Mr
Crewe several votes were divided between Mr Grosvenor
& Mr Crew but scarcely any between Mr Bootle & Mr
Crewe—The former may therefore be left out of the
question & the latter be deemed to give the true state of
the strength of each party. You can not be unacquainted
with the nature of Corporation–influence which goes
(with the exception of a very few individuals of the
Body) in favour of the Grosvenor family; & their long
possession of the representation & their repeated tri-
umphs over an hitherto ill-conducted opposition are circumstances which of themselves give additional strength
to their cause. Besides these they had the good fortune a
few years ago to get a lease from the Crown of several
tenements in the City which they let at very low rents &
since the last election have taken care that they shall be in
the hands of freemen *only*. The Corporation also immediately after the election created a considerable number
of honorary freemen, of such as they thought attached to
their interest so that it must be confessed they have apparently an accession of strength since the last contest.
The arguments they urged in opposition to us (& it must
be owned there was some weight in them) were the impropriety of turning out an old member & a man of respectable character, for such Mr Bootle certainly is to
make room for one whose principles were unknown &
who from his relationship to Mr Crewe of Crewe might
be suspected of favouring Mr Fox against whom you
must remember there was at that time an almost universal outcry— I must also tell you candidly that if an
opposition were now attempted, no dependence ought to
be placed on receiving pecuniary assistance from the inhabitants. What they did at the election & have since done
in support of the Quo Warranto cause has run pretty far
into their spare Cash—& you must observe that this is a
place of very little trade & consequently moneyed people

among us are very rare—or if there be any of that description they are mostly such as would as soon part with an ounce of their blood as a single guinea in a cause to which they might *wish* never so well—

Let me now give you the per contra state of the Account— The Election of Members is, by a vote of the house in 1747 confined to *resident* freemen only so that the charge of bringing voters from a great distance is entirely avoided— Yet notwithstanding this material narrowing of the ground of contest the successful party obtained their majority at the last election at no less a charge than 24,000£ while the expense on the side of the opposition did not much exceed 5000, of which it was afterwards found much might have been spared. Of the 24,000£ above mentioned there is still remaining full 5000 unpaid to different persons chiefly Innkeepers to the number of 50 or 60 who were all obliged to give receipts in full for the composition paid them, so that in all probability the Grosvenor family would have to discharge all or the greatest part of these arrears or lose the votes, & probably the interest which would be considerable, of the persons to whom they are due— Mr Crewe's friends lost many votes even by their honourable proceedings upon the canvas— Being avowedly the friends of liberty it would have been inconsistent in them to use any methods but those of fair persuasion— But no sooner was ground broke by the other side but threats & promises were dealt about without reserve, & if we may judge by the magnitude of the sum expended *other* measures still more exceptionable were resorted to in no common degree, so that I do not think *popularity* has much weight in their scale, & I believe many would have voted against them had it not been for the fear of oppression. I think their influence in these matters as well as in the King's tenements might receive a heavy blow, if previous to an election 1000£ were deposited in the hands of a banker with a public & general intimation that out of that fund redress should be afforded to any person who could bring sufficient proof of his having been oppressed for giving his vote according to his conscience.

From *popular argument* (so far as that would go) opposition would have every thing to hope. The plea of attachment to old Members would be urged with very little propriety if, as I am informed, Mr Grosvenor & Mr Bootle retire to make room for Lord Belgrave & Mr Thos. Grosvenor— Perhaps Mr Grosvenors withdrawing may depend upon the circumstance whether there be a contest or not, but of Mr Bootle's there is no reason to doubt. The transactions developed in the course of the cause would give their opponents every handle against them that could be wished for, and I do believe would have weight with several independent men who voted with them last time merely from considerations of something like gratitude & respect to which it now appears they have not the least title & something might be expected from several freemen who did not vote at all in the last election & who may be supposed if their minds were unbiassed to join that party which appears to have most reason & justice on its side. As to the honorary freemen there is strong reason to doubt of their title to vote as I am informed by a Gentleman of the Law on whom I can safely rely for a good opinion on the case.

There are a few circumstances of a general nature which it may be proper to mention. The question concerning the residency of voters with other incidental enquiries protracts the election considerably the whole being a continued scrutiny—that in 1784 lasted 11 days & expences were incurred in opening houses of entertainment a week before it began—The Sheriffs are the officers

John Coxe Hippisley *to* Duke of Portland [1789 *or* 1790]

Address: His Grace / the Duke of Portland
Found in a bundle of Adam's correspondence and papers relating to the
general election of 1790.

My Lord Duke
    I just left Ransoms Bank in Pall Mall where Mr. Robert Frazer (a Broker at the Hungerford Coffee House) left a Note intimating that He had 4 Seats to dispose of— 2 at £5000 each for 7 Sessions & reelections— 2—at 3500 but contested, & if *un*successful which *was scarcely* probable—at a risque of £500 only.

I am Your Grace's
very faithful ⟨Obedient⟩
J Coxe Hippesly.

Harriet Fawkener Bouverie *to* William Adam—[1790]

Endorsed: Mrs. Bouverie / about / Northampton / 1790.

Edward Bouverie (1738–1810), of Delapre Abbey, Northamptonshire, M. P. Salisbury 1761–1771, Northampton 1790–1810. In 1764 Bouverie had married Harriet Fawkener, and both he and his wife were close social and political friends of Fox. Charles Compton (1760–1828), styled Lord Compton, eldest son of Spencer, 8th Earl of Northampton, was M.P. Northampton 1784–1796. The Earls of Northampton had a dominant interest in Northampton and usually returned one member for the borough during this period. There does not seem to have been a contest at Northampton in 1790. Williams has not been identified.

Dear Sir

Mr Bouverie desires me to say how much obliged to you he is for the trouble you have taken about Northampton, he thinks the best thing to be said to Mr. Wms is, that *you* imagine from what *you* know of [the] Town of Northampton that a third Candidate would be to the full as troublesome to Ld Compton as to Mr Bouverie, and that it would only be making a disturbance, without a chance of success, which I really believe is the true state of the case. I find the account I gave you this Morning of the four People Mr Williams mentioned was a true one. I must once more thank you for the trouble you have had, am dear Sir

Your Sincere Humble Servant
H Bouverie

Saturday *Old Bur Street*

Memorandum *by* Charles Stuart
[1789 *or* 1790]

Endorsed by the writer of the memorandum: Mr Stuarts / Easy / and almost / Certain / Plan / For securing a strong / Party in / The New Parliament
Endorsed by Adm. Sir Charles Adam: Papers relating to the / General Election / 1790

For information on Charles Stuart, who was a journalist and newspaper editor, see Aspinall, *Politics and the Press,* and Werkmeister, *London Daily Press.* It is not entirely clear whether Stuart's plan was implemented, but some correspondence from Stuart to Adam published by Aspinall (pp. 447–448), in which

Stuart claims payment from the party of "£50 for the Excise business," gives some ground for believing that it was. Compare Murray of Broughton's plan for regularly inserting columns in the country newspapers in the event of a Regency, also published by Aspinall (pp. 445–446). Excise was a theme much played upon in the Westminster bye-election of 1788; and the Opposition had recently made an attack upon the shop tax, for example, a cardinal point in their strategy against Pitt in the House. Perhaps an examination of local newspapers would reveal that excise was an issue in various constituencies during the general election of 1790, but there is no evidence of this fact in the private papers of the leaders and men of business of the party.

Mr Stuart's Plan for an auspicious General Election.

It may be perceived that as the Period approaches, all schemes to operate generally upon the public mind, are likely to be absorbed in the partial attention of candidates, and ⟨thus⟩

While it is highly necessary to attend to particular canvassing, it is surely as necessary to embrace every plan that can bias the public mind.

Of all schemes able to effect this, there are none equal to holding up the Minister's Intention of

A General Excise.

The most effectual method to make this answer, is, by having all the Public Bodies in Britain meet, to Declare, "that they will not support any Candidate, who will not solemnly affirm, that he will not give his vote to any measure of the Minister, until he has not only repealed the Tobacco Act, but until he and his partizans recant their destructive doctrine, by declaring, that they will on no pretence whatever introduce any more laws of Excise, and that they will support any feasible code that may be introduced, for softening the rigour of those now existing."

To obtain such Meetings, and such Declarations, it

might in a great measure be accomplished in three weeks, by some such scheme as this: (Mr Bell [1] is of this opinion.)

Let there be Posting-bills, and Hand-bills printed, on which are Mr Dundas's [2] Declaration, and underneath a Test to the Candidates similar to the above.

Let there be likewise three or four good caricatures done.

Let four persons be appointed to go with some thousands of each to the country.

One all down the west to Exeter, Bristol, and from thence to Birmingham, Liverpool, Manchester and Leeds.

Another to go the Midland, as far as York.

A third to take the Norwich, Hull, Durham, and Newcastle route.

A Fourth, Winchester, Southampton, Portsmouth, Chicester, Canterbury, Rochester, Chelmsford, Colchester, and Ipswich.

Mr Bell would furnish letters of introduction to the Tobacco manufacturers in all these places. A certain number of each to be left with every one to be properly distributed, and pasted up by him, but not till a day after the Courier leaves him.

Besides this,—bold, good queries, &c. to be put in all the capital country papers, but not by the courier, but by the manufacturer, after the courier is gone, he leaving money with him for that purpose.

These queries, &c. should be local, not general—For instance. For the Hereford paper, the Excise on Cyder. For the Gloster paper, the Excise on woolens in the loom —and so on—speaking home to the feelings of every county by the idea of excizing their staples.

The tobacco-manuf. in all parts, after the courier left them, to call meetings themselves for the Test, or to influence for instance, the cloathiers in Glostershire, the cyder-makers in Herefordshire, to stand forth, with indignant declaratory Resolutions against Excise, and proposing a Test to their parliamentary candidates.

In a few weeks, and this is Mr Bell's opinion, by such a plan, numbers of public bodies would assemble, to Declare their abhorrence of Excise-laws, and to propose the Test to their candidates.

Excise, besides, is so odious, that Mr Pitt could not procure one body in the island to meet for counter-declarations, unless Excisemen themselves!

The minds of the People being thus prepared—what a vast acquisition that would be, whenever the Dissolution happened?

About Two Hundred Pounds would effect all this mighty purpose, which might certainly be accomplished in a month!

Irish Test

Mess. Ogilvie, Curran,[3] and Forbes[4] could carry a Test for Ireland, "That each candidate solemnly should declare,

"That they would never support the introduction of any Excises, and that they would do every thing in their power to soften the rigour of those in existence.

"That they would vote for a Declaratory Law, that extreme Bail was unconstitutional, and censuring the Judges for the excessive Bail, in the case of ⟨Macpherson⟩.

"That they would vote for a Law to put Ireland on the footing of England, in respect to Members vacating their seats, on accepting any place, or pension.

"That they would not support the measures of any Minister, until he acceded to these terms, in the beginning of the New Parliament, as questions of Privilege to the People, before he entered on any other business."

The above gentlemen could get Dublin to declare, and the rest of the Kingdom would soon follow.

Mr S[tuart] at the time of the Propositions,[5] made every county, city, borough, and volunteer company in the kingdom meet in three weeks, and declare their abhorrence of them, as Mess. Ogilvie, Forbes, &c. will know.

Remarks.

Without some such plans as the above are immediately put in execution, that millstone, Excise, now about the Minister's neck, will be of little detriment to him at present;—but, properly used, it certainly could be made to weigh him down, and pinion him.

If the popular mind be not rouzed before the Dissolution, the odious hue and cry at the General Election will be of small avail.

The New Parliament and his Majority will appear before the popular indignation can in such a case take place.

Now is the time;—and with submission S. thinks not a moment ought to be lost, after the Repeal of the Tob. act is thrown out.

The Dissolution cannot be put off longer than a twelvemonth; therefore the sooner the public mind is rouzed, the better, for a chance of a Majority, or such a very strong minority as may shake ministry in the first sessions.

NOTES

1. John Bell (1745–1831), the printer and bookseller in the Strand, was a highly experienced publicist. See Aspinall, *Politics and the Press,* and Werkmeister, *London Daily Press.*

2. Henry Dundas.

3. John Philpot Curran (1750–1817), a leading Oppositionist in the Irish Parliament.

4. John Forbes (*d.* 1797), also an Oppositionist in the Irish Parliament.

5. Pitt's Irish commercial propositions of 1785.

Memorandum—[1789]

Endorsed: Friends who lose / their present seats & still / unprovided
                    for—
The memorandum and endorsement are in Adam's hand.

Ten of the nineteen members listed below did not find seats during
the Parliament of 1790. Some may not have seriously wished to do
so, of course; that is, they may not have been willing to pay the
price.

    Anstruther John [1]
    Cooper Sir Grey [2]
    Cunnyngham Sir W. A.
    Cotsford E— [3]
5   Downe Lord [4]
    Ellis Rt Hon. W.[5]
    Francis Ph— [6]
    Greville Hon. Chas [7]
    Lee John [8]
    Melbourn Ld [added later] [9]
10 North G. A.
    Ord John [10]
    Osbaldiston G.[11]
    Nedham [added later] [12]
    Palmerston Lord [13]
    Parker Sir P.[14]
15 Scott Thos [15]
    Spencer Lord Rt [16]
17 Wrightson Wm— [17]

NOTES

1. Anstruther contested Pontefract and petitioned against the
return (Oldfield, *History of Boroughs,* 2nd ed., II, 287), both
without success. He was returned for Cockermouth while awaiting
the outcome of the petition.

2. Sir Thomas Dundas required Cooper's seat at Richmond for his eldest son, Lawrence Dundas (1766–1839), later 1st Earl of Zetland. No seat was found for Cooper at the general election and he never again sat in the House.

3. Midhurst, for which Cotsford sat in the Parliament of 1784, had been sold to Lord Egremont in 1787 for £40,000, and at the general election Egremont brought in two family members, Percy Charles Wyndham (1757–1833), who had been one of "Fox's Martyrs" in 1784, and Charles William Wyndham (1760–1828), both of whom supported Opposition 1791–1792. Cotsford did not again sit in Parliament.

4. John Christopher Burton Dawnay, 5th Viscount Downe (1764–1832), M.P. Petersfield 1787–1790 on the Jolliffe interest, Wootton Bassett 1790–1796 on the St. John interest. In 1790 Downe simply exchanged with G. A. North, who found Wootton Bassett too expensive.

5. Welbore Ellis, who could no longer be returned for Weymouth, was unable to find a seat at the general election. He was returned for Petersfield in April, 1791, when Lord Titchfield succeeded Lord Verney as member for Buckinghamshire.

6. Philip Francis (1740–1818), the antagonist of Warren Hastings and at this time close friend of both Fox and Burke. He had been member for Yarmouth (I.o.W.) since 1784. In 1790 Leonard Troughear Holmes, the patron of both Yarmouth and Newport (I.o.W.), returned Lords Melbourne and Palmerston (who also appear on this list) for Newport. Edward Rushworth (1755–1817), Holmes's son-in-law and a supporter of Opposition, was moved from his seat at Newport to the one seat at Yarmouth over which Holmes had control. A seat was found for Philip Francis at Bletchingley, where he was returned with the incumbent patron, Sir Robert Clayton.

7. Charles Francis Greville (1749–1809), younger brother of George, 2nd Earl of Warwick. M.P. Warwick 1774–1790. Lord Warwick was the natural patron of his borough, but he frequently had difficulty with a strong independent party. In 1784 Charles Greville had broken politically with his family when he resigned his office in the household and followed the Coalition into opposition to Pitt. He decided to stand for Warwick despite this, and in 1784 he was returned with another candidate on the independent interest. "Greville seems to have canvassed Warwick at the general election of 1790, but retired before the poll" (*H of P; cf.* Oldfield, *History of Boroughs,* 2nd ed., II, 172). He had been in serious

financial difficulties for a number of years, which may explain why
the party was unable to find him another seat.

8. John Lee (?1733–1793), M.P. Clitheroe 1782–1790,
Higham Ferrers December, 1790–1793. An old connection and
legal adviser of Rockingham, he had been solicitor general April–
July, 1782, and April–November, 1783, and attorney general
November–December, 1783. His patron at Clitheroe, the staunch
Oppositionist Thomas Lister (1752–1826), had in 1780 captured
both seats in the borough from the Curzon family, with whom he
had previously shared the return of one member each. By 1790
Lister had agreed once again to share the borough with the
Curzons, who were Pittites. The Curzons returned a family mem-
ber for Clitheroe at the general election; Lister returned Sir John
Aubrey (1739–1826), 6th Bt. Aubrey, who had been returned for
Buckinghamshire in 1784 as a supporter of Pitt and was a lord of
the Treasury, had deserted Government at the time of the Regency.
He voted with Opposition in the Parliament of 1790. Lee was
without a seat at the general election. In December, 1790, Lord
Fitzwilliam brought him in for Higham Ferrers when Lord Dun-
cannon elected to sit for Knaresborough.

9. Melbourne's patron at Malmesbury, who had deserted to
Opposition in 1784, had taken once again to returning Government
nominees by 1789.

10. Ord did not sit in the House after 1790.

11. George Osbaldeston (?1753–1793), M.P. Scarborough
1784–1790. He was a Yorkshire friend of Lord Fitzwilliam and it
had been assumed that he would support Fitzwilliam's friends
when in Parliament—indeed Fitzwilliam had offered him a seat at
Hedon in 1784, but Osbaldeston had chosen to stand for Scarborough on his family interest. At the general election, however, he
denied his opposition to Pitt; and in Parliament he supported Government until the time of the Regency, when he began to veer
towards Opposition. The two principal patrons of Scarborough had
been the Duke of Rutland and Lord Mulgrave, both members of
Pitt's Government; Mulgrave and the Duchess of Rutland, who
managed the family interest after the death of the 4th Duke in
1787, undoubtedly made it impossible for Osbaldeston to be returned for their borough in 1790, and he did not again sit in the
House.

12. William Nedham (?1740–1806), M.P. Winchelsea 1774
and 1775–1780, Pontefract 1780–1784, Winchelsea 1784–1790.
He had opposed North and Shelburne and supported the Coalition

(though not very frequently by his attendance and vote) both in and out of office. He lost his seat at Winchelsea when Nesbitt, his patron, sold his interest in the borough to Barwell and Darlington. He did not find another seat.

13. Palmerston was unable to stand again for Boroughbridge, where his patron, the Pittite Duke of Newcastle, had withdrawn his support.

14. Sir Peter Parker (?1721–1811), 1st Bt., M.P. Seaford 1784–1785 and 1785–1786, Maldon 1787–1790. A prominent naval officer during the American War, Parker had been brought forward at Seaford as a Government candidate, as he was again at Maldon in 1787. But Parker voted against the Government on Richmond's fortifications plan in 1786, and by November, 1788, he had been won over to Opposition at least partly through the good offices of Lord Sandwich. He did not find another seat in 1790.

15. Thomas Scott (1723–1816), M.P. Bridport 1780–1790. A brickmaker by trade, he had opposed North's government, supported Shelburne, and opposed the Coalition until its fall, from which time he voted steadily in Opposition. He had been returned for Bridport on the Sturt interest; but Sturt was unable to return more than one member in 1790, and Sturt himself and a Government supporter were returned at the general election. Scott did not again sit in the House.

16. A seat was finally found for Lord Robert at Wareham, which was a pocket borough in the hands of John Calcraft (1765–1831). The borough had been managed during Calcraft's minority by his uncle, who had returned Government nominees; but Calcraft, when he came of age, replaced his stepfather in one of the seats and voted with Opposition during the remaining four years of the Parliament. Gen. Richard Smith (1734–1803), the other member returned for Wareham in 1790, had been one of "Fox's Martyrs" in 1784 and he supported Opposition during 1791–1792.

17. For some reason, perhaps because of the enormous expense required, Wrightson did not again contest Aylesbury in 1790. Another Oppositionist, Gerrard Lake (1744–1808), was returned in his stead. Wrightson instead contested Downton on Robert Shafto's rather shaky interest; he and Shafto lost their Downton contest, as they did again in 1796. Shafto (?1732–1797) had been reputedly Oppositionist as late as 1788, but he had voted with Pitt on the Regency.

Memorandum—[1789 *or* 1790]

Endorsed: Candidates / Unfixed—
The memorandum and endorsement are in Adam's hand.

Eighteen of the thirty candidates appearing on this list (Aston, Blair, Calvert, Campbell, Cunynghame, Horseley, Jodrell, Ironside, Mackey, Morant, Pocock, Prescott, Scott, Assheton Smith, Tollemache, Hume, Harford, and Daer) did not sit during the Parliament of 1790. Of those eighteen only four (Cunynghame, Jodrell, Tollemache, and Daer) are definitely known to have canvassed or contested a constituency at the general election, and one of the four (Jodrell) seems to have contested as a Government candidate. Two of the candidates were eventually returned (Payne and Tempest), but not until late in the Parliament.

      Aston Hervey [1]
      Blair Alexr [2] [crossed out]
      Bradyll Wilson
      Byng G. Junr [3] [crossed out]
5   Calvert Felix [4]
      Campbell J. Fletcher [5]
      Cunningham Wm [6]
      Clive Edwd–
      Grey Lord
10 Horseley
      Jodderell R. P. [7]
      Ironside
      Lushington St. [8]
      Macky Robt—Q. who. [9]
15 Morant E. [10]
      Payne Sir R.
      Pocock [11]
      Prescott
      Scott Robt [12]

20   Smith T. Ashton [13]
      St Leger J.[14] fixed Oakhampton
      Tarlton [15]—Liverpool [16] fixed Seaford
      Tempest—Junr
24   Tollemache Hon Wm
      Tarlton Colonel— [17]
      Hume— [18]
      Harford— [19]
      Lord Daer fixed Canterbury
[added aslant and upside down]
      Bodmyn [20]
      Wm Popham
      J. Purling [21]

NOTES

1. Col. Henry Hervey Aston, of Clarges Street (in 1788) and Portman Square (by 1792), had joined the Whig Club on 16 July 1788. He had campaigned for Townshend during the Westminster bye-election of 1788, and in 1795 he was appointed a Groom of the Bedchamber to the Prince of Wales. He never sat in the House. See *Whig Club,* 1788 and 1792 eds.; Aspinall, ed., *Correspondence of George, Prince of Wales 1770–1812,* II, 539 n.

2. Alexander Blair, of Portland Place, had joined the Whig Club on 17 January 1785. He may be the same Blair for whom the party attempted to find a seat in 1784. He was never returned to the House. His profession and connection with the party are unknown.

3. The younger George Byng was returned for Newport (I.o.W.) on 28 January 1790. At the general election he was returned for Middlesex. His name might have been crossed out when he became fixed for Newport, or later when he decided to stand for Middlesex.

4. Felix Calvert, of Portland Place, had joined the Whig Club on 6 February 1787 (*Whig Club,* 1788 ed.). His profession and connection with the party are unknown; he was never returned to the House.

5. John Fletcher Campbell was promoted Lt. General in 1793. Possibly this is the Gen. Fletcher for whom a seat was sought in 1784. He was never seated.

6. Sir William Cunynghame.

7. Richard Paul Jodrell (1745–1831), classical scholar and

dramatist, stood for Seaford at the general election as a Government candidate and in opposition to Tarleton, who is also on this list. Tarleton was finally returned on petiton in the place of Jodrell. *DNB;* Oldfield, *History of Boroughs,* 2nd ed., II, 389.

8. In 1790 Lushington was returned for Helston with Sir Gilbert Elliot.

9. Presumably the same Robert Mackey who sought a seat in 1784. He was never returned to the House.

10. Edward Morant (1730–1791), M.P. Hindon 1761–1768, Lymington 1774–1780, Yarmouth (I.o.W.) 1780–1787. An independent supporter of Opposition in the Parliament of 1784, he had been returned for Yarmouth on the Clarke Jervoise interest and had vacated his seat in 1787 when the latter's son came of age. He did not again sit in the House.

11. Not identified, unless this is George Pocock (1765–1840), son of the admiral, who was returned for Bridgwater in 1796.

12. Probably Robert Scott (?1746–1808), a wealthy wine merchant, who in 1782 had married Emma, daughter of Thomas Assheton Smith. He was M.P. Wootton Bassett 1774–1780 as a Government candidate on the St. John interest. While in Parliament he had voted with Opposition. He was not returned to the House after 1780.

13. Thomas Assheton Smith (*c.* 1751–1828), M.P. Caernarvonshire 1774–1780, Andover 1797–1821. He had voted consistently with Opposition during the Parliament of 1774.

14. John St. Leger (1756–1799), Lt. Col. 1782, Maj. Gen. 1795; a Groom of the Bedchamber to the Prince of Wales. M.P. Okehampton 1790–1796. He joined the Whig Club on 16 November 1790 (*Whig Club,* 1792 ed.).

15. John Tarleton (1755–1820), younger brother of Banastre Tarleton. He was returned on petition for Seaford.

16. Adam must have jotted this note hastily. It may be that John was at one time intended for Liverpool, but it was his brother Banastre who contested the city at the general election. In 1796 John contested Liverpool in opposition to his brother.

17. Banastre Tarleton (1754–1833), a distinguished cavalry officer during the American War. Lt. Col. 1782; Col. November, 1790; Gen. by 1812. Tarleton was the 3rd son of John Tarleton, a merchant and mayor of Liverpool in 1764. He had unsuccessfully contested Liverpool in 1784. Oldfield maintains that in 1790 he was nominated in his absence by an independent group of freemen, who returned him without expense to himself in opposition to Bamber Gascoigne and Lord Penrhyn, the Government and Opposition candidates respectively, who had united their interests in the

hope of avoiding a contest. Tarleton topped the poll with 1257 votes to Gascoigne's 887 and Penrhyn's 716. Penrhyn seems indeed to have withdrawn early in disgust. Tarleton was member for Liverpool 1790–1806 and 1807–1812. During the Parliament of 1790 he staunchly supported Opposition. *Annual Register,* 1833, pp. 198–199; Oldfield, *History of Boroughs,* 2nd ed., I, 342–343; *DNB.*

18. Perhaps Sir Abraham Hume (1749–1838), 2nd Bt., M.P. Petersfield 1774–1780, Hastings 1807–1818. In 1780 Hume had asked the Rockinghams for a recommendation to a seat, and Portland had endorsed his application; but Rockingham doubted "his patriotic principles" (*H of P*).

19. Perhaps Henry Harford, of New Cavendish Street, Westminster, who joined the Whig Club on 10 November 1789 (*Whig Club,* 1792 ed.). He was never returned.

20. Bodmin, where the Opposition candidates were Sir John Morshead and Roger Wilbraham.

21. Purling stood for Tregony.

Memorandum—[1789 *or* 1790]

Endorsed: Scheme of / Certain Seats
The memorandum and endorsement are in Adam's hand.

1. Aldborrough—Suffk.[1]
1. Bletchingley
2. Malmesbury [2]
2. Newport Hants
1. Petersfield
1. Winchelsea Lord Robert–by Fox)
1. Wooton Basset

4000 & upwards

Lord Grey 4500£
Mr Byng 4000£ [crossed out]
Lord Down 4000 G[s]
Mr. North 4000£ [crossed out]
Mr Tempest 4000 G[s]

Ld Robt Spencer 4000 G^s

NB. not at } Ld Melbourn 4000 G^s
Malmesbury }

8. Ld F.Wm's friend 4000 G^s

3500

Ph. Francis } in case fails
at Hindon ^{3}

Morant
Ld Palmerston
Sir R. Payne [crossed out]

Welbore Ellis.

M. A. Taylor.^{4}
Tollemache

NOTES

1. Two Opposition candidates (Thomas Grenville and Lord Grey) were eventually brought in for Aldeburgh.

2. Wilkins did not bring in Opposition nominees at the general election.

3. Hindon was principally in the interest of the Calthorpe family and of William Beckford of Fonthill, whose interest was managed by Lord Chancellor Thurlow. At the general elections of 1780 and 1784 each patron had returned one member; but "outsiders could not be kept out" of the borough, though "their chances of success were small" (*H of P*). Francis does not seem to have gone to a poll in 1790. Beckford and a Government supporter were returned at the general election.

4. In 1784 Taylor had successfully contested Poole, but as a Government candidate on the recommendation of Lord Howe and Pitt. In 1790 he stood as an Opposition candidate and was doubtless looked upon by many as a turncoat. The appearance of his name here indicates an awareness of his danger and need of alternatives. Taylor lost the poll at Poole by a single vote, petitioned against the return, and had to await the decision of a committee of the House of Commons. In December, 1790, he was able to come in for Heytesbury in the place of William Pierce Ashe A'Court, an Oppositionist, who vacated his family seat. In February, 1791, when his petition had been decided in his favor, Taylor retired from Heytesbury and elected to sit for Poole.

Hunter, Peter, 113, 114
Hutchings Medlycott, Thomas, 19, 100, 215, 216
Hyndes, Charles, 222–223

Independent Friends, xli, 46, 91
Innes, Charles, 32
Irish propositions, xxv, xxxiii, 46, 250
Ironside, [Mr.], xli, 258

Jackman, J., xxxv, xxxvii, 177–178, 179; letter from, 167–173
Jackson, [Mr.], 81
Jackson, George, 233
Jarvis, J., 100, 105
Jenkinson, Robert Banks, 2nd Earl of Liverpool, 172, 211
Jervoise. See Clarke Jervoise
Jodrell, Richard Paul, xli, 157, 255, 256–257
Johnston, Alexander, 60
Johnstone, James, 59–60
Jolliffe, William, 207, 232, 252
Joweld, [Mr.], 206

Keating, Thomas, 13, 16, 19
Keene, Whitshed, 97, 98
Kellie, Earl of. See Erskine, Archibald
Kennedy, David, 10th Earl of Cassillis, 4, 5, 28, 29, 68, 84–85, 174
Kennedy, Thomas, 81, 84; letter from, 68–70
Kenrick, John, 99
Kent, Edward, 186, 201, 221–222, 222–223
Ker, John, 3rd Duke of Roxburghe, 56, 59, 91
Kerney, [Mr.], 87
Kimber, John, 87, 88
Kinnoul, Earl of. See Hay Drummond, Robert Auriol
Knatchbull, Edward, 8th Bt., 196, 197–198

Ladbroke, Robert, 153
Lake, Gerrard, 254
Lamb, Peniston, 1st Viscount Melbourne, xli, 13, 14, 71, 252, 253, 259
Lamb, Thomas, 167, 169–170, 172

Lamb, Thomas Phillipps, 170, 172
Lane, Mr., 141
Lauderdale, Earl of. See Maitland, James
Laurence, French, 94
Laurie, Robert, 5th Bt., 71, 205
Lavender, J., 103, 130, 131, 132
Lee. See Dillon Lee
Lee, John, 251, 253
Lee, Sir William, 19
Leeds, Duke of. See Osborne, Francis Godolphin
Legge, William, 2nd Earl of Dartmouth, 63, 64
Leicester, John Fleming, 5th Bt., 215, 216
Lemon, William, 1st Bt., 200
Lenox, [Mr.], 119
Levenson Gower, George Granville, styled Viscount Trentham and Earl Gower, 46–47, 48, 114, 117, 118, 162
Lichfield, Earl of. See references under Dillon Lee, Charles
Lindsay, Alexander, 6th Earl of Balcarres, 90, 91, 93
Lindsay, Robert, 91
Lister, Thomas, 253
Liston, Sir Robert, 60
Lock, of Kirkaldy, 125
Lockhart, Thomas, 7, 8
Lockhart Ross, Charles, 7th Bt., 115, 116–118, 121, 122, 199, 200, 219, 231
Lockhart Ross, John, 6th Bt., 117, 122, 182, 183
Lockyer, Thomas, 18
Long, Charles, 170, 172
Long North, Dudley, 76, 78, 79, 81
Lonsdale, Earl of. See Lowther, James
Loughborough, Baron. See Wedderburn, Alexander
Lowten, Thomas, 144, 165; letter to, 237–239
Lowther, James, 1st Earl of Lonsdale, 73, 146–147, 211, 214, 220–221
Lowther, Col. James, 211–212
Ludlow, Peter, 1st Earl, 165, 166
Lushington, Stephen, xli, 11, 12, 13, 18, 81, 82, 171, 213, 225, 226, 255, 257
Luttrell. See Fownes Luttrell
Luxmoore family, 153

CONSTITUENCY INDEX